HOW TO MAKE MONEY
IN A RETAIL STORE
OF YOUR OWN

CANADIAN SMALL BUSINESS SERIES

The Canadian Small Business Series represents a
unique library of information designed to assist the
independent business owner in the practical aspects
of daily business operations. It is the first such
series written for and by Canadians. Its goal is to
help you do better, whether you are now running your
own business or want to.

One of the greatest contributions of this series is its
recognition that, indeed, "SMALL BUSINESS" is the
biggest and most vital business in this country.
The series has made a giant step towards meeting
the needs of the largest contributor of Canadian
economic well-being.

Endorsed by and featured in seminars
presented in co-operation with

The Society of
Management Accountants
of Canada

La Société des
comptables en management
du Canada

HOW TO MAKE MONEY IN A RETAIL STORE OF YOUR OWN

A.P. Kneider

A FINANCIAL POST/MACMILLAN BOOK

To the memory of Edward R. Kneider,
truly an independent merchant

Canadian Cataloguing in Publication Data

Kneider, A. P., date
  How to make money in a retail store of your own
(Canadian small business series)
Bibliography: p.
Includes index.
ISBN 0-7705-1645-9 pa.
1. Retail trade—Canada—Management.
2. Stores, Retail.   I. Title.   II. Series.
HF5429.6.C3K54   658'.91'65887   C78-001297-6

Printed and bound in Canada for
The Macmillan Company of Canada Limited
70 Bond Street, Toronto, Ontario M5B 1X3

CONTENTS

INTRODUCTION

Retailing in Canada has become extremely complex and increasingly sophisticated since the days of the trading post and the general store. Since the retail industry has always operated in a constantly changing environment, these market variances have resulted in both revolutionary and evolutionary developments in the trade. As a result, the competitive pressures of these changes have caused retailers to become more concerned with the daily problems associated with store planning and management. *How to Make Money in a Retail Store of Your Own* is offered to the many independents facing these changes.

It is the objective of this book to provide independent retailers with current, practical, and operational tools that can be implemented in the management of their stores. To this end, the discussion which is offered on each of the topics is specifically directed to applying the principles discussed to the small retail establishment. The charts, exhibits, and forms have also been included to provide the independent with the foundation needed to define the data required for effective decision making.

With this goal in mind, the format of the book has been designed to allow you to logically follow the steps encountered in establishing and operating a retail store. Because of length limitations, it has not been possible to include all areas of store operation, but all fundamentals have been included to assist you.

Chapter 1 has been presented to allow the independent to continually assess and appraise the environment in which the store operates. A brief outline of the history of retailing is offered to motivate existing merchants to seek ways of improving their operations before being replaced by a newer evolutionary institution.

Chapter 2 offers you a look at the main reason for the existence of the independent merchant. Successful retailers operating in today's competitive market must seek to define and understand their target markets before budgeting funds that will capture those markets. Apply the concepts presented here to the community in which you are located so you can better satisfy the needs and wants of your customers.

Chapters 3 and 4 examine the spatial aspects of retailing. One of the primary tasks of the successful retail operator is to ensure that the store has the most productive location in the community. The various location factors you need to explore are examined to illustrate the need for constant appraisal of the changing values of store locations. Chapter 4 is provided to outline some of the practical solutions to the planning of the exterior and interior of the retail store. The chapter seeks to offer the basics of providing a store environment that will maximize sales and profits by inducing customer patronage.

The next six chapters outline and explain the various merchandising and operating functions of managing a retail business. The aspects of buying, promoting, pricing, selling, and controlling are each examined to assist you in adapting the principles to your store.

The final chapter is offered as a summary of the retail-management principle. But more importantly, the chapter includes an examination of some of the important elements of operating a retail store not dealt with in the other chapters. While the discussion is therefore brief on these topics, you are asked to further investigate those areas that have special significance for your store.

This book is offered to the many independent retailers, existing and potential, male or female, large or small, who seek to improve the profitability of their operations. Since the field of retailing is so diverse in type and nature of merchandise—and in the capabilities and knowledge of the merchants—I have attempted to write this book to satisfy the many independents I've had the privilege of serving professionally over the years.

This book is dedicated to the many independent retailers who constitute the nucleus of the Canadian retailing environment. Thank you for your courage, your ideas, your individuality, and your service.

A. P. KNEIDER

HOW TO MAKE MONEY IN A RETAIL STORE OF YOUR OWN

1

THE RETAILING ENVIRONMENT IN CANADA

THE CANADIAN ECONOMIC SYSTEM

The economic system in Canada is a private- and free-enterprise system. As such, entrepreneurs are free to follow their own inclinations in conducting their operations, with those that serve their customers most efficiently being successful. It is obvious that the inefficient operator soon fails. This freedom of choice for the Canadian entrepreneur is the foundation on which the private-enterprise system has been built.

Traditionally, Canadians have shown a great affinity for this freedom and independence and have subsequently shown a great desire for business ownership. Often Canadians with initiative, ability, and economy can establish a small business; with stamina and insight, the business can be developed into an operation of considerable size. Reading the success stories of many of our giant retail operations, from their early beginnings to the present, continually spurs the imagination and excitement of the entrepreneur.

An important derivative of this free-enterprise system is the rivalry generated among businesses for buyers of a product or service. Freedom of choice exists for the buyers of merchandise as well as for the sellers, so competition becomes a very important and dynamic element of our system. It is because of this element that one person will be more successful than another. It is essentially this drive for success among rival firms and individuals in our society that has resulted in the overall economic progress we have seen.

In addition to the resulting changes that competition has brought to our system, this rivalry has also led to an invisible control of business by ensuring that successful merchants remain alert to the economic environment in which they operate. It induces stores to become more efficient, to provide better services and products, to modernize their facilities, and to offer better values to their customers. Merchants who don't modernize obviously do not share in the growth and success of the environment.

This keen competition in the retail sector of our economy has led to the growth of price competition among our discount stores and supermarkets. They assume that price will be the determining factor in the consumer's decision to patronize a particular store. At the other end of the spectrum, it is common in our system to find retailers of fashion merchandise or other shopping goods competing on the basis of style, quality, service, and assortment rather than price. Thus, both price and non-price competition have stimulated the demand for efficiency in the retail trade.

While we have noted that our private-enterprise system offers freedom of choice inducing some degree of control through competition, our governing bodies have passed certain laws regulating the operation of businesses in Canada. These laws of our municipal, provincial, and federal governments were enacted to protect the public and to protect the ability of each entrepreneur to compete. While some government and labour intervention exists in our economy, merchants are still free to operate retail stores, to decide what to sell, and to set their prices and policies, provided they work within the framework of the laws designed to further competition and to provide consumer protection.

THE EVOLUTION OF RETAIL INSTITUTIONS

Retailing has been developing for thousands of years, as is evidenced by the earliest written records of mankind. In this time frame, the history of retailing has really been one of changing institutions which have developed to satisfy the demands of the particular era in which they were created. In each case these retail institutions have reflected the economic, social, technological, and political environment of the times.

For almost every type of present-day retail outlet there is a counterpart or forerunner in ancient and medieval civilization. For centuries, such retail outlets have been serving people, by procuring for them the necessities and luxuries which they desire to own.

However, these developments in retailing were not a matter of physical growth alone. In contrast with the present-day high standards and practices of progressive retailers stand the fraudulent and dishonest methods of bartering practised by the early traders. But it is from these early adventurous merchants that retailing has developed over the years to the vital role it plays in the economy of this country.

While it is not necessary for purposes of our understanding of small retailing in Canada to trace the historical aspect of the industry to biblical times, it should be noted that the early merchants and traders were responsible in great measure for procuring goods which contributed to higher standards of living for each succeeding generation.

In addition, many retail institutions have evolved out of ideas and techniques presented by an existing operation. This section has been included with the hope that you may discover some unique or different means of retailing a product or service by observing the historical developments in the industry.

Before the beginning of the twentieth century, retailing in Canada essentially served a rural economy by offering goods and services through the general store, the major retail institution at the time. As the forerunner of today's department store, the general store carried a wide variety of merchandise to satisfy the needs of the immediate community in which it was located.

From the turn of the century to the outbreak of World War II, Canadians witnessed a rapid expansion in mass production, a growth in urban centres with the move to an industrialized economy, and the subsequent development of the importance in the marketplace of the distribution of these goods and services. These developments led to the early stages of large-scale retailing as the population tended to concentrate in specific geographical areas. As a result of this shift in population, department stores soon discovered that it would be economically feasible to operate their large multi-line units in these areas. It was also during this time period in our history that the smaller urban markets provided the setting for the rapid growth of the chain store as an important retailer in this country. With these larger population densities and the demand for more goods and services at popular prices, the chain store was able to carve out its niche in the marketplace.

After World War II, Canada's economy began experiencing the rapid and exciting developments in retailing that we have today. The growing prosperity of the middle class made it possible for a larger segment of our population to spend substantial sums of money on merchandise that was not classified as necessities. At the same time, new product developments, new methods of sales promotion, quality control, and warranties, as well as the impact of mass communication through television, have greatly changed the needs and wants of the general consumer market.

But perhaps more than anything, the changes in the environment and structure of retailing have been influenced by the rapid increase in ownership and use of the automobile after World War II. This factor has led to the introduction of a large number of new products and outlets catering to the motoring shopper. The car's effect on all sectors of the retail trade has been evidenced through the widening of trading areas—the geographical area that encompasses the potential customers for a store, the possibility of eliminating delivery services to customers, the development of one-stop shopping, the acceleration of large-scale retailing, and, most importantly, the rapid evolution and expansion of suburban shopping centres.

Essentially, the history of retailing has been marked through the years by individuals able to discover a need in the marketplace and able to adapt the techniques of existing retail operations to this need. This process has led to the development of many of our retail institutions.

THE STRUCTURE OF RETAILING IN CANADA

Modern retailing in Canada is a complex process in which many different kinds of merchants can prosper. Because of the wide variety of goods and services demanded by consumers in the marketplace, retailers have evolved over the years in an effort to satisfy these requirements. While some consumers are seeking quality and prestige from the stores they patronize, some seek low prices, some seek convenient location, and some seek a wide assortment of merchandise under one roof. Therefore, within this framework of consumer demand, many different types of retailers can and do exist in our competitive environment.

This structure is composed of small independent retailers, department stores, and chain stores. All these forms of retailing operate in Canada, with each striving to maintain or increase its share of the total retail sales.

Because of the process by which large retail organizations have developed over the years, it's interesting to note the evolution of the various types of merchants in Canada in their quest to establish a more unique method of satisfying a market demand. For this reason, you'll want to note the process by which one type of retail institution has evolved from its predecessor or how each evolved to meet the demands of the particular era in which it was created. The following paragraphs briefly trace the evolution of the various retail institutions.

Trading Posts

The establishment of the Hudson's Bay Company by royal charter in 1670 signalled the start of retailing in Canada. At the end of the winter season, trappers would visit the nearest Hudson's Bay Company trading post to exchange their furs for foodstuffs, guns, ammunition, and other supplies.

The trading posts—and the itinerant peddlers who also operated at this time—served the primary function of distributing goods among the various settlements on the frontiers. Goods made in one community were exchanged for different products made in neighbouring settlements.

The General Store

As the number and sizes of these settlements increased, these itinerant merchants and trading posts gave way to the general store. These stores, as we noted earlier, were the early 1900s version of a department store, carrying a wide variety of merchandise with little concentration in depth of assortment. While the general store carried a variety of foods, dry goods, notions, hardware, and so on, little effort was made to offer customers a choice within these items. Very little attention was paid to merchandise arrangement or display in the presentation of goods to the customer. In addition, since prices were seldom marked on the items or shelves, each customer was responsible for negotiating the best deal he or she could.

The general store was the centre of the community. It sold merchandise brought in from larger centres, housed the local post office, and (because everyone in the area had to go there to buy whatever was needed) it was the meeting place for most people in the community. As a result, people gathered at the general store and discussed the social and political issues of the day—as well as the weather and crops.

While the general store has since given way to more efficient means of merchandising, Statistics Canada reports in the 1971 census that over 4000 general stores still operate in Canada, accounting for approximately $611 million in retail sales.

The Limited-Line Stores

As communities began to develop in size and the consumer began to make more demands on the general store, the limited-line store was established. Recognizing the limitation of the general store in offering the consumer any depth of merchandise assortment, these new institutions of retailing were formed to provide the consumer with a limited line of merchandise in depth of assortment. With this philosophy came the development of hardware stores, food stores, clothing stores, and variety stores.

The limited-line store really became the forerunner of the specialty stores predominant in today's retail environment. Obviously, the family clothing store provided the basis for the men's and boys' apparel store, women's clothing, children's shoes, hats, handbags, and similar stores allied to the apparel trade. In similar fashion, the hardware store gave rise to paint and wallpaper outlets, toy and sporting-goods stores, automobile accessories, lawn and garden equipment centres, and many other types of retail specialty units. Therefore, the specialty store became a further development of the limited-line store in which the consumer was provided with a concentration of both depth and breadth of merchandise assortment in a selected group of items.

The Department Store

Prior to the development of the specialty store in Canada, the shrewd merchant realized a need to offer the consumer both breadth and depth of assortment in a wide variety of items that was neither available from the general store nor from the limited-line units. Therefore, in the latter part of the nineteenth century, department stores began to emerge in Canada.

Three essential factors led to the growth of the department store. The growth of communities into cities induced retail stores to expand into a group of small shops under one roof. Secondly, the increased industrialization of the economy brought the need for ways and means of providing a mass distribution system. Finally, and perhaps most importantly, a group of entrepreneurs saw the need and place for this type of store in Canadian retailing.

Interestingly, many of the department stores that exist today grew out of dry-goods stores which subsequently added other lines such as hats, shoes, and clothing. Essentially, this entrepreneurial awareness led the department store to capitalize on the limitations of the limited-line stores.

It is therefore not surprising to discover that on December 8, 1869, Timothy Eaton opened a dry-goods and haberdashery emporium on the southwest corner of Queen and Yonge streets in Toronto. This store, with a 24-foot frontage, was purchased for the cash price of $6500, representing the humble beginnings that would make Timothy Eaton "the merchandiser to a whole nation" in only 30 years.

Similar discoveries can be made regarding the entrepreneurial talents of such men as Robert Simpson, of the Robert Simpson Company, or Donald Smith, governor of the Hudson's Bay Company. We have all become familiar, as well, with the names of R. H. Macy, John Wanamaker, Marshall Field, and Adam Gimbel in the United States.

Mail-Order Houses

While department stores were established to offer the consumer both breadth and depth of merchandise, they were too large to locate in the smaller rural communities of Canada. Therefore, in order to capitalize on this widely dispersed market, Eaton's and Simpsons sought to take their merchandise to rural consumers by means of mail-order catalogues.

In 1884, Eaton's published its first catalogue and arranged to have it distributed free to visitors of the Canadian Industrial Exhibition in Toronto. This modest 32-page booklet gave birth to mail-order retailing in Canada. In 1894, Robert Simpson joined his major competitor by offering customers a 130-page fall-winter catalogue. Before the turn of the century, then, Canada's two major department stores had embarked on an evolution in retailing that took their stores to the customer.

In 1953, the Sears, Roebuck Company of the United States joined forces with the Robert Simpson Company to form the Simpson-Sears organization that now operates in Canada under the Sears name. This organization took on responsibility for the mail-order operation of the Robert Simpson Company as well as establishing retail stores across the country. Beginning with the spring-summer catalogue of 1953, the Robert Simpson catalogue became the Sears catalogue.

In 1976, a further change in mail-order retailing came to

Canada with the demise of the Eaton catalogue operation. The mail-order field was thus left solely in the hands of the Sears organization, which has since recorded significant sales increases in this division of the company. Therefore, even with our mass transportation, mass communication, and our large urban society, the mail-order catalogue for general merchandise remains a viable means of retailing.

Chain Stores

Along with the development and growth of department stores in the early twentieth century, the chain-store organization emerged and grew. A chain system is a group of four or more stores which are centrally owned and managed and which offer similar lines of merchandise to their customers.

The chain store originated as an outgrowth of the independent limited-line store by providing customers with a wide assortment of brands in a restricted group of items. Its appeal was essentially for the price-conscious customer. For this reason, its primary growth centred around the variety-store merchandise and groceries. Better prices to the consumer resulted from more efficient buying because of the volume discounts.

Based on the success enjoyed in this merchandise field, chain stores began to develop in fashion merchandise of men's, women's, and children's apparel. The primary appeal emphasized at their inception was that of bringing the consumer popular, up-to-date fashions at economical prices. Further developments of chains followed in the fields of automobile accessories, tobacco and confectionery stores, and pharmacies.

The growth of the chain-store movement in Canada continued, and within a decade accounted for almost 20% of all retail sales by 1930. While price was the primary impetus for acceptance of the chain as the newest large-scale retailer, its development was enhanced by the environment which now existed. By 1930 the shift from a rural to an urban society had begun. The automobile was accepted as a major means of transportation, with increased ownership and use on Canadian roads. And finally, these merchants with their suppliers had developed new merchandising techniques associated with self-service retailing.

In the early 1950s the chain-store movement experienced a renewed impetus with the exodus of consumers to the suburban areas of our cities. The development of the suburban shopping centres as a result of this population shift provided new locations for these merchants. In addition, the landowners and developers of these centres needed the support and drawing power of these chains to make the suburban centres economically viable. As a result, chain stores were eagerly sought as tenants in these ventures, providing an accelerated growth pattern for this form of Canadian retailing.

Voluntary Chains

While chain stores experienced a rapid and exciting growth from 1920, this expansion was largely at the expense of the independent merchant. In an effort to meet this competition from both the chains and the department stores, the independent merchant became associated with voluntary chain organizations.

Realizing that much of their success was dependent on the success of the independent retailer, wholesale organizations sought to organize small merchants in an effort to combat this competition. The voluntary chains were therefore formed by a sponsoring wholesaler who recruited members for the organization from the existing retailers in the company's merchandise line. Membership was obviously voluntary, but for those merchants who sought to join, a contract was required indicating the percentage of merchandise which must be purchased from the sponsoring wholesaler, and specifying adherence to the operating and merchandising policies of the company.

Originally, the voluntary chain became the source by which the independent grocer might survive the fierce competition of the large corporate grocery chains. As a result, Independent Grocers' Alliance (IGA), Clover Farms, Red and White, and similar grocery operations were formed to assist the independent with store operations and to provide a form of group buying. Subsequent developments and expansion took place in other merchandising fields. Hardware stores such as Crest, Pro, Dominion, and Home Hardware were organized. Drug stores also found themselves united against the chains and department stores by forming Independent Druggists' Alliance (IDA) and Rexall.

The voluntary chain represents a significant development in the historical evolution of our retail trade. It provides an effective vehicle for organizing independents in their battle for survival against the giants.

Franchising

A major evolution of the voluntary chain movement in Canada has been the success of the franchise system of distribution. While franchising is essentially the grant of a right to operate a business with a specific trade name or mark and a designated format, it does differ from the voluntary chain.

The franchise system was also developed to unify and provide the independent retailer with the tools required to effectively compete in the marketplace. However, since the franchise system generally succeeds by recruiting new entrepreneurs rather than existing retailers, it does differ from the voluntary chain. In addition, the franchise system normally requires that the retailers pay a percentage of their gross sales to the wholesalers. The voluntary chain, on the other hand, seeks to record profitability by requiring the member merchants to purchase a specified percentage of their goods from the sponsoring wholesaler.

The basic objective of granting franchises is to allow wholesalers to increase their market coverage. To this end, the many different types of franchise systems have been successful in providing lucrative opportunities for many independent merchants across the country. While franchising is not new in Canada—it dates back to the nineteenth century—it has enjoyed an extremely rapid growth since the early 1950s.

Franchising is indeed an effective alternative for the prospective independent retailer. However, each franchise opportunity must be thoroughly explored before establishing a business under this retailing system.

The Supermarket

The supermarket was essentially the outgrowth of the limited-line stores and the chain stores in the early twentieth century. Excitement was generated with its development since it offered consumers low prices, a wider assortment of product lines, mass merchandising, self-service, and cash-and-carry retailing. However, it was not until the late 1940s that the supermarket experienced significant growth. Similar to the effect on other types of retailing at this time, the mobility of the population, the use of the automobile, the development of suburban shopping complexes, and the informality of Canadian lifestyles led to the rapid expansion of the supermarket.

The supermarket chains found themselves competing with each other on a price basis, thus depressing overall profit margins. Consequently, in the late 1950s and early 1960s, the supermarkets turned to non-price promotions such as trading stamps, bonus tapes, extended hours, and other promotional tools. However, consumers expressed dissatisfaction with the rising costs resulting from these promotions, by boycotting some supermarkets. Provincial legislation ultimately restricted the type of non-price competition that supermarkets could engage in.

Following the success of the supermarket in its ability to attract a large consumer segment, the discount food store, the combination store, the convenience store, the food emporium, and the hypermarché have evolved.

The discount food store has evolved to fill a void by offering consumers brand-name merchandise at discount prices without the frills of the traditional supermarket. The combination store developed to provide the consumer with one-stop shopping by allowing for the purchase of all types of food products and, subsequently, non-food items that would carry higher markups. As the name implies, the convenience store evolved to allow consumers to purchase necessity items at a place and time convenient to them. The food emporium capitalized on the experience of the supermarket in the merchandising of non-food items and sought to expand these merchandise lines to improve its profit picture with higher markup items. In addition, it sought to take the one-stop shopping concept further in its implementation. The hypermarché is a European innovation that was attempted in Montreal in 1974 providing a large self-service outlet with a mixture of foods and general merchandise in a warehouse atmosphere.

In recent years the supermarkets have shown their ability to innovate and to seek new ways of increasing market share and profitability. Some have added larger general merchandise departments, drug sections, small exclusive specialty boutiques for meat, bakery, and produce, as well as lunch counters, and plant and flower sections. One of Canada's leading grocery chains has expressed a desire to expand into the small convenience-goods stores by developing a franchise system to capture this market. On the other hand, the five major supermarket chains in Canada have also indicated their intention to build larger stores accommodating far more customers and a greater volume and variety of inventory.

The Discounter

While the supermarket brought food products to the consumer at lower prices than the traditional grocery store, the discount department store evolved in the early 1960s to offer the same consumers brand-name merchandise at reduced prices. Such stores operated with a policy of higher turnover and lower margins.

Again, the movement of the population to the suburban areas and the effect of the automobile provided the foundation for the development of the discount store. In addition, the enactment of legislation in 1951 made resale price maintenance illegal in Canada. On this basis, the manufacturer was no longer allowed to dictate the retail price at which the merchant must sell the item. This legislation opened the way for the discounter who sought to sell national brands of merchandise at lower than suggested list price to attract volume traffic.

Since manufacturers realized the opportunities to be gained by preselling their branded merchandise, by offering product performance warranties, and in some cases by offering to ship merchandise from their warehouses directly to the customers, the stage was set for limited-service retail institutions similar to the supermarket. The discounter also became aware of a void in the marketplace: Canadian department stores were both reluctant and slow to move to the suburban shopping centres. As a result, suburbia provided the discounter with a growing population with increasing demands for general merchandise required to establish and furnish its new homes.

However, while the discount store entered Canadian retailing with much fanfare, its success as a retail operation was to be shortlived. It did indeed do battle with the traditional department stores, but the latter were quick to react to this new form of competition. The two major department stores in Canada extensively promoted their policy, stating that they would not knowingly be undersold on identical items. This claim gave rise to head-on competition in which consumers opted to purchase the same item at the traditional department store if the price was identical. Consumers made this decision on the basis of all the additional services they could receive from the department store, including satisfaction guaranteed or money refunded.

While the major department stores offered fierce competition to these discount stores, the pioneer discounters were generally real-estate developers or promoters rather than merchants; as such they had difficulty coping with this rivalry. From its early beginnings, the discount department store was unable to capture the confidence of the Canadian consumer in the image it projected.

By the middle 1960s, the surviving discounters realized that it would be necessary to add some customer services if they wanted to establish a niche in the marketplace. As a result of more services, better quality merchandise, and more attractive outlets, the discount department store became more like the traditional stores. These outlets then dropped the term discounter from their advertisements and stores, preferring to be known as promotional department stores, in an attempt to regain the confidence of the Canadian public but still emphasizing the lower prices available. With the addition of more and more services, the improvement of merchandising techniques, and the overall philosophy of these operations, the term promotional has since been dropped from their names. Such organizations now refer to themselves as department stores only.

The discount department stores, then, have been caught on the "wheel of retailing," for in adding more services they have increased their costs and ultimately have been forced to increase the prices on their merchandise items. They have thus lost the competitive advantage that gave rise to their early acceptance in Canada. However, after more than 15 years, customer confidence in this type of retailing is being restored by the entry into the field by the major food chains and variety chain organizations.

Showroom Retailing

While the discount department store showed a merchandise turnover of ten times per annum compared to four for the traditional department store, the showroom retailer sought to capitalize on increasing sales per square foot of selling space. The merchandising policy was to eliminate selling costs as far as possible by limiting customer services. The main selling tool is an annual or seasonal catalogue which allows customers visiting the outlet to select the item they wish. The catalogue illustrates and describes the merchandise and shows the list price of the item while giving the actual price of the item in code. The purpose of this form of retailing is to convince the consumer that the items are priced at wholesale or very special prices, since the coded price is always less than the suggested list price of the manufacturer.

The customers' orders are filled from an adjacent warehouse or stockroom, where the inventory can be handled efficiently and without the frills of a traditional retail store. The claim of such retailers is lower prices for branded merchandise.

In the late 1950s Consumers Distributing Company of Toronto was formed, offering a variety of brand-name merchandise including electrical appliances, sporting goods, jewellery, toys, and home-entertainment products. In a 20-year period this company has expanded to some 160 stores across Canada, doing an annual volume in excess of $178 million.

In recent years, this type of retailing has been adopted by one of the major department stores and a large variety chain organization. However, the rapid growth of this form of retailing has shown a stabilizing trend that would seem to indicate that, for the present at least, the competitive strategies of other retailers have made it difficult for the showroom retailer to capitalize on its original advantage. Operating these showrooms in recent years has proved more difficult than anticipated; as a result, many companies in the field are suffering disappointing results.

SURVIVAL OF THE SMALL RETAILER

The evolution of the various types of retailing institutions has had a profound effect on the operation of the small independent retail establishment. With the advent of large-scale retailing in this evolution, the department store became known as the giant that had been established to bring about the demise of the small retailer. In turn, as each developed and created an impact on Canadian retailing, the chain store, the mail-order house, and the discounter were also designated as the big-business operations that would finally destroy the independent merchant.

This prophecy of doom has been evident in the industry since the turn of the century. Now, almost 80 years later, the small independent retailer is still a very significant part of the total retail trade. In the last major census, in 1971, Statistics Canada reported that 96.8% of all retail establishments in this country were single-unit operations. These one-store firms accounted for almost $17.5 billion in sales; which represented 55.9% of the total retail trade in Canada.

From these statistics, it is evident that the small independent retailer is a vital element in the economy of Canada.

However, the survival of the small merchant will indeed be as gloomy as some forecast unless independents become aware of the reasons for their existence. The remainder of this book is aimed to assist small retailers in developing their strengths to the fullest, while at the same time including, where possible, the positive elements of the large-scale organization that can effectively be used by the small entrepreneur.

It is not sufficient for the independent merchant to withdraw from competitive battle by assuming that the store's customers will remain loyal to it regardless of the aggressive efforts of its competitors. History has shown that consumers have become less loyal, more educated, and more sophisticated about the environment in which they shop.

The negative attitudes that generally prevail in independents' minds need to be rectified. No longer can they suggest that they can't compete with the larger merchants on the basis of price, assortment, and services. Their survival as retail merchants will depend on positive, well-defined attitudes that outline their retail strategies and provide their potential customers with the reasons for patronizing their stores.

In general, the large retail operators are attempting to do battle with each other for market share and competitive advantage, rather than concerning themselves with the impact of the small merchant. These large merchants depend for survival and market share on concentrated population densities and large sales volumes. For these reasons, large retail operations have tended to dominate the food, variety, and discount fields. Once independents recognize this fact and are able to capitalize on the advantages they are likely to possess over the large-scale merchant, they will be better able to create room for themselves in the marketplace. Obviously, we find independent merchants succeeding in bakery shops, hardware stores, apparel units, and many other merchandising areas where the customer seeks personal service, individuality, and convenience of location.

As small, independent retailers, then, you must learn to demonstrate and communicate to the consumer the advantages you possess. As small retailers you are very active in the day-to-day operation of the merchandising function of the store; therefore, you are better able to adjust your strategies to the specialized and changing needs and wants of your customers. In addition, because of the size of the small retail operation, you can enter and move out of a market more quickly than any large-scale competitor, who has a much larger capital investment in plant and equipment.

In the fight for survival and success, the independent must seek to develop the store's own character rather than attempting to outdo the large merchant with lower prices or wider assortments. The store must establish a unique image in the minds of its customers, one which will attract them on the basis of specific merchandise or service features.

Since the small store is generally limited to fewer employees and a more personalized service between customer and retail representative, this face-to-face relationship tends to strengthen the independent's position over the larger, impersonal, self-service operations. Very often it is difficult to distinguish between the personality of the owner of the store and the image of the store itself. This unique benefit of the small firm needs to be further emphasized in stressing the human and personal nature of the independent retail store.

Therefore, the small stores that select merchandise for certain people, that buy with individual lifestyles in mind, and that have a one-to-one relationship with their customers provide themselves with the opportunity to meet the needs of their market.

FAILURE RATES IN RETAILING

While the small retailer can and does enjoy success in Canada, many independent merchants also fail in their efforts every year. This section has not been included to scare prospective retailers from entering the field, but rather to induce you to adequately prepare for your retailing careers. Perhaps through this analysis you will acquire the proper merchandising tools that will ensure success.

It is often stated that the failure rate in retailing is generally high due to the ease with which one may enter the field. When an individual needs only to find a location, a limited amount of money, and a merchandise line to set up a retail store, it is obvious that the chances of success are likely to be very slim. Since no apprenticeship, no formal training, no management expertise, nor any specific financial resources are required to enter the field, retailing generally attracts the incompetent as well as those who have successfully planned and researched their proposed outlet.

Perhaps the foremost authority at reporting the numbers and reasons for failure in Canadian business is Dun and Bradstreet Canada Limited, an international credit agency. It is by reporting these facts that existing and potential merchants seek to more effectively prepare themselves for the demands of building a strong and healthy retail organization.

The information given in Exhibit 1-1 classifies the reasons given for failure in all types of businesses in Canada, as indicated by informed creditors and the credit reports of Dun and Bradstreet. The specific reasons for failure in retailing have not been segregated, but, due to the proportion of total failures in Canada in the retail trade, the table will give you the fundamentals required to protect yourself against premature bankruptcy.

While we have noted the reasons for failure in Canada, for our purposes it is also important to note the significance of the failure rate in the retail trade when compared with all businesses in Canada. Exhibit 1-2 has been taken from information compiled by Dun and Bradstreet. It is significant to note that over this 13-year period, retailing accounted for approximately 43% of the total number of business failures in Canada, yet only represented some 20% of the total liabilities of these bankruptcies.

It is therefore plain that the largest number of business failures in this country is derived from the retail trade. Consequently, it is vital for any prospective merchant to conscientiously plan an entrance into the field and to continuously avoid the pitfalls that have been detailed as the reasons for business failures.

While significant dollar losses have occurred as a result of retail failures, the largest share of liabilities resulting from all collapses were generated by the manufacturing enterprises. The records show that many of the business failures have occurred with liabilities of more than $100,000, and many, in fact, with losses in excess of $500,000. Since many of the retail failures come from small operators, with smaller dollar investments, the proportion of numbers of casualties is high. But while total retail liabilities fall behind manufacturing, they are ahead of the construction, wholesaling, and commercial services liabilities.

Perhaps another important fact that should be noted regarding the unfortunate problem of failure rates in retailing is the proportionate number of casualties that occur in their first five years of operation. Statistics illustrate that in 1975, 63.9% of all businesses that failed had been in operation five years or less. The first few years of operating a business are usually more

Exhibit 1-1

Classification of Causes of Business Failures in Canada
All Lines of Businesses, 1975

Number	Per Cent	Underlying Causes	
28	1.0	Neglect	Due to:
10	0.3	Fraud	On the part of the principals, reflected by:
921	32.2	Lack of experience in the line	
439	15.3	Lack of managerial experience	Evidenced by inability to avoid conditions which result in:
231	8.0	Unbalanced experience*	
1216	42.5	Incompetence	
13	0.5	Disaster	Some of these occurrences could have been provided against through insurance.
5	0.2	Reason unknown	
2863	100.0	Total	

* Experience not well rounded in sales, finance, purchasing, and production on the part of an individual in case of a proprietorship, or of two or more partners or officer constituting a management unit.

Apparent Causes	Number	Per Cent
Bad Habits	9	0.3
Poor Health	14	0.5
Marital Difficulties	1	0.0
Other	4	0.2
Misleading Name	—	—
False Financial Statement	—	—
Premeditated Overbuy	—	—
Irregular Disposal of Assets	9	0.3
Other	1	0.0
Inadequate Sales	1829	63.9
Heavy Operating Expenses	699	24.4
Receivables Difficulties	92	3.2
Inventory Difficulties	101	3.5
Excessive Fixed Assets	66	2.3
Poor Location	31	1.1
Competitive Weakness	129	4.5
Other	8	0.3
Fire	8	0.3
Flood	—	—
Burglary	—	—
Employees' Fraud	—	—
Strike	—	—
Other	5	0.2

Because some failures are attributed to a combination of apparent causes, the totals of these columns exceed the totals of the corresponding columns on the left.

Source: Dun & Bradstreet Canada Limited, The Canadian Business Failure Record (Toronto: 1975). Reprinted by permission of Dun & Bradstreet Canada Limited.

hazardous as•a result of the testing period of ability, stamina, and management alertness.

The figures also indicate that 14.7% of the business casualties in 1975 had been in operation for more than ten years. So the need for constant supervision, awareness, and management know-how is the key to an effective and healthy organization carrying on business in the Canadian environment.

Exhibit 1-2
Failure Rates in Retailing, 1963-1975

Year	Number of Retail Failures	Total Business Failures (%)	Liabilities of Retail Failures (in $1000s)	Liabilities of Total Failures (%)
1975	1216	42.5	114,720	24.3
1974	1073	42.7	84,419	22.4
1973	1183	43.5	63,270	19.8
1972	1271	44.6	50,879	20.4
1971	1203	45.8	58,838	17.9
1970	1077	47.1	52,806	19.9
1969	816	43.8	41,482	28.4
1968	725	42.7	26,428	20.3
1967	789	40.1	35,535	16.4
1966	1024	42.3	37,247	21.3
1965	1132	43.6	37,129	21.1
1964	1209	48.4	38,017	23.0
1963	982	45.5	29,234	25.0

Source: Dun & Bradstreet Canada Limited, *The Canadian Business Failure Record* (Toronto: 1975).

2
THE CONSUMER
IN RETAILING

THE CUSTOMER RULES

The success of any retail store operating in this country depends on its ability to satisfy the needs and wants of its customers. Truly, customers are sovereigns. Our most successful merchants recognized very early in their development that the growth and expansion of their companies would depend on their ability to capture market share by customer satisfaction.

Shortly after the opening of his store, Timothy Eaton announced a unique policy for the times by stating that he would offer "goods satisfactory or money refunded". This policy leaves very little to interpretation in its ability to attract a large customer segment. While Henry Birk offered quality and prestige wrapped in a distinctive blue box, Honest Ed Mirvish offered a wide assortment of merchandise at discount prices in a unique setting. Sam the Record Man offered customers the largest selection of phonograph records and tapes available, at lower prices. All of these retailers—and the many large-scale merchants throughout this country—have grown from their original one-store operations to the giants of today because of their policy of adapting their merchandising strategy to a defined customer grouping.

Therefore, in order for the retailer of today to enjoy success in this competitive environment, it is essential that the market to be served be first defined. In addition, an understanding of the purchasing patterns and habits of this market is required before an effective merchandising program can be established.

Thus, to be a successful merchant you must define your potential market in an effort to establish a customer profile for your store. While much research has been undertaken recently on the psychological, sociological, and behavioural techniques of analyzing the market, it is our intention here to illustrate those basic means of understanding the market that can best be used by the independent retailer. If you wish to have more detailed information on understanding consumer behaviour the Bibliography at the back of this book has a list of books on this subject.

THE TARGET MARKET

One common mistake many individuals who have opened up retail stores make is the assumption that the total population of the area constitutes the store's market. But it's virtually impossible for one retailer to be all things to all people. As large as our major department stores are, they are unable to satisfy everyone. Because you want to attract one portion of the market with a particular strategy, you will no doubt alienate another. By appealing to the teenage market, a retailer may be eliminating the middle-age market. By seeking to attract the price-conscious customer, those who are seeking extensive personal service will be put off, and will patronize another retail outlet.

It is, therefore, essential for you to define that portion of the market which you consider will constitute the bulk of your primary customers. These are the customers who will provide the store with the sales volume it will require to survive in the marketplace.

Marketing and retailing firms refer to this group of customers as the firm's target market. The store's merchandising efforts will be directed toward this market. The advertising, the pricing, the merchandise assortment, the location of the store, and the personnel must all be planned with this group in mind. Your store must satisfy the needs and wants of this market in order to succeed.

To the small retail firm, the definition of this market is vital. Since you do not have the wide merchandise assortment of your large-scale competitors, you must be careful in selecting your merchandise lines and target market. In selecting this market you must ensure that you can achieve sufficient volume from this group to make your operation profitable. In a small operation there is less margin for error; therefore a constant review of the store's target market needs to be undertaken. On the other hand, this smallness provides you with the advantage of flexibility in being able to adjust to the market you serve much more quickly than larger firms.

MARKET SEGMENTATION

In selecting this target market, the retailer is required to proceed through a series of activities known as market segmentation. This is the process of breaking down the total market for a product or service into relatively homogeneous groups. Through this process we can list market segments such as the teenage market, the middle-income group, the French-speaking segment, the northern market, or the professionals. It should be noted at this point that there are probably as many market segments in this country as there are Canadians. However, in order to develop a general understanding of the various customer segments, the total population has been grouped according to specific characteristics. It is from this group of homogeneous segments that you select your target market.

Various means have been established by marketing people in their efforts to break down the total market into meaningful segments. Four methods of market segmentation are being explained in this section with the hope that you will undertake an analysis of the market you decide to serve.

Demographic Segmentation

Perhaps the most common—and certainly the easiest—method for retailers to segment their markets is by the population's characteristics. This process of demographic segmentation establishes market segments based on age, sex, marital status, education, occupation, income group, religion, ethnic origin, or any other characteristic of the general population that would establish a relatively homogeneous group. The principle behind demographic segmentation is that a merchant catering to the educated, middle-income consumer should find that their needs and wants, as well as their purchasing patterns, are similar. In this way, the retail store is able to plan and direct its merchandising strategy directly to this market.

Geographic Segmentation

A second means by which retailers have sought to segment the market is on the basis of the geographical location of the market. This process operates on the premise that the buying patterns and motives of the various markets in Canada will differ according to their location. Generally, the rural market differs from the urban market, the suburban customer is different from the city dweller, the northern market is as different from the southern market as the western consumers are from those who live in the east. Each market requires separate analysis on the part of the retail organization.

From the point of view of the small retail firm, geographic segmentation illustrates its importance when linked with the findings of demographic analysis. Independent merchants in a specific area of a town or a city may find that their market is much different from the market of a similar store in another location. Location in a suburban shopping centre will affect the market segment in a different way than will location downtown.

While the independent retailer who locates in a small town has fewer problems with geographical segmentation, the need to segment the overall market is just as important.

Therefore, in tying the geographical segment to the demographic segment, you should attempt to establish a definitive customer profile. For this reason, many merchants keep mailing lists of their customers to determine the geographical location of their market as well as defining the group demographically.

Volume Segmentation

While this method is not uniformly used by all retail firms, it does provide another way to define a target market for the retail store. Essentially, volume segmentation points out that in most merchandise lines half of the consumers account for approximately 80% of the consumption. Retailers recognizing this factor would tend to concentrate their merchandising efforts on this segment only. For example, the independent merchant who has opened a tennis boutique would concentrate all merchandising efforts on tennis players rather than on inducing non-players to take up the sport in order to expand the total market for the boutique.

Not all retailers have opted to accept this principle of segmenting the market, of course. Surely the recent expansion of large home-improvement centres has facilitated the means by which the inexperienced customer may now become competent through do-it-yourself merchandise. Large efforts have been made by cross-country ski shops to expand their markets by offering lessons and package deals to the non-skier.

Benefit Segmentation

A fourth means of segmentation that has been developed in the process of analyzing the total market is benefit segmentation. This process seeks to break down the market into causal factors rather than into the descriptive factors of demographical and geographical segmentation. Such a means of selecting a market suggests that the benefits people seek in consuming a product or service are the only true reasons for the existence of a market segment.

This approach measures consumer value systems in detail, together with what consumers think about the various brands in the merchandise assortment. While this process seems simple enough, in actual fact it is rather complex, requiring the handling of large volumes of data. However, each segment is identified by the benefit it is seeking. The total of the benefits sought differentiates one segment from another, while individual benefits are likely to have appeal for several segments.

In benefit segmentation analysis, you attempt to determine what benefits the various segments would receive by patronizing your store and how your store would satisfy those benefits sought by the consumer. Consumers who purchase sportswear seeking high style, top quality, large selections, and personal service form a different segment from their counterparts who seek the benefits of serviceable quality at popular prices in a convenient self-service store.

While few retailers take the time to analyze their markets on the basis of benefit segmentation, most firms have intuitively established the benefits generally sought by their market. The advantages to be gained by thoroughly understanding and analyzing the market cannot be overemphasized.

It is certainly to your advantage to attempt to analyze your store's target market on the basis of the four means of segmentation given. In this way you will be able to clearly define and understand the complexities of the market and to use this information to direct all merchandising efforts to this market.

Such information will lead you to the proper decisions regarding the brands to carry, the price lines to include, the advertising media and messages to select, the customer services to be offered, and the location for the store. Once the target is defined in these terms, then and only then have you planned to satisfy the needs and wants of the store's customers. It is not surprising to see the number of small retail firms which make false assumptions about their targets and soon discover that their market has either changed over the years or was never really the market it was anticipated to be.

It is to your advantage to constantly analyze your store's market to determine its characteristics and the total benefits that are sought by this group of customers.

UNDERSTANDING THE CUSTOMER

Once the target market has been defined, it's important to understand the buying behaviour of these customers. This understanding results from an analysis of the buying motives and buying habits of the store's market. In this context, look for answers to the questions: Why do customers buy what they buy? Why do they buy from where they buy? and How and when will the customers buy the merchandise the store proposes to sell? With this information you are better equipped to design a successful merchandising strategy.

BUYING MOTIVES

An analysis of the customers' buying motives will lead you to a better understanding of why your market buys what and where it buys. A study of buying motives is therefore an analysis and understanding of the "why" of consumer behaviour. Product motives seek to describe why consumers buy the products and brands they buy, whereas patronage motives seek to explain the reasons for purchasing the items from particular retail stores.

Product Motives

Knowledge of the product motives of your customers facilitates the selection of merchandise for your store. If you can determine what causes buying action from your customers, you'll be better able to decide price, brand, colours, fabrics, styles, sizes, and the many other selection factors available in most merchandise lines.

Here are several product motives which explain some of the reasons why consumers buy what they do.

Rational Product Motive With this motive, the consumer seeks to purchase an item or brand by analyzing the advantages and disadvantages of the purchase. Such motives include economy of operation, economy of purchase, safety features, dependability, and convenience. If the merchandise line tends to generate rational buying, then these features should constitute the primary appeal of the promotional strategy.

Emotional Product Motive At the other extreme, consumers make decisions without considering the arguments for or against the proposed purchase. Obviously, promotions for such merchandise will be based on an emotional appeal. Prestige, conformity, pleasure, individuality, and creativity are appeals that you can use to stimulate emotional purchasing. Most items purchased by the consumer are bought for emotional reasons like status, sex appeal, or emulation. Effective use of this fact should be evident through your advertising, interior displays, window displays, and personal selling presentations.

Dormant Product Motive This consumer motive represents those desires that are unrecognized by buyers until brought to their attention through the instruments of the retailer's strategy. This is perhaps the greatest opportunity for you to increase sales per square foot, average sale and the number of transactions. With point-of-purchase displays, effective sales presentations, exciting window displays, and efficient buying, you can capitalize on the elements of suggestion selling and impulse purchasing by the store's customers. An alert retailer plans to activate the dormant product motive in all customers.

Conscious Product Motive The conscious motive represents those desires which are clearly experienced by the customer without being aroused through a retailer's strategy. In essence, the customer has been presold on the item by the manufacturer or the retailer before entering the store. The customer who enters a men's apparel store seeking to purchase a 15½-33, white, long-sleeve shirt with a button-down collar in a specific brand is functioning on a conscious product motive. In order for you to capitalize on the demands of such customers, effective buying and inventory controls are mandatory in your store.

Primary Product Motive This refers to that which causes an individual to buy a certain kind or classification of a product category. As an example, consider the purchasing decisions of the woman who decides to purchase a pant suit instead of a dress for a dinner party, the college graduate who opts for a sports car instead of a standard automobile as a means of transportation, and the homemaker who selects broadloom instead of tile as a floor covering. Since all of these purchases have been made to solve a particular problem, the successful retailer must be able to offer the consumer solutions to these problems in the store's merchandising strategy.

Selective Product Motive When consumers select an item from within the classification of items presented, they are said to have exercised a selective product motive. In the primary motive example above this would refer to the woman selecting a three-piece, blue pant suit, the graduate selecting a convertible, four-speed Fiat, and the homemaker's choice of a plush, nylon carpet. It is the retailer's responsibility to have these choices available for the customer, and, at the same time, to direct the purchase decision.

Not all small retailers will be able to analyze the motives of each customer who enters the store in such detail, but you must understand these motives in your effort to appeal to the wants and needs of your target market. For example, the hardware merchant who wishes to appeal to the rational, selective, conscious motives of buyers might design an advertisement promoting a portable hand saw with a unique safety feature, at a special anniversary price. Such concepts and ideas are also used by merchants in the preparation of display signs and point-of-sale messages by employees.

Patronage Motives

While product motives explain the reasons why consumers purchase the merchandise they do, an analysis of patronage motives seeks to define why consumers purchase these products at particular retail outlets. In an effort to attract your target market, you must understand what will induce your market segment to patronize your store rather than those of your competitors.

Customers give many reasons for selecting a particular store. The successful and alert merchant combines as many of these

Exhibit 2-1

Positive and Negative Factors of Customer Patronage

Customer Likes	Customer Dislikes
1. Price-value relationship	1. Limited assortment of merchandise
2. Store specialization	2. Too much pressure to buy
3. Quality of merchandise	3. Mistakes and indifference of salespeople
4. Salesclerk service	4. Prices out of line with what customer thinks is fair value
5. Store location	5. Long waits for service, change, parcels
6. Variety of assortment	6. False promises about delivery
7. Guarantee, exchange, adjustment policies	7. Carelessly wrapped parcels
8. Customer habit or routine	8. Being told they are hard to fit or hard to please
9. Legitimacy of sales	9. Overheated, under-heated, poorly ventilated stores
10. Other convenience factors (delivery, parking, store hours etc.)	10. Dark or poorly-lighted stores
11. Credit and billing policies	11. Evidence of poor and careless housekeeping
12. Store layout and atmosphere	12. Lack of courtesy
13. Merchandise displays	13. Idlers inside and outside the store
14. Suitability of advertising	

Source for Customer Likes: Marvin A. Jolson and Walter F. Spath, "Understanding and Fulfilling Shoppers' Requirements," *Journal of Retailing,* Summer 1973, p. 41. Reprinted by permission of *Journal of Retailing,* New York University.

Source for Customer Dislikes: Harold Shaffer, Herbert Greenwald, *Independent Retailing: A Money-Making Manual,* © 1976, p. 8. Reprinted by permission of Prentice-Hall, Inc., Englewood Cliffs, New Jersey.

features as possible into the store's merchandise offering in an effort to develop a customer following.

Exhibit 2-1 lists what shoppers have indicated as their reasons for shopping at certain stores, as well as those features which they dislike about some operations. The responses to this survey have been listed in order of importance to the shoppers and should point out what areas of your merchandising strategy may need to be improved in your store.

You will note that the results of the survey are not all-inclusive; such information would vary significantly with the type of merchandise, the type of customer, and the sample size selected for the survey. Nevertheless, you should be able to compare these factors with those presently offered in your store to determine if your strategy is likely to motivate your market to patronize your operation.

Consumers have also been specific in listing the following reasons why they choose to patronize certain retail operations. In some cases similarities exist with the previous chart of positive and negative factors; this overlap tends to strengthen the importance of these classifications. You should never lose sight of the fact that you are in business to serve your customers, and must be alert to those factors which induce your market to patronize your store. The classification of patronage motives of consumers which are frequently noted are listed in Exhibit 2-2 for easy reference.

Exhibit 2-2
Patronage Motives—Selected Classifications

1. Reputation of the seller
2. Customer services rendered
3. Breadth and depth of merchandise assortment
4. Price-quality combinations
5. Convenience of location
6. Effective window displays
7. Habit
8. Prestige
9. Friendly, efficient personnel
10. Relationship to owner or employees

Use every facility available to appeal to the buying motives of your customers in influencing their purchasing behaviour.

BUYING HABITS

In the preceding paragraphs we have noted that the study of buying motives illustrates the reasons *why* consumers buy what and *where* they buy. To understand *when* and *how* they will make their purchases as a result of these motives is explained in the analysis of the customers' buying habits.

When the Customer Buys

Customers' buying will vary with the season, the day of the week, and the time of day. This variation in purchasing generates a significant adjustment to the store's operating and merchandising strategy. Adjustments must be made to promotions, inventory levels, business hours, personnel schedules, and the other vital elements that constitute the store's appeal to its target market.

In Canada, climatic changes are responsible for much of the seasonal variation in customer purchasing. However, social customs, such as the giving of gifts at Christmas, play a very significant role in the buying done in the fall-winter season in most merchandise lines. It is generally true that most lines of merchandise generate more sales in the fall-winter season than during the spring-summer months. Exhibit 2-3 shows the variation in the sales of selected merchandise classifications during the months of the year. You will note that piece goods and fabrics, for example, do particularly well in January as a result of the traditional textile sales, while men's and boys' wear do well in November and December indicating their importance as gift-giving items at Christmas.

The hours which tend to be favoured by consumers for patronizing retail stores will also vary with the kind of store, the preferences of the retailer, and the operating procedures of the shopping area or centre in which the store is located. Generally, the business hours of retail stores are under municipal jurisdiction, which explains why the same stores in different communities are open for business at different hours. Some stores operating in the same business district also illustrate a variance in the hours that they are open, with some opting for early closing every night of the week. In an effort to eliminate this confusion, the suburban shopping centres have designated the hours that the retailer must be open as a condition of the lease. In such commercial complexes, retailers have discovered that approximately 60% of their business is generated after 6 PM. Obviously, such retail centres have then opened their establishments at least five nights a week for shopping.

At the other extreme, the peak number of arrivals in the central business district of a town or city is frequently near noon. On a shopping expedition to the central area of the community, the

Exhibit 2-3
Total Retail Sales by Types of Stores

Per cents of year's total sales done each month

Retail sales total	Jan	Feb	Mar	Apr	May	June	July	Aug	Sept	Oct	Nov	Dec
Department Stores	5.7	5.3	6.8	7.4	8.1	8.1	7.3	7.8	9.2	8.6	10.8	14.9
Drug Stores	8.1	7.7	7.6	7.5	7.9	8.3	8.0	8.1	8.2	8.6	8.5	11.5
Family Clothing Stores	6.0	5.4	6.9	7.6	8.1	8.7	7.0	7.0	8.5	9.2	10.5	15.1
Fuel Dealers	12.5	14.4	11.2	8.4	6.3	3.6	3.4	3.5	4.1	7.8	10.4	14.4
Furniture, Appliances & Radio Stores	8.4	5.6	7.0	8.4	8.6	8.2	8.3	8.0	9.5	8.5	9.9	9.6
Garages & Filling Stations	7.4	7.2	7.3	8.2	9.4	8.7	9.7	8.9	8.1	8.0	8.6	8.5
General Stores	6.4	6.7	7.3	8.0	8.6	9.2	8.6	8.8	8.5	8.9	8.6	10.4
Grocery & Combination Stores	7.7	7.6	8.3	8.0	8.8	8.8	8.2	8.0	8.8	8.2	8.3	10.0
Hardware Stores	5.4	5.8	6.3	7.0	10.5	9.9	8.9	8.5	9.4	9.2	8.3	10.8
Jewellery Stores	5.2	5.7	5.9	6.8	7.4	7.5	6.6	6.7	8.2	6.2	8.4	25.4
Men's Clothing Stores	7.6	6.2	6.7	7.2	8.5	9.8	7.5	6.9	7.5	8.5	9.5	14.1
Motor Vehicle Dealers	5.9	6.6	8.6	9.4	10.6	10.0	8.3	7.1	7.2	9.7	9.3	7.3
Shoe Stores	6.7	4.5	5.7	8.7	8.8	8.5	7.2	6.7	9.9	10.0	10.8	12.5
Variety Stores	5.1	5.1	6.3	6.7	8.6	9.2	8.4	7.9	8.4	8.5	9.8	16.0
Women's Clothing Stores	7.1	5.7	7.6	7.3	9.0	8.8	7.9	7.6	8.6	8.3	9.2	12.9

Source: *Newspaper Advertising Planbook* (New York: Newspaper Advertising Bureau, Inc., 1974), p. 56. Reprinted by permission of the Newspaper Advertising Bureau, Inc.

consumer often visits several retail stores. Also, retail firms located in the shopping concourses of high-rise office buildings in the core area have found their operations dependent on workers from the area who shop during their lunch time and immediately after work.

Therefore, to use your personnel in the most efficient manner be aware of the variations that exist in the time of day that your customers wish to shop.

Just as the time of day varies among the different types of retail establishments and locations, so too will a variation exist in the days of the week that a customer wishes to shop. Generally, consumers vote in favour of Friday and Saturday shopping. Since Friday is often payday for a large number of workers, and Saturday has generally been a free day from employment, these days have tended to generate the largest sales volume. For these reasons, and in areas of merchandising where the consumer was offered the choice, Sunday retailing also showed some significant success.

In some provinces like Ontario, however, the provision of shopping seven days a week met with opposition from various groups, so that provincial legislation was enacted in 1976 prohibiting the retailing of many items on statutory holidays and Sundays. Because many communities are close to one another, the jurisdiction to enforce such a regulation became provincial rather than municipal. Similar legislation exists in the provinces of Quebec and New Brunswick, with pending controls in British Columbia.

Customers, therefore, are restricted in their shopping days in part by provincial legislation, in part by the availability of time, and in part by their incomes.

How the Customer Buys

In addition to being aware of the time that consumers wish to patronize stores, merchants are constantly attempting to induce customers who have been attracted into the store to buy while in the store. In this manner, you can increase the incidence of impulse purchasing in your store.

Impulse purchasing results from decisions made by consumers on the spot in the outlet where they see the product displayed. By appealing to as many senses as possible, the retailer tries to stimulate buying action on the part of the customers. This inducement to purchase generally results from the effective point-of-sale presentations that the retailer has planned either in the form of interior displays, sales presentations, or window treatments.

The amount and proportion of impulse purchasing to total purchases continues to increase, due in part to the increase in self-service retailing. These increases have also been generated by retailers who have recognized that customers can be induced to buy impulsively by either reminder-buying or suggestion-buying. Reminder-buying refers to a purchase made by the consumer upon seeing a product displayed and remembering a need. Displaying shoe polish at the cash-wrap desk of the shoe store induces reminder-buying. Suggestion-buying, on the other hand, refers to impulsive purchases made by customers who see a product displayed and visualize a need for it. Creativity in the point-of-sale presentation will maximize the benefit of impulse buying. Demonstration of the many alternative uses of several household products has stimulated greatly the suggestion-buying of these products in retail stores.

WHAT CUSTOMERS BUY: CLASSIFICATION OF CONSUMER GOODS

The classification of consumer goods is a process by which the retailer attempts to further understand the buying process of the store's customers by analyzing what the consumer buys. Consumer goods have been categorized according to the merchandising strategy required to attract the desired market. Retailers and marketers have traditionally classified consumer products into convenience goods, shopping goods, and specialty goods.

Convenience Goods

Merchandise items which the consumer wishes to purchase frequently with a minimum amount of effort are classified as convenience goods. Such products and services must be easily accessible to customers, providing them with convenience in their purchase. Since these items are usually fairly inexpensive, the consumer does not spend much time or effort to plan their purchase.

From the retailer's point of view, the merchandising of convenience goods implies that they are available at many retail outlets. Therefore, the merchant seeks to display these items in heavy traffic areas of the store—near the cash-wrap desk and main customer aisles, for example. Because many retailers carry identical or similar items, the trading area for the convenience items of each store is small. In addition, due to the frequency of the purchase and habitual request for such items, brand preference by the consumer usually plays a very significant role, with brand substitution by the retailer somewhat difficult.

Merchandise items such as cigarettes, candy bars, pantyhose, facial tissues, sandpaper, greeting cards, tennis balls, shoe polish, and many other items are classified as convenience goods.

Shopping Goods

This classification represents goods which the consumer will shop for by comparing price, quality, style, fabric, colour, or other selection factors which the buyer deems important. In comparison with convenience goods, the consumer is much more deliberate in planning the purchase, exerts more effort in making comparisons prior to selection, and expends a larger amount of money in acquiring the merchandise.

In making the selection, customers are willing to visit many stores and are prepared to travel farther than in the purchase of convenience items. The trading area of such items will therefore be larger, with accessibility of the merchandise less important than it is with convenience goods, since the consumers are prepared to make the effort to locate the products or services demanded.

In general, brand loyalty is not extremely relevant and the customer's practice of visiting many stores before a selection is made indicates an inability to make a quick decision. This buying process provides an opportunity for a retailer to test the effectiveness of the store's sales presentation. The most effective merchandising strategy will pay close attention to satisfying the customer's patronage motives.

Items of clothing, furniture, sporting goods, appliances, automobiles, and many other consumer products are classified as shopping goods.

Speciality Goods

Merchandise which the consumer exerts a considerable amount of effort to obtain as a result of some unique characteristic or designated brand is known as specialty goods. As a result of this brand preference by consumers, substitution by a retailer for an out-of-stock item is generally very difficult.

Specialty goods are usually of high unit value, infrequently purchased, and normally associated with the better-quality retail shops. For these reasons, shoppers are likely to spend a considerable amount of time in planning the purchase and acquisition of the item. Often consumers become aware of retail stores which carry the item and go directly to this outlet with a minimum amount of time and effort.

For this merchandise assortment, you must maintain effective inventory control procedures and efficient buying plans, since substitute selling is not likely, due to the brand loyalty established in this category.

Classification Overlap

You should note that the same product may be in a different category for one customer than for another, or for the same customer at different times. An Arrow shirt may be a specialty item for one person, but a convenience item for another. When a person's status changes, his or her impression of the classification of a product also changes.

A product can move from the specialty goods classification to the convenience goods designation if it becomes more available, better known, and gains consumer acceptance. It is more difficult, though, to move an item from the convenience goods group to the specialty goods category. Nostalgia items, memorabilia, and antiques, however, are some of the items that have gone this route in their quest for exclusivity and consumer demand.

Your merchandise assortment will include items from all of the three classifications mentioned. The effective merchandising of the store's total assortment will depend on your ability to recognize these differences and to develop a means of catering to the variations in your store's overall strategy.

THE CHANGING CONSUMER MARKET IN CANADA

Any discussion of the management of a retail enterprise must by necessity involve an analysis of the changes which are taking place in the consumer market. Since the customer is the primary reason for the continued existence of any retail store, significant changes in this market must be constantly monitored to determine the effect on the store's operation.

In order to look at the environment of the independent retailer, it is necessary to be concerned with the changes that are occurring in both the population and the income of the country. For a retail store to prosper, it must have willing customers who have the purchasing power necessary to satisfy their needs and wants. The following paragraphs analyze the implications that population and income shifts might have on your retail operation.

General Population Growth

While the total Canadian population has been increasing, the rapid growth experienced during the 1950s has been reduced to an overall expansion of approximately 2% per annum. Thus, we are likely to have a total population of some 26 million people by the mid-1980s.

While independent retailers are more concerned with the growth rate of their communities, making comparisons with the country as a whole will provide you with the basis for more effective management decisions. General increases in the overall population of the country and a particular community will signify a resultant increase in the demands for food and clothing. The current general increase in population has been the basis for optimism in the consumer market and the continued growth of the retail sector of the Canadian economy.

However, while the population has continued to expand, not all retailers have shared equally in this growth. In order to more effectively prepare for future expansion of our economy, a knowledge and understanding of the changing character of this population is vital to the successful merchant.

Population Shifts

Just as the population growth has not been shared equally by all retailers, the expansion has also varied by province, by city, and by sections of the same city. The provinces of British Columbia, Alberta, Ontario, and Quebec have shown the greatest growth, with the concentration of the Canadian population in the latter two provinces.

However, an analysis of the shifts in population in Canada reveals that the market in the last 25 years has moved from essentially a rural market to an overwhelming concentration in urban centres. Further shifting has caused significant implications to the retailer, as consumers have opted since the mid-1950s for a suburban environment. This explosion of suburbia, coupled with the impact of the automobile, has played a very significant role in the establishment, growth, and success of many retail operations.

It is essential that you carefully note these shifts to determine if the composition of your market is changing and subsequently to determine if an alternative location for your operation is now required. Many retailers who have avoided this analysis have found that the market has shifted without them—resulting in declining sales and profits for their stores.

Changes in Age Groups

Every retailer must be concerned with the trends in population changes that result in variations in the growth of the different age groups which constitute the market. The merchant catering to the teenager, the young executive, or the senior citizen, will be greatly affected by changes in the size of these groups in the community.

Statistics, forecasts, and analyses have shown the following changes anticipated through the 1980s in the Canadian market. They are presented to alert you to study the factors that make up your communities and subsequently your market.

Under 5 Years of Age The size of this market will obviously depend on the fertility rate, with variations in the family size seriously affecting it. This market must constantly be reassessed by you, as changes in the fertility rate will affect the store's merchandise assortment. Such changes will affect the potential for such items as baby food, toys, baby clothing, and such facilities as day care centres and nursery schools.

5-14 Years of Age (Elementary School) The current decline in this market in Canada has been noticed in the educational system, in the sale of sporting goods for this age group, and in the formation of such activities as hockey leagues, Guides, and Scouts.

While this market is showing a moderate decline, the rising affluence of Canadian consumers has made more disposable dollars available by way of larger allowances for these children. As such, this group will have money to spend on soft drinks, potato chips, records, and many other items. In addition, the increasing awareness of the 10- to 14-year-olds to fashion should affect the market for up-to-date styles in clothing and accessories. The market is filled with examples, from jeans to skateboards, that have caught on with this group and subsequently moved to older age groups.

15-19 Years of Age (Teenagers)   The secondary school population has begun to show a decline in the late 1970s as a result of the low birth rate experienced during the 1960s. This will have widespread implications for the retail merchant.

As consumers, teenagers are interested in variety and uniqueness in their selections. As a result, many boutiques during the teen boom experienced such success that large mass-merchandise stores developed special departments to cater to these consumers.

With this market, records, sports equipment, cameras, cars, and apparel have done exceptionally well during the 1970s. Despite the fact that this market will decline during the 1980s, its members will want to be recognized as individuals with constantly changing needs and wants. A growing number of teens have been staying in school because they seek the economic advantages of an education, and because of the lack of employment opportunities for the unskilled dropout.

20-24 Years of Age (College)   The college market will continue to make great demands on society with regard to the high unemployment rate, the values of a higher education, and the economic structure itself. Social trends also become extremely important in evaluating this market. Their lifestyle decisions regarding marriage and establishing households will play a very significant role in the marketing and merchandising of many items requiring discretionary income.

Generally, this group is interested in clothes, automobiles, travel, and entertainment. Their higher level of education and broader experiences will influence their tastes and value scales. As a result, quality and style in the merchandise assortment is important.

25-44 Years of Age (Family Market)   This group represents the fastest growing age group in Canada, with large purchasing requirements for the total family. Whether these young people marry and have children at the same rate as earlier generations, the sheer increase in their numbers will guarantee a rapidly growing family market.

Whatever changes occur, the family market will continue to engage in heavy consumption of food, clothing, appliances, home furnishings, and cars. In addition, those in this age group without the responsibilities of a family will have more discretionary purchasing power and different consumption patterns than their counterparts with families. This age group, with its rising affluence, will continue to offer independent retailers their greatest potential for growth during the next decade.

45-64 Years of Age (Mature Market) This age group has generally been characterized as having more than one income earner in the household. The increasing number of women who have entered the labour force, and the possibility of working siblings, create higher family incomes. In addition, adult earning power tends to reach its peak at this age, while family responsibilities have been greatly reduced. Consequently, high discretionary spending tends to be evident with the mature market.

In general, these consumers will establish demands for more personal hobbies, travel, participation in community activities, and for entertainment and cultural interests. With the additional discretionary dollars available as a result of limited family responsibilities, this group also seeks to refurnish their homes, may purchase services rather than do-it-yourself items, and may opt for the convenient advantages of apartment life as their occupancy requirements are altered by family size.

Over 65 Years of Age (Seniors) Our senior citizens represent the second largest growth market among the Canadian population. As long as this age group does not have its spending power eroded by inflationary pressures, a significant combined purchasing power can be attributed to these consumers.

As consumers, their expenditures tend to be concentrated on food, clothing, shelter, and health care. Their discretionary purchases tend to centre around hobbies, travel, and the role of being a grandparent.

Changes in Income

The market for your merchandise is determined by both people and their ability to purchase your products. While the significant changes in the Canadian population have been noted, you should also notice that both personal disposable and personal discretionary income has been increasing in Canada over the last several years.

Personal disposable income refers to the income the customer has available to spend after deductions have been made by the employer for personal income taxes, pension plans, unemployment insurance, and other fringe benefits. Personal discretionary income represents the income available after the purchase of the basic necessities of food and shelter. On this basis, merchants of food products must be concerned with analyzing the changes in their markets' disposable income. On the other hand, the retailer of sporting goods, appliances, or clothing observes closely the discretionary purchasing power of the store's customers. In many market segments of this country, retailers have discovered that discretionary income is increasing at a faster rate than disposable dollars, and consequently their customers have more income to spend on non-basics.

Consumers have historically shown variations in their spending and saving patterns as their income increases. Engel's law illustrates that as income increases, 1. the proportion of income spent for food decreases; 2. housing and household operation remain in about the same proportion; 3. the proportion spent for clothing, automobiles, recreation, and education increases; and 4. the proportion which is saved increases. (B. S. Loeb, "The Use of Engel's Law as a Basis for Predicting Consumer Expenditures," *Journal of Marketing*, XX:1 [1955], p. 23.)

Alert retailers attempt to adapt these principles of expenditure patterns to their analysis of the target market they have selected for their stores. Such adaptions may result in trading up to better quality goods as income increases or alternately trading down to meet the demands of their market segment.

You must be concerned with changes in income in the selection of the location for your retail store. The income per family, the discretionary income, and the various income groups will all affect the importance of a trading area for your merchandise assortment.

In general, then, you must be aware of what is happening in the country as a whole, but most importantly, you must be able to analyze the trends in the community you've opted to serve with your store. Valuable information can be obtained from the municipal offices, the local chamber of commerce, local media, and the trade associations that cater to the various merchandise lines. The information is available; it is to your advantage to employ the facts in operating your store.

The merchant operating in today's environment must accept the challenge of being able to serve the customer well in light of the rapid changes being encountered. Such a challenge can best be answered by the creative and analytical abilities of the retailer in determining the appeals that can be made to the various lifestyles of the different customer groups.

3

RETAIL STORE
LOCATION FACTORS

It has frequently been stated that good retail locations will often overcome deficiencies in management, but poor locations will seriously handicap even the most skillful merchandisers. To a large extent the location selected for the operation of the retail firm will determine the volume of sales that can be realized and the subsequent profits that can be generated. The success of many small independent retailers is virtually dependent upon their ability to obtain a desirable site for their operations. Yet, for the most part, independents have opened up their stores where space has been available rather than as a result of any planning or analyzing. This chapter offers you some insight into the various factors that you should consider in evaluating your present location or potential location for future store units.

LOCATIONAL CHANGES

It should be emphasized that the discussions which involve the selection of a site for a retail store are not restricted to the opening of new outlets. Population shifts, the development of suburban shopping centres, and changes in the buying habits and motives of consumers can seriously affect the compatibility of an existing store with its immediate market area. The history of retailing is filled with examples of retail stores which have been literally stranded in the downtown core while their market moved to suburban areas. In some of these cases the core of the city has been left to deteriorate, and as a result so have the sales and profits of merchants who have opted to remain in these locations. I will discuss the efforts which are presently underway to improve these downtown shopping districts of our towns and cities in a later chapter.

Ideally, locations should be evaluated at frequent intervals to determine if they are meeting the firm's expectations at the present time and to estimate their impact on future sales and profits. Constant reassessment of a store's location must also be applied to the community in which you have chosen to do business. I have chosen to analyze the community factors of location before evaluating the specific site for the retail operation.

CHOOSING THE COMMUNITY

In many cases the independent retailer is at a serious disadvantage when choosing a city in which to locate an operation. While large firms engage in expensive scientific location research, the independent frequently selects a community on the basis of climate, health, relatives, or the general environment. Some independent retailers have successfully capitalized on their stores' size by locating in communities where their large-scale counterparts do not go because of the limited population concentration in the area. Many retailers across this country have chosen locations in communities which have provided them with very successful operations.

Nevertheless, while independents generally rely on intuitive reasoning for selecting a community in which to locate, an analysis of the following criteria may lead you to more accurately assess, plan, and operate an outlet as a successful store unit for many years. Much of the information required for community evaluation is available from your local chamber of commerce, municipal office, local newspaper and other advertising media, trade associations, manufacturers, wholesalers, and local bankers and business people.

Social Characteristics of the Community

Population The number of people that can be expected to buy clothing, food, and shelter represents for the retailer the store's potential customers, the trading population, the market. But knowledge of those currently living in the area is not sufficient information to evaluate a community. It is much more useful to determine whether the population has been increasing, decreasing, or has remained constant. Obviously, if the population has been increasing, with other factors remaining equal, the sales of the retail store can also be expected to increase. Therefore, the merchant who finds a community which has been increasing— over a period of years—faster than the population of other areas of the country in general, may have found an ideal location for a store. An understanding and analysis of the reasons for these changes in the community's population will allow the merchant to make a more effective analysis of the area as a profitable site for a store.

Much like the consumer market, the community must be evaluated through the consideration of the age groups within the total population. While the importance of the various age groups will be dependent upon the goods being carried, it has been established that the larger the concentration of young people in the community, the more active is its purchasing commitment. In contrast to the older population, younger people are frequently considered to be heavy consumers for most products. Therefore, it will be to your advantage to determine what proportion of the community's population is concentrated in each of the various age groups.

From these factors and the other characteristics of the population of the community, you should be able to develop an effective demographic profile of the potential market. From this analysis you can select a target market for the store. The breakdown of the population by sex, ethnic origin, religion, marital status, education, occupation, age, and similar characteristics can be of particular significance to various retail stores when a trading area is being considered. It is to the advantage of all merchants to analyze the trading areas of their communities to determine their composition and potential as store locations. Obviously, the more retailers know about their population mixes, the more successful will they be in meeting their requirements as retailers of goods and services.

Feature Attractions The trading area that attracts people from unusual distances offers you as a retailer a more economical market for your store. Consumers can be attracted to these communities for such features as resort and recreational facilities, festivals, museums, zoos, universities, historical monuments, theatres, and special topographical features of the area. These and many other community elements have been responsible for increasing the size of the flow of customers into a trading area.

It is important for you, though, to analyze these attractions on the basis of the traffic that is generated on a seasonal basis only.

Such fluctuations will seriously affect the merchandising strategy of any retailer who opens a store in an area such as this.

Community Progressiveness Communities that have an active and progressive chamber of commerce, an effective industrial commissioner seeking new industry, and adequate school systems provide an effective environment for a retail store. More specifically, the activities of the merchants' association of the community are vital in promoting the facilities of the trading area, especially in light of the heavy competition being generated by the suburban shopping centres. Such activity and progressiveness is important to the retailer who opts for a downtown location and who subsequently becomes concerned with the plans that have been made for rejuvenating the area as a shopping district.

This progressiveness is generally indicated in a community by the attitude and interest of local government, school, and civic projects, and the activities of business associations.

Economic Characteristics of the Community

Industry Composition In order to ensure an adequate volume of sales and profits for the store, it is necessary to determine the source of the income of the consumers in the trading area. The number, type, and character of the industries in the community will determine the amount and stability of the population's income. Generally, it is much more advisable to seek a location in a community with a diversified industrial base rather than one which depends on one industry or one firm for its employment.

In addition, it is important to note the growth potential of these industries, since an expanding industry will obviously benefit the sales of the merchants in the community. In this analysis, you should also observe that industries involved in the production of durable goods may be characterized by wide fluctuations in sales. This can seriously affect the potential of the retailers in the immediate area, as layoffs and slowdowns occur.

Income The purchasing power of the people in the area is perhaps the single most important factor in qualifying a community as a place in which to locate a retail store. Statistics have shown that the total retail sales in an area are closely related to the purchasing ability of the population, since the income received by the people becomes the retailers' potential sales dollars.

To the retailer, the dispersion of wealth among the various income groups in the community plays a significant role in determining the potential sales and profit opportunities. In this evaluation of the income of the trading area, you attempt to determine the proportion of consumers in each of the various income groups, the extent of disposable and discretionary income, and the overall family income of members of the community. Only in this way are you able to determine the profitability of your proposed target market, and your means of appealing to this market.

Competition   Retail firms seeking a community in which to locate a store must also analyze the quantity and quality of competition that exists in the area. As a result of the increasing incidence of scramble merchandising—in which retailers carry merchandise outside of their major lines—all retailers selling similar items to those planned by the prospective merchant must be surveyed for their degree of competition.

In this analysis and evaluation of competition, similar stores must be carefully scrutinized to determine the services offered, their ability to react to the present and future demands of the consumers, and their merchandising techniques in general. In this way, you will be able to capitalize on your store's competitors' weaknesses and to seek more effective methods of combatting their strengths.

Miscellaneous Factors   You should be concerned with the facilitating services available in the community that will allow you to effectively execute your merchandising strategy. The adequacy of the banking system, the availability of various media for promotional purposes, and the economics of acquiring and transporting merchandise into a store's inventory are some of the facilities required in the community to allow for the implementation of the merchandising strategy.

SELECTING A SITE WITHIN A COMMUNITY

In the past several years, changes have taken place in the structure and position of locations as well as in the shopping patterns of consumers that will significantly affect the location of your retail store. Historically, location has always played a very important part in the merchandising strategy, but the sites which were allocated for this purpose also served the consumer in other ways.

In almost all early towns and cities, and to some extent those of today, such merchandising areas provided the communal meeting place where social, political, and ceremonial activities took place. This fact has become relevant in today's planning and design of the promotional activities of the downtown areas and the modern shopping centres. Interestingly, the most successful retailing districts have been those which have initiated a series of events and activities which generate a great deal of consumer participation.

Every town or city has designated specific districts or centres where retail activity is permitted to take place. The smaller the community, the fewer choices will be available to the merchant, since some small towns only have a shopping district on their main street which is only two blocks long. At the other extreme, large metropolitan areas offer you an enormous range of possibilities in selecting a specific site for a retail unit.

In an effort to analyze the various alternatives available to you, site locations have been conveniently classified into the central business district, string-street locations, and suburban shopping centres.

Central Business District

The effectiveness of the downtown area of each community as a retail site location depends on the impact that the suburban shopping centre has had on the purchasing patterns of the area's consumers. For many years, the hub of business activity of the town or city has been concentrated in the central business district. Much of this has been changing over the past 25 years, due to new developments which have taken place in the suburban areas of our cities and towns.

Traditionally, department stores and other large retail establishments joined the financial and governmental institutions in establishing the importance of the downtown area as a shopping district. In the larger towns and cities, great concentrations of workers enter and leave the core area every day by public transportation or private car. To this group is added the large number of shoppers, both residents and tourists, who patronize the downtown core each day. As a result, this shopping district exhibits a high degree of consumer activity during the business hours of the six-day week.

In addition to the commercial, financial, and governmental services available in the central business district, the entertainment, cultural, and convention facilities of most of the larger cities tend to be concentrated in the core area. On the basis of this activity, the majority of business in the downtown area is designated as local business coming from people living or working in the central business district. A slightly smaller proportion of business tends to come from the metropolitan area, or consumers living within the metro boundaries who make infrequent visits to the downtown area to shop. The remaining business that is generated in the core area tends to be regional, made up of consumers living outside of the metropolitan area who visit and shop in the area on occasional trips to the city.

As developments change our towns and cities, the bulk of the business will continue to be local. In the past two decades much of the metropolitan downtown business has been intercepted by the large suburban complexes. However, in those communities where the downtown areas have been rejuvenated and have projected a unique image, regional consumers and additional metro customers have sought to patronize the retailers in these areas.

In most downtown areas where commercial activity has remained a vital element of the core of the community, retail space is at a premium. As a result, the rental or purchase rates for such sites continue to escalate, requiring your careful analysis with regard to the potential profitability of the location. In general, these factors tend to restrict prime locations in downtown to merchandise lines that will generate a high sales-productivity ratio per square foot of selling space. At the other extreme, retailers of bulky items like furniture, automobiles, or building and lumber supplies should avoid the high rent locations of the core area. The retailer must first determine the restrictions imposed by the by-laws of the community designating where retailing activity may take place. You will note that in the downtown areas of some communities, furniture or automobile dealers do operate. In such cases, possibly these prime locations have been owned by the operator for many years, making it an economical site for the firm.

String-Street Locations

String-street locations for retail stores developed in towns and cities as a result of the population growth and the dispersion of these consumers over a broader trading area. As the population moved to residential areas away from the downtown core, retail shopping facilities began to appear on the main thoroughfares leading from the central business district to these newer populated districts.

On the basis that these retail areas developed to intercept customers on their purchasing expeditions to the downtown areas, these string-street locations became known as the interceptor rings of the decentralization of the city. In addition, further retail space became available on neighbourhood streets to satisfy the needs of the consumers in the immediate vicinity. Both of these developments of decentralization had a significant impact on intercepting the business that was destined for the downtown shopping area.

In many of the larger towns and cities, such string-street developments ultimately expanded until they became a mere extension of the older shopping district. Because of these interceptor rings, merchants have been provided with sites for selling merchandise in a more limited assortment than is normally available in the major shopping areas of the city. As a result, independent merchants have found these locations to be particularly advantageous to their needs and goals since their overhead tends to be low, their market easy to define, and their locations readily available to customers.

Jug milk stores, dry cleaners, restaurants, drug stores, service stations, and similar operations tend to constitute the bulk of retail establishments operating on string-street locations. But many other types of retail establishments also locate in these areas in an effort to capitalize on the advantages of the interceptor location.

Suburban Shopping Centres

The suburban shopping centre has been the most significant institution through which decentralization of the urban retail trade has proceeded. The shopping centre has generated continual discussions and evaluations among retailers regarding the economies of various store locations.

Unlike other retail sites, the suburban shopping centre is planned, developed, and designed as a unit with a minimum of five retail establishments operating during any part of the current year. In this Statistics Canada definition a requirement also ensures the proportion of free parking that will be made available to patrons of the centre. In addition, shopping centres have attempted to avoid the pitfalls of other site locations by requiring all tenants of the centre to belong to the merchants' association. Such a requirement is specified in the lease and is designed to ensure the co-operative promotion of the total centre. In this way most suburban shopping centres are able to more effectively generate traffic than other retail locations where the area merchants are neither organized nor concerned with co-operative efforts.

While the development of suburban shopping centres has largely been attributed to the population shifts in the 1950s and the increased ownership of cars, its growth has continued at a spectacular rate throughout the country. From the first shopping centre in Vancouver in 1950, these merchandising complexes grew to 664 in 1973 and accounted for approximately 20% of the total retail sales in Canada. Their effect throughout the country has been felt in various ways, by both consumers and retailers.

No two shopping centres are alike, since each has been designed to best serve its particular trading area. However, in an effort to analyze the effect of shopping centres on the site locations for retailers and their impact on the consumer, Statistics Canada, in *Shopping Centres in Canada, 1951-1973*, (Cat. No. 63-527, Appendix A), has classified all centres into one of the three types listed below.

Neighbourhood Centres   These are centres with five to 15 retail establishments, providing the everyday needs of the people in the immediate vicinity. In this type of centre, the emphasis is placed on food and other convenience goods that will satisfy the wants and needs of the neighbourhood. As a result, such centres can operate efficiently and economically with a population of approximately 5000 people. In the neighbourhood centre a fairly large proportion of the consumers walk to the centre.

Community Centres   These complexes have 16 to 30 retail establishments serving a wider area than the neighbourhood centre, and drawing on markets of up to 50,000 people. Such centres usually contain one or two major tenants such as a chain variety store, a supermarket, or a discount department store. An assortment of smaller specialty stores and convenience goods stores round out the tenant mix. More customers are likely to drive to the community centre than would drive to the neighbourhood centre.

Regional Centres   These shopping centres have more than 30 retail establishments operating during any part of the current year and serve as many as one million people, with many from outside the immediate community. Such centres correspond to the downtown shopping districts, supplying once-a-year as well as day-to-day needs of the patrons. Good-sized department stores, chain stores, and supermarkets are a natural part of such centres.

Ancillary Centres In addition to the three traditional types of suburban shopping centres, you will notice the development in most of the cities in this country of shopping centres in the downtown area.

These centres have been referred to as ancillary centres, or downtown malls. They differ from the conventional shopping centre in that they are located downtown rather than in suburbia, they do not necessarily have an anchor store, free parking is not provided to the patrons, and the majority of outlets are not entered directly from the street.

Such centres must have at least ten retail and service establishments located in a complex which has usually been designed for some other purpose such as offices, apartments, hotels, or carrier stations.

While these are the various types of shopping centres that have been developing in Canada, it should be obvious that tremendous changes have taken place in these complexes since their inception in 1950. The regional centres are getting larger, with many well over the hundred-store mark and others reaching close to 300 retail and service establishments under one roof. In addition, some of the older regional and community centres are beginning to enlarge their facilities and to enclose the plaza in order to become more competitive with the newer facilities.

The neighbourhood centre, which provides the day-to-day needs of the consumer, has also continued to represent the largest number of shopping centres in Canada. Such centres represent over 60% of all centres in this country and are likely to continue to be a dominant factor because of their convenient nature. Since they depend on walk-in trade, the neighbourhood centre has found it economical to locate in new residential areas and near high-rise apartment developments. Also, many such centres have moved into smaller towns and communities where the impact of the shopping centre has yet to be felt and where the downtown area remains the only shopping facility for the population.

In the midst of this growth is the community centre which has had difficulty competing with the large drawing power of the regional centres and the convenience and accessibility of the neighbourhood centres. As a result, some community centres have chosen to expand their facilities and improve their tenant mix to establish the characteristics and drawing potential of the larger regional centres. While not always economical or advisable, the community centre, in its efforts to survive, has opened up site locations to independent merchants who previously found it difficult to secure locations in the large regional centre.

While statistics have shown that the regional centres have expanded greatly in the past and have received a great deal of publicity with each opening, their continued rapid growth may be somewhat restricted for a number of reasons. Rigid zoning by-laws, obtaining adequate mortgage financing for these costly ventures, and the large population required to support these centres are some of the significant factors which will impede their development. Such large centres require well-known department stores as their anchor tenants, but since Eaton's, Simpsons, Sears, and the Bay are now fairly represented in most market areas, their expansion to additional units may be difficult to induce. Therefore, in some metropolitan areas, we have reached the saturation point of the large regional centres. Both the land-owners' and the retailers' objective in these locations will now be to make each of their units more productive.

Much of what has been said with regard to the growth and development of suburban shopping centres is centred upon the large retailer as opposed to the independent merchant. This has been especially true regarding the ability of the independent merchant to obtain a site in a new regional centre. However, it should be noted that in the future large regional centres will have to attempt to attract more independent merchants into their complexes to provide some individuality in their tenant mix. Generally, the large shopping centres in this country have been filled with the same merchants, so that the various regional centres offer the consumer little in the way of a unique shopping experience.

The process of attracting independents into shopping centres in the future is likely to be hampered by the increased construction costs, the soaring real estate taxes, and the ensuing rental rates that will need to be charged. But shopping centre developers have begun to realize that it will be necessary to attract that unique and fresh approach to retailing that the independent can offer. Therefore, developers must seek new ways to make it economical for independent merchants to take locations in these centres.

LOCATIONAL CRITERIA

The principles for selecting a site for a retail store are essentially the same as those used to determine the location of a suburban shopping centre. But because of the size and nature of the facility required by independent retailers, only those principles that relate to these operations will be discussed. There are many sophisticated techniques and formulas used by developers of shopping centres to establish the potential of the complex. But the basics of accessibility, possibility of interception, prominence of location, character of the neighbourhood, and traffic must all be taken into consideration by both the independent merchant and the large shopping centre developer. In most cases the independent is faced with acquiring an existing space rather than undertaking the problems encountered in the selection of a site on which to build.

In analyzing the factors which affect the selection of a site for a retail store, you will note that the criteria reaffirm those elements evaluated when choosing the community in which to locate.

Population In analyzing the existing and future population, it is important for you to determine the relative proportion of pedestrian traffic in comparison with those who will drive to the site. Apartment buildings or large residential complexes next to the store will play a large role in generating walk-in trade and hence will lessen the dependence on parking facilities.

Car Ownership If the families in general have two cars per household, both spouses will theoretically have six days of shopping available to them. In cases where one or the other spouse works in an industrial area isolated from stores, shopping will generally be limited to evenings and Saturdays. In locations where the automobile plays a significant role in the purchasing habits of consumers, parking facilities will have to be available.

Personal Income The personal income of the population in the area will tend to signify the character of the neighbourhood and the quality of the image and merchandise assortment to be presented to the market. An analysis of the income groups of the total population is more useful to an independent seeking a site in a smaller community than in a large metropolitan area.

Personal Expenditures An examination of the spending patterns of the consumers in the trading area tends to indicate the proportions of the consumers' income which is being dispersed among the various merchandise categories. With this information, you should be able to assess the potential sales volume the store may secure.

Retail Competition   While independent merchants are concerned with the type and nature of existing competition in their trading area, they must make every effort to attempt to determine the potential competition that might arise. By using the facilities of the municipal planning offices, they may be better able to prepare for future developments of shopping centres that will present additional competition to their store.

Accessibility   One of the primary criteria in selecting a site for a retail store or shopping centre is the accessibility to the operation. Ideally, a shopping centre should be located as close as possible to major transportation routes and, ideally, at the intersection of these arterial roads. The ability of a store to handle vehicular and pedestrian traffic, the facilities available for delivery to and from the store, and the location of traffic signals play important roles in determining site accessibility. In addition, the availability of parking as a significant motivator of accessibility is being demanded on the basis of the competitive pressures of the suburban shopping centres.

Local By-Laws and Zoning Regulations   In many areas the local by-laws and zoning regulations specify parking ratios to gross ground floor areas, types of businesses that can and cannot be operated in certain areas, and hours that retail establishments may open for business in specified locations. Since these municipal restrictions, as well as others on the books, may affect the merchandising strategy of a retailer, awareness of these factors will assist the entrepreneur in determining the desirability of the site.

Cumulative Pull   This principle has been established and used extensively in the merchandising strategy of most of the large regional shopping centres as a means of attracting customers to the complex. The premise is that a group of stores will exercise a cumulative drawing power far exceeding the sum of their individual appeals. Shopping centres with two large department stores, for example, will attract many more customers than centres with only one department store. Similarly, independent retail stores which have located close to other merchants with complementary or supplementary lines experience a significant cumulative pull on their trading area to this site. The degree of their cumulative attraction depends on how well balanced the tenant mix is.

Negative Factors Pedestrian interruptions are negative factors which must be considered in assessing the suitability of a site for a retail store. Dead spots, driveways and other physical breaks in the sidewalks, as well as cross traffic, either vehicular or pedestrian, can seriously reduce the effectiveness of a store site. Areas that are identified with hazard, noise, odour, unsightliness, pornography, vagrancy, or other pedestrian-inhibiting qualities provide less than desirable sites for retailers. Finally, business firms whose customers' average parking time is extremely long seriously affect the accessibility of other retail firms located in the area.

TYPES OF RETAIL SITES

The selection of a site for a retail store will to a large extent depend on the type and nature of the merchandise lines carried. When the merchandise assortment is compared to the purchasing habits of the customers decisions regarding location are made more accurate. Following are three categories of types of retail sites.

Generative Business

A retail operation designated as a generative business represents one to which the consumer is directly attracted with the express purpose of shopping at that location. Supermarkets, home improvement centres, automobile service centres, and lawn and garden operations are all types of generative businesses which attract the consumer directly from home. For this reason a retail store which classifies itself as a generative business will not require a prime location for its operation.

Recipient Business

This operation is one to which consumers are impulsively or coincidentally attracted while away from their places of residence for any purpose other than shopping at that store. The recipient retail business tends to receive rather than generate its own patrons. The primary examples of such operations are the cigar store in hotels, newspaper stands in airports, and drug stores in office buildings. Such merchants tend to feed off the population which is in the area for other reasons and which patronizes the store because of convenience. The independent merchant selling items designated essentially as recipient in nature will seek the best and generally most expensive location since the store depends on other operations to draw the population to the area.

Shared Business

In general, most retail stores represent some combination of these two types of businesses. They neither totally generate nor do they completely receive business. Apparel, hardware, department, and sporting goods stores are all examples of merchandising units that generally combine the elements of both generative and recipient businesses.

RENT-ADVERTISING RATIO

To determine the importance of a site for a retail store with relation to the type of business designation, a rent-advertising ratio has been established. This principle simply states that rent and advertising are reciprocal items in a retail store's operating budget. The higher the percentage of money spent on advertising, the lower the percentage of money which can be spent on rent, and vice versa.

The application of this principle is appropriately related to the type of business classification of a retail store. Since location is vital to the success of the recipient business, the proportion of money spent on rent or occupancy will far exceed the proportion spent on advertising. You will note that many recipient businesses, in fact, spend little or no money on advertising. The opposite applies to the truly generative business, where location is less vital, and rent is not as high. For the majority of retail firms, a blending of advertising and rent is required to effect the optimum drawing potential for the store.

THE 100% LOCATION

Retailers generally talk about finding the best location for their operation. The 100% location has been defined as the most ideal location from every point of view for that particular store. Each retailer must judge each site on this basis and select that which comes closest to satisfying the requirements for the store.

Proximity to similar stores, corner locations, the side of the street, terms of the lease, condition of the building, and similar factors all play important roles in determining the value of the site for the retail merchant.

Consequently, the recipient business seeking the best possible location will be prepared to pay the premium rental to secure what is considered to be the 100% location.

OCCUPANCY TERMS

As previously indicated, the terms of occupancy will play a significant role in establishing the desirability of a particular site for a retail store. Many existing independent retailers operating small stores or located in small communities own their own store buildings, but the majority of retail merchants are required to lease premises for the operation of their businesses.

Retailers have tended to lease rather than own the space since it has been assumed that the funds designated for real estate can be more effectively appropriated to merchandising strategies. In addition, the changing values of retail locations have prompted merchants to take the more flexible position of leasing space.

Lease Variations

There are two common types of leases that appear in the rental of retail space. One lease requires the payment of a fixed amount of rent per month or year, while the other type calls for a payment of a percentage of the retailer's gross sales as rent.

Of the two lease alternatives, you will find that in the new shopping facilities, and certainly in the larger communities, the percentage lease has become almost standard in the leasing of retail space. Such a lease may require the tenant to pay a specified percentage of the store's gross sales with no minimum and no maximum dollar amount designated as the annual rental charge. However, in the more common percentage leases, a retailer is required to pay a percentage of the sales over a specified minimum rental charge, which has been calculated on the basis of the amount of square feet occupied. Thus, the merchant who has leased 2000 square feet at $10 per square foot is committed to a minimum rental of $20,000 per annum. If the lease also stipulates a percentage clause of 7% above the minimum, the break-through sales figure will be approximately $285,715.

Therefore, should this merchant achieve a sales volume of $350,000, the annual rental payment for this period would be $24,500 or $4500 greater than the minimum stipulated in the lease.

The principal advantage of the percentage lease is that it makes the occupancy expense of the store's operating statement a variable item rather than fixed. As a result, when business improves the retailer will be required to pay higher rent and the landowner will share in this prosperity.

Arguments are generally raised from both sides on the advisability of percentage leases. Merchants generally prefer fixed rental leases where they are confident of their ability to produce a large volume of sales, while owners prefer the percentage lease with a minimum rental, for obvious reasons. It would seem realistic to assume that the inflationary pressures will result in an increasing popularity of the percentage lease among all landowners in the future.

Rental Rate Variations

You must also be aware of the fact that the rental rates for space available will vary with each site and within different uses for the same space. Varying profit margins and different sales volumes place merchants in negotiating positions with different leverages.

The rental rates for these sites may vary with the space productivity of the merchant. A retailer who is able to achieve high sales per square foot of selling space will be able to negotiate a better rate based on the percentage return to the landowner. Also, entrepreneurs owning businesses of a recipient nature are willing to pay a higher rental rate to achieve the 100% location.

Another variation in rental rates that has received significant attention in many shopping centre leases has been the services provided and the extra charges to the tenant. Such variations are now being adopted by owners of other retail space. In many cases the retailer is required to occupy the building as it is, whether it be a new structure or the re-lease of an old one. Depending on the capabilities of the tenant and the policy of the landowner, a completion allowance for the store interior on a square foot basis may be negotiated, causing a variation in the rental rates.

In addition to the rental rate per square foot, landowners are now attempting to obtain leases on a net, net basis. Such a lease requires that the tenant, on the basis of the square footage occupied, pay the store's share of all utilities, maintenance of common areas including parking lots, real estate taxes on the complex, and membership in the merchants' association for group promotion. While these items are required under the terms of a lease in a shopping centre, many of the factors included here have been adopted by the landowners of free-standing units and retail store sites in the downtown and string-street shopping districts, as well.

This implies that in the larger centres especially, the frequency of the net, net lease is increasing. The amount of space available in the community for retail use will determine the impact of the negotiations on the rental rates between the owner and the tenant.

It should also be stressed here that those tenants who the landowner seeks, particularly in a shopping centre, to act as anchor stores and to provide drawing power to the complex are able to negotiate more favourable rental rates and lease terms than other retailers. Since the independent merchant generally is not in this position when seeking a location in a shopping centre, the small retailer will be required to pay a premium rental until the store has established itself as a viable operation.

Duration of Leases

Independent retailers in downtown or string-street locations of smaller communities tend to sign short-term leases of five years or less. In retail areas which have been designated as prime locations, and certainly in the larger shopping centres, leases of less than ten years are rarely available. On buildings which have been designed and constructed for a particular retail tenant, a lease exceeding 15 years may be common.

While some retailers tend to lease premises on a month-to-month basis, this form of occupancy generally only occurs in sites of questionable value or with the very small retailer.

In your negotiations of the length of the lease be cognizant of the fact that demolition clauses are beginning to appear in many leases. Such clauses give the owner of the property the right to terminate the lease with specific notice given to you, so that demolition of the premises can take place. In downtown and string-street areas where redevelopment and rejuvenation is occurring, such clauses are common and deserve the attention of the merchant seeking space.

TRENDS IN RETAIL LOCATIONS

In recent years new developments have been taking place in the environment in which retailers operate. These factors have led to changes, innovations, and opportunities for the independent merchants in their selection of a location for their retail store. While the developments vary considerably within each provincial jurisdiction and specifically within each community, the trends which are discussed below will have serious implications for evaluating sites for retail stores in almost all areas of the country, both now and in the future.

Rejuvenation of the Central Business District

The decentralization of urban retail trade had such a significant impact on the deterioration of the downtown areas of most communities that efforts are now being made at all levels to restore the prominence of the core area as the primary business district.

Much of the declining importance of the downtown has been attributed to the advantages perceived by the consumer to shopping in the suburban centres. Accessibility difficulties by customers, limited parking, traffic congestion, high occupancy costs of land, building, and taxes, as well as the general deterioration of the older building structures have led to the lack of support given to our core areas. In some communities, the central business district has all but disappeared, as both large and small merchants have vacated the premises and moved to the outlying areas. In other cases landowner-tenant situations exist in which neither party is willing to undertake the expenses involved in restoration or improvement of the premises. In those communities where major retail establishments vacate the core, the drawing power of the central business district as a primary shopping area has been seriously weakened.

However, in many towns and cities the downtown merchants, in co-operation with municipal and provincial governments, are making efforts to restore and increase the attractiveness of shopping downtown. Direct transportation routes to the heart of the city, improved public transit services, better parking facilities, and the general beautification of the area have all been instrumental in revitalizing interest in the retail sector of the core. In the larger metropolitan areas, major department stores, financial institutions, and developers have played significant roles in attracting a larger shopping population to the core by the construction of modern shopping complexes in these areas. Communities like Toronto, Montreal, Halifax, Ottawa, Sudbury, Winnipeg, and Vancouver have all seen major rejuvenation in their central business districts.

As part of this rejuvenation program, retailers must modernize their stores and merchandising strategies to induce customers to return to their outlets. Too many merchants have operated on the assumption that beautification of the core area alone will increase the sales volume of their stores. While the shopping area is being improved and is attracting a larger number of people, it is the responsibility of the retailers to improve their operations in order to capitalize on this increased potential.

Co-operative efforts will be required by the downtown merchants with regard to joint promotional programs similar to those found in the suburban shopping centres. Perhaps even more than the large-scale retailers with branch outlets in the suburban malls, the independent retailer must take advantage of joint promotions, merchants' associations, and the efforts of the governmental authorities.

While many downtown areas have suffered badly from continual neglect, the downtown business districts in most communities can continue to be vital shopping areas for most consumer goods. However, this will only occur in those communities where the downtown merchants and other local business owners solicit the co-operation of government agencies in their efforts to rejuvenate shopping areas which have been deteriorating for almost a quarter of a century. But in the final analysis, it will be the self-help programs of the merchants in the downtown areas that will return the core and its shops to its previous role as the major shopping area for the population of the community.

Trends in Suburban Shopping Centres

As we noted earlier, the regional shopping centres are getting larger in size and as a result are being restricted in their growth. While these centres only represent 15.2% of the total number of shopping centres in Canada, they account for more than 47% of the retail sales attributed to shopping centres. These large regional centres will most likely continue to take the lion's share of these sales in the future since their population draw is similar to that of the drawing power of the downtown areas. In actual fact, the large regional centres in some metropolitan boroughs have become the downtown areas of the suburban community.

In addition to the great convenience of the neighbourhood centres, their lower capital costs and their smaller population requirements will allow these shopping facilities to increase in number in the future.

The large growth of the ancillary centres in most metropolitan areas has had a significant impact in recent years on the available retail space within the boundaries. Increases in such space has been witnessed in the downtown areas and at the intersections of major transportation and public transit routes. Such locations have provided a built-in market for the retailer in the complex. In some areas a number of these complexes have been connected by underground tunnels, expanding the market potential further and at the same time providing a controlled shopping environment for the consumer. However, you should note that these locations are generally limited in the time of day and days of the week that they can attract customers. Generally, such malls generate the bulk, if not all, of the traffic at lunch hour in office complexes, or after working hours in apartment complexes. Such restrictions are not apparent in those ancillary centres which have a major drawing power outside the complex.

Further developments in suburban shopping centres are noted by retailers as community and regional centres attempt to expand in size and to enclose their facilities to provide a complete climate-controlled mall. In the past few years, many centres have adopted this strategy in their efforts to recapture market share which has been lost to newer shopping centres. This is particularly true in the community centre's fight for survival among the giant centres of today.

Due to the success experienced by the shopping centres in Canada, new centres as well as established areas are making serious efforts to attract more and more independent retailers to provide some individuality to their centres. As more centres open their doors to the small retailer, the merchant will need to determine the optimum location for the store's limited resources.

The constant acceleration of operating costs of the shopping centre—costs which are ultimately passed on to the tenants of the centre—are now being monitored by a joint committee of the Retail Council of Canada and the International Council of Shopping Centres in Canada. This new committee has been established to design guidelines for budgeting common area costs and to investigate a possible system of incentives to encourage shopping-centre developers to minimize these rechargeable costs. This committee is considered to be a major development in the co-operation between owner and tenant for the ultimate benefit of the shopping centre.

Independent retailers seeking locations in suburban shopping centres or the ancillary centres must take careful consideration in their projections of sales and profits. Such opportunities may in many cases seem to be too attractive to reject, but a financial analysis may reveal a commitment far beyond the means or capabilities of the independent. While many small retailers have experienced success operating in suburban shopping centres, a great many have also found themselves overextended and unable to meet the heavy competition and progressiveness of these locations. You must individually assess your requirements and capabilities before committing yourself to a lease in these complexes.

4

PHYSICAL PLANNING
FOR THE RETAIL STORE

Once the site for the retail operation has been selected, you must critically review all of the physical aspects of the store building. Such an analysis is vital to ensure that the store has the characteristics necessary to function profitably. Therefore, the prospective and existing retailer must be concerned with the store planning activities of the exterior and interior design, and the physical layout and presentation of the merchandise assortment.

If you have selected a location in a new shopping centre you will generally find your plans regarding the store different from the merchant who has opted for a site in the downtown or string-street area. Shopping centres generally provide the tenant with three cement block walls and the delivery of essential services to the premises. The merchant is required to complete the store front and the interior—with the basic design requirements needing approval by the developer of the centre. On the other hand, unless it is a new building, the merchant who opts for a downtown location is generally faced with adapting the existing characteristics of the building to the store's requirements. Renovations to existing structures can be very costly unless they have been properly designed and planned. The merchant who opens a store in an older shopping centre may also find renovation problems in the outlet.

Regardless of the situation, the successful merchant will soon discover that effective store design will significantly influence the store's ability to appeal to its designated market segment. In addition, such importance placed on store planning and design pays tribute to the success some merchants have experienced by offering a unique shopping environment. Retailers have also found that the high rates of rent, utilities, taxes, and leasehold improvements have led to the maximum use of the space available for merchandising the inventory.

You should realize that many technical decisions will be required to make the store ready for operation. Such decisions will require the services of architects, interior designers, engineers, and other technical experts. While large retail organizations usually have extensive planning departments, the independent retailer will find such technical assistance available from manufacturers of fixtures and equipment, merchandise suppliers, and trade associations. To ensure that the concepts presented by the specialized counsel satisfy the merchandising strategy of the firm, you must constantly assess the design stages from the retailing point of view. The store plan must provide for the efficient operation of the outlet as well as the aesthetics contributed by the store design.

In this context, the following principles of store planning are outlined to give you the basics of providing your potential customers with an appealing shopping environment. Obviously, these factors need to be continually reviewed by both existing merchants and new retailers. This is particularly true in those communities where rejuvenation of the downtown areas are being undertaken. The merchant who continues to operate an outdated store is merely prolonging the inevitable. Rather, independent merchants should lead the way to store modernization in the improved downtown areas.

Retailing literature is filled with what aspects should constitute a well designed store. "A well designed store is one embodying features that attract customers and facilitates their movement inside the store, provides a pleasant environment in which they may shop, makes possible economical operations and maintenance, and has adequate space for selling and sales-supporting activities currently and in the foreseeable future." (Delbert J. Duncan and Stanley C. Hollander, *Modern Retailing Management, Basic Concepts and Practices* [Illinois: Richard D. Irwin, Inc., 1977], p. 122.) The many elements of this definition of the effectively planned and designed retail outlet will be discussed in the remainder of this chapter.

THE EXTERIOR OF THE BUILDING

The exterior of the building represents the first impression the consumer has of the projected image of the retail store. As a result, the store front should suggest stability and permanence as well as provide an inviting and appealing look that will attract customers on the basis of confidence and goodwill.

In planning the exterior of the retail store, the merchant attempts to maximize the advertising value of the store by establishing a unique and attractive front that will strengthen the defined image of the store.

Store Front Materials

The selection of a particular material for the store front depends on the funds available, the character of the store, and the income group to which the store wishes to appeal. Effective merchandising presentations of the façade have been illustrated with such materials as wood, brick, aluminum, glass, marble, stone, and various combinations.

Marquees or Overhangs

Retailers who find themselves housed in older buildings have tended to modernize the facility by the construction of a marquee above the entrance and windows. The use of this design concept directs attention away from the unsightly upper parts of the building. In addition, the marquee provides customers with protection from bad weather and acts as a permanent awning for the protection of merchandise featured in the window displays.

Recessed Fronts

In some stores, retailers have found it advantageous to recess the front of the building by several feet from the property line. Such a recession provides similar benefits to the consumer as does the marquee but at the same time permits customers to window shop without being jostled by pedestrians in front of the store.

There are several variations in the type of recessions that can be used by merchants in planning their stores. Some of the variations of angled, squared, or splayed recessions that have been effectively adopted by retailers are outlined in Exhibit 4-1.

Perhaps the most important reason for recessing is that it permits integration of the exterior and interior of the store. However, as retail space becomes more expensive, the use of

Exhibit 4-1
Recessed Store Fronts

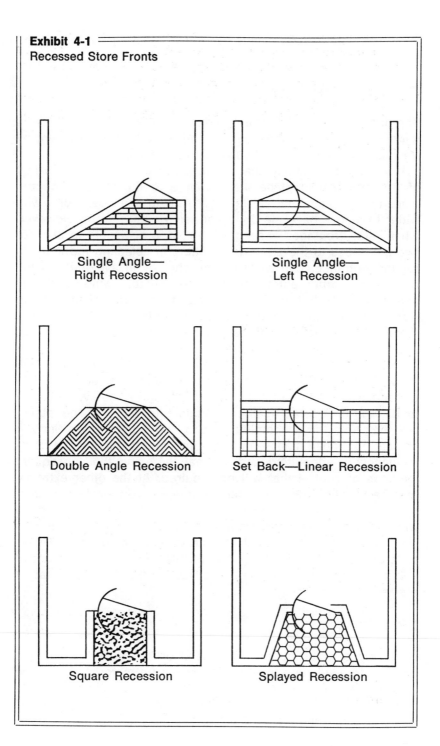

Single Angle—
Right Recession

Single Angle—
Left Recession

Double Angle Recession

Set Back—Linear Recession

Square Recession

Splayed Recession

such valuable selling space for a recession may indeed be uneconomical.

Customer Entrances

The density and direction of entering traffic and its circulation in various parts of the store can be influenced to some extent by the number and location of customer entrances.

It is generally agreed that retail stores with less than 25 feet of frontage should place the entrance to the store off-centre, since the main customer aisle is normally to one side. Stores with wider frontages have the option of using centre doors. However, when retail frontages exceed 75 feet, it is advisable to plan for two entrances to the store. In addition, in selecting the location for the entrance, corner entrances should be avoided. On the one hand, corner entrances take up valuable window display space; on the other hand, it is difficult to integrate aisles leading from corner entrances into a general floor plan.

Entrances should permit easy access for the customer. Steps, ramps, and other hindrances to entering the store tend to deter customer traffic. Further, the selection of the type of door such as push doors, automatic doors, revolving doors, or air curtain entrances will depend on the size of the store, the availability of funds, and the overall weather conditions in the area. The retailer who has selected a completely open entrance—as one finds in climate-controlled malls—must pay special attention to the rising incidence of shoplifting and internal theft and the subsequent methods of control that will be required. At the other extreme, merchants who have attempted to create a very exclusive atmosphere by using solid wooden doors and closed-background windows deter customers from entering since they are unable to see into the store at all. Such customers fear the unknown. Therefore, the store entrances need to be planned with the impact of enhancing the store's image and attracting the designated target market.

Signs

Large signs which have been placed on the upper part of the store or free-standing towers inform passing motorists about the existence of the unit, but are of little value in appealing to people who pass immediately in front of the store. For this reason it is helpful to have the store's name imprinted on the window, door, and display cards in the windows. Window-shoppers should immediately associate the name of the store with the items they have taken the time to evaluate in the display. In large downtown areas and the growing regional centres, the number of merchant assortments tend to confuse the customer; as a result, this name-merchandise association becomes even more important.

You will observe that shopping centres and municipal by-laws in some communities regulate the types of signs that may be erected. In selecting a sign to designate the store, you must carefully choose the letter style and the colour combinations to be used in the sign to ensure that a unified image is being projected. Those signs which must be read vertically are difficult to read and are not recommended except for very simple or familiar names and only when very large block letters can be used. In selecting the sign for the store, specialists in the manufacture of these products generally offer a service to help the independent retailer choose an effective design.

Window Displays

Window displays represent an identifiable feature of the store exterior that may largely determine whether a customer will enter a store.

The size and type of windows used in a particular establishment will be determined by the type and nature of the goods and the image desired by the store. In department stores, most windows have a closed background which completely shuts off the store interior from the window shopper. This is essential in the department store, since the merchandise located behind the window display is generally significantly different from the items placed in the window. Independent merchants of men's and women's apparel have also extensively used the closed-back window to provide more exciting and effective display treatments for these specialty stores.

The open or visual front store display which has no formal window treatment is, on the other hand, used by supermarkets and drug stores. In such stores the customer views the entire store as the window display. Retailers employing this concept operate on the premise that the window display is not an important element of their merchandising mix, and as a result the space required, and the time and expense of putting in window displays, can be more effectively used in different types of promotion.

Some retail merchants have chosen to combine the advantages of both the closed- and open-back window displays by placing screens or partial enclosures in the display. Merchandise is then featured and emphasized on these partitions, while, at the same time, the window shopper is able to view the interior display of the store. Such window treatments are frequently found in hardware stores, some independent drug stores, gift and jewellery stores, shoe stores, and many other operations seeking these benefits. A more thorough discussion of window displays is offered later as an important element of the promotional mix.

PLANNING THE STORE INTERIOR

While the retailer is concerned with the first impression customers receive from the store exterior, a continuing projection of the store's image through the interior is also important. The overall interior must provide an atmosphere that will help execute the store's merchandising strategy. It should also be designed with flexibility in mind so that it can be altered frequently to accommodate seasonal changes and future developments in the store's strategy. With limited selling space available and the need to project a modern appearance, flexibility for the small retailer in planning the store's interior is essential.

In selecting the different aspects of the store interior, consideration must be given to their desirability, the initial investment, and the continuing operating costs. The combination of these factors must be analyzed in selecting the most effective merchandise presentation for the store interior.

Floor Materials

The type of flooring that will be selected becomes an important consideration since this will represent a sizable investment both initially and in general maintenance. The flooring in a store influences the comfort and appeal experienced by both customers and employees. While you can select from marble, terrazzo, carpeting, wood, linoleum, tile, or combinations, different types will be required for different purposes within a store and for the many images a store wishes to create.

You should note, then, that it is possible to project varying images throughout the store by using several flooring materials and various colour schemes. These variations may also be used to differentiate departments from one another. In a men's apparel store, the clothing department might be broadloomed, while furnishings can be placed on vinyl tile, and the shoe department located on quarry tile.

Colour and Interior Finishes

Many colour combinations are available from paint and wallpaper companies that can assist in the sale of specific merchandise and at the same time emphasize the character and image of the retail store. Colour selections have been effectively used to visually alter the physical dimensions of the store, as well. A long, narrow store can be made to appear wider by using darker colours on the end walls than those used on the side walls. To further the illusion of pulling the side walls outward, the strategic placing of mirrors on the side walls visually offers more width to the store. Obviously, the opposite is true for locations that are characterized by wide, shallow space. Similarly, the high, un-sightly ceilings in many old stores can be made to visually disappear by painting these a darker colour than the walls, assuming that suspended panels are not used.

Just as there are hundreds of colour combinations, you can also select from a wide variety of wall and ceiling finishes that enhance the store's image and increase sales. The choice to be made will vary with the type and nature of the store, but flexibility must also be considered in retaining a modern in-store ap-pearance.

Lighting

The most important function of store lighting is to attract customers to the merchandise and to induce them to buy. It is also important that customers be visually able to evaluate the merchandise and read the labeling. Thus the quantity, quality, and effect of the light reaching the merchandise, as well as the appearance of the area, are determining factors in the effective-ness of the sales technique.

In planning the in-store lighting, retailers are required to provide two different levels of brightness. On the overall sales floor, diffused overhead lighting should be used to create a pleasing atmosphere for shopping. To complement this, lighting must also be tailored to the merchandise display. These two systems must be balanced to avoid any annoyance to the customer from the glare or disharmonious levels of brightness.

In their selection of lighting, retailers generally make use of two types of lamps. Fluorescent lamps are popular with stores because of their economical means of general lighting and their adaptability to inclusion in display fixtures and signs. Secondly, incandescent lamps are used to provide good colour and light control with a low initial cost but generally a shorter life and higher heat production. Such lamps are often used to emphasize special displays or departments.

Just as colours may alter the visual dimensions of a store, so too can the arrangement of the lighting fixtures in the store. A narrow store might place the ceiling fixtures running the width of the store rather than along the length in an effort to visually widen the appearance. In addition, in order to attract customers to secluded sections of the store, merchants have discovered that intensifying the lighting in these areas has tended to draw many more customers.

Continued exposure of coloured fabrics to high levels of illumination is likely to result in fading or discolouration. The degree of fading is dependent on the time of exposure, the level of illumination, the fastness of the dye and, to a lesser extent, the spectral characteristics of the light source, temperature, and humidity. To avoid such losses, place the more delicate articles farther away from the light source, shift merchandise regularly, and select equipment that will provide as uniform a distribution of light as possible.

Modernization

With the widespread success of the suburban shopping centres and their new modern retail stores, independent retailers must ensure their survival by bringing and keeping up to date the physical appearance, the fixtures, and the equipment of their stores.

To fight this suburban competition, as mentioned before, many downtown and neighbourhood areas have sought to improve their shopping districts by revitalizing the environment. Independent retailers operating in these areas must capitalize on these improvements by undertaking their own store modernization program. While large retailers can obtain the funds for store renovations and the expertise required, the independent merchant is generally left to personal ingenuity and creativity to ensure modernization. Assistance is available from trade associations, trade magazines, manufacturers of fixtures, equipment, and decorating supplies. Providing a modern store environment for the customer's shopping experience is as vital to the profitability of the store as is the right merchandise assortment.

INTERIOR LAYOUT

In planning the layout of the merchandise in the space available, you must be concerned with the efficiency of the flow of the assortment into and out of the store. As a result, store layout has been defined as "the arrangement of selling and non-selling departments, aisles, fixtures, displays, and equipment in the proper relationship to each other and to the fixed elements of the building structure." (William R. Davidson *et al.*, *Retailing Management* [New York: Ronald Press Co., 1975], p. 523.)

While this definition generally represents the areas that need to be explored in planning the layout of the interior of your store, it is important to outline the objectives that you should consider in establishing your plan. Obviously, the primary objective of designing the store layout is to increase sales by maximizing the customer-merchandise contact. In this way, the merchant attempts to show the greatest amount of merchandise in the space available in an attractive manner. At the same time, you must plan the direction and extent of the customer circulation throughout the store.

In addition to maximizing sales, you should attempt to minimize your expenses through effective planning of the layout. By efficiently using the available space to facilitate customer selection and suggestion selling, you can reduce the handling costs and the selling expenses per transaction.

As a means of satisfying the needs of the customer through store layout, retailers attempt to provide convenience and service to the patrons of the store. To achieve this facility, stores have been designed to imply to customers that useless effort is not being expended in their shopping trip through the store.

In an effort to accomplish the objectives which have been established for the layout of the store, appropriate steps are needed to ensure effective planning and customer satisfaction. In analyzing and appraising these steps, it is usually advantageous for the retailer to seek the services of a store architect or merchandising consultant to obtain objective and professional assistance. While small independent merchants tend to avoid the

expense associated with these specialists, a competent professional can often recommend cost savings that more than offset
the fee charged.

Departmentalizing

This step in store layout represents the process of classifying
merchandise into somewhat homogeneous groups known as
departments. While department stores have made extensive use
of this procedure by keeping separate records of purchases,
sales, inventories, and operating expenses, independent retailers
also adopt this system. Almost every type of independent merchant is capable of being departmentalized to provide the information needed to more effectively buy and sell the merchandise assortment.

Retailers may form departments by putting related merchandise together—such as golfing equipment in a sporting
goods store. Merchandise which appeals to specific groups by
sex, age, social status, or any other characteristic has been
successfully departmentalized in many stores. A gift department
in a women's apparel store can simplify the purchasing decision
of the male customer who has a selection problem.

This procedure of grouping the merchandise into departments
should not be relegated to the confines of the large store. Small
retailers who have undertaken the step have been able to effectively control and merchandise their inventory. Such a process
can inform you of the productivity of the merchandise line in
relation to the total assortment of your store. With the limited
space available in the independent store, the maximum use of
every square foot of selling space is essential.

Types of Arrangements

Once you have determined the number and type of departments
you wish to offer the customer, you must choose one general type
of arrangement for the fixtures and merchandise in your store.
The type of arrangement will play a significant role in projecting
the firm's image to customers who enter the store. Generally,
store layouts are designated as either gridiron or free-flow
arrangements based on fixture locations and customer aisles.

The gridiron layout This is an arrangement of fixtures and aisles
that is generally found in our mass-merchandise outlets. In this
type of arrangement, the secondary aisles run perpendicular to

Exhibit 4-2
Basic Layout Patterns

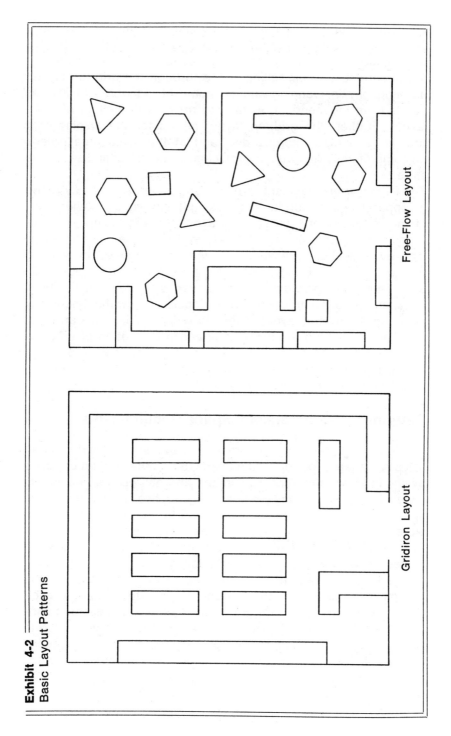

Gridiron Layout

Free-Flow Layout

the main customer aisle. Large retailing outlets like supermarkets, variety stores, and department stores have effectively used this arrangement, and many small independents have also made maximum use of their selling space through the gridiron layout. Its simplicity in planning and economy of standardized fixtures has led the independent, in fact, to prefer this method of store layout. Further, the gridiron layout allows for the display of a greater amount of merchandise and at the same time breeds customer familiarity with the placement of merchandise in the store.

The free-flow arrangement   This arrangement is generally found in apparel stores, furniture stores, gift stores, and other merchandise operations seeking to avoid the monotony and uniformity of the gridiron layout. Such an arrangement is characterized by a deliberate absence of uniformity created by varying fixture shapes and aisle patterns. The obvious advantage such an arrangement provides to the retailer is its inherent flexibility in expanding or contracting certain departments without seriously affecting the overall layout of the store. In addition, this arrangement allows for more effective use and presentation of different images and departments within a store. Retailers have found that this arrangement creates a unique look for their stores, which is an advantage over their competitors.

Determining Departmental Space Requirements

All retailers, both large and small, are seeking to maximize the sales per square foot of selling space. Since the amount of space available to each merchant is limited and has become extremely expensive in most communities, the effective allocation of this space to each merchandise line is vital to the profitability of the store. The independent merchant operating in very limited space must evaluate every department's contribution to the total store to determine how much space to allot to each.

One technique which has been applied by existing merchants in their determination of the amount of space to allocate to each department is based on the anticipated sales volume per square foot of selling space in that merchandise line. This technique is referred to as the department's space productivity ratio since it attempts to measure the effective use of the space in the operation.

In Exhibit 4-3, which follows, sample productivity rates are indicated for various merchandise lines. While an established

Exhibit 4-3

Sales Per Square Foot of Selling Space,
Selected Merchandise Department

Merchandise Lines	Median	Superior
Women's Dresses	$ 58.20	$ 97.90
Separates and Co-ordinates	118.20	147.40
Corsets and Bras	113.60	167.50
Lingerie and Sleepwear	95.90	108.40
Jewellery and Watches	189.80	328.30
Costume Jewellery	147.20	297.40
Hosiery	143.80	203.70
Handbags	106.50	159.30
Men's Clothing	101.50	168.10
Men's Furnishings	97.90	185.10
Children's Apparel and Accessories	59.30	118.10
Stationery and Office Equipment	55.50	96.30
Cosmetics and Toiletries	185.40	253.50
Hobby and Recreation	49.10	93.20
Home Furnishings	37.30	62.30
Floor Coverings	28.70	61.80
China and Glassware	40.70	70.30
Gift Shop	40.90	58.40
Housewares	36.40	68.30
Linens and Domestics	93.10	112.80
Sewing Notions	31.60	94.70
Fabrics	26.40	41.60

Source: National Retail Merchants Association, *Department Store and Specialty Store Merchandising and Operating Results* (New York: 1975).

retail store will be able to compare its productivity with that of other merchants, prospective merchants can use such a table as a guideline in determining the amount of space for each department.

If the planned sales of a men's suit department are forecasted to be $180,000 and the planned space productivity is designated by the merchant to be above that of the better merchants' productivity (Exhibit 4-3: $168.10) at $200 per square foot of selling space, then the amount of space required to achieve these goals will be 900 square feet.

The prime advantage of this technique is its simplicity of application. As such, it can act as a guideline in the allocation of space to the various departments in the store when the space productivity ratio for each department is known.

A more effective means for determining the amount of space for each department is referred to as the model stock approach.

Such a procedure allocates space to a merchandise line based on an inventory assortment which is balanced with regard to consumer demand. Using the model stock approach the merchant can plan the merchandise line in detail, taking into consideration breadth and depth of assortment and the facilitating services required.

The model stock approach requires the merchant to determine at the outset the composition of the inventory both on display and in reserve. This will be balanced with respect to the potential sales for the department. Once the decisions regarding the numbers of each size, colour, style, fabric, price, and other customer selection factors have been made, then the manner in which the merchandise will be presented to the customer must be determined. The choices which are available range from highly personal selling to complete self-service retailing.

Once the store's selling technique is established, the merchant can determine how many and what types of fixtures are needed, as well as the facilities that will be required for the services of the department. The sum total of all of these estimations will determine the amount of space that is needed for any one department, based on a thorough planning of the merchandise assortment.

Of the two methods for determining the amount of space to be allocated to each department, the model stock approach is better because it induces proper planning on the part of the retailer. Its use has increased inventory turnover, reduced overbuying, and minimized excessive price lines and out-of-stock conditions.

Departmental Locations

In the assessment of any retail store you will notice that some areas attract more customer traffic than others. As a result, the merchandising values of different parts of a store vary significantly, and generally tend to decrease the further the department is removed from the main entrance.

Obviously, in those areas of the store where the customer-merchandise contact is maximized, the value of the space is much higher than other areas. In larger stores and multi-floor operations, the values of the selling areas tend to be determined not only by the entrances to the store but also by the proximity to the vertical transportation system.

It is difficult to establish a general rule that can be applied to every retail store in its quest to determine the value of the various parts of the store. While the front portion of the store is assumed to have higher value because of the customer traffic, merchants have drawn customers to the rear corners of the store by the strategic placement of various merchandise departments. For this reason customers find the pharmacy at the rear of the drug store, the meat department at the back of the supermarket and the post office in a similar position in a variety store.

You will also observe that customers generally move to the right upon entering a store, unless prohibited by some obstruction. This section of the store tends, as a result, to have a higher value than its counterpart on the left. The following guidelines are helpful in allocating space to various merchandise departments.

1. Merchandise which generates a high gross margin per square foot of selling space as well as high sales per square foot should be located in the most valuable space.
2. Items which are frequently purchased on the basis of impulse should be located in heavy traffic areas, while those which customers seek out can be placed in more remote and less valuable space.
3. Convenience goods of low-unit value which are purchased frequently demand locations in retail stores which are easily accessible to the customer, and thus require prime locations.
4. To establish customer convenience in shopping and to increase the incidence of suggestion selling, related departments should be placed in close proximity to one another.
5. Merchandise lines need to be allocated space on the basis of the seasonality of the items and ability to expand or contract the available space for these departments.
6. Certain sections of the store are more suitable than others for displaying particular types of merchandise for sales or demonstration purposes. Wall space may be required for one department, while centre floor space is more beneficial for other lines.
7. Merchandise which requires careful evaluation by the customer should be placed away from heavy traffic areas.

Merchandise Arrangement and Presentation

One major decision that must be made by you with regard to the layout of the interior of the store is the quantity and quality of sales assistance that will be given to the customer. The following methods of merchandise arrangement are included for your analysis. Keep in mind that a retail store may offer a combination of four of these types to the customer in the various departments of the store.

Salon selling Salon selling presupposes that the customer is helpless—and as a result all merchandise is hidden under glass or in stockrooms. In this selling situation the customer must be served by a sales person who, by the nature of the selling situation, must be an experienced professional. This is obviously an expensive way to sell merchandise and is generally offered to customers who are seeking service and atmosphere rather than price in their patronage motive. Diamonds, furs, bridal wear, and expensive apparel may be effectively merchandised in this manner.

Sample selling Sample selling is used in a retail store where the merchant does not wish, or does not have the space, to show all of the merchandise. In this method of arranging the merchandise, the customer selects from samples on the floor but requires the services of a sales person to satisfy specific selection requirements. Shoes, carpets, sweaters, and furniture are offered to the consumer in this manner.

Pre-selection selling Retail stores which prominently display all merchandise available for sale so that customers can select what they wish without assistance from a sales person are using the technique of pre-selection selling. The sales person is necessary in pre-selection selling to offer guidance, demonstration, and information before the sale can be completed. The majority of apparel merchandise for men, women, and children is currently being offered for sale in this manner among our retail stores.

Self-selection Self-selection is a merchandise arrangement which is employed when customers are expected to do all of the buying themselves. In this selling situation, the sales clerk is merely used to complete the sale—a process which must be done in the department concerned.

Self-service Self-service retailing has been adopted by retailers who have chosen to allow customers to do all of their shopping without the services of store personnel. The completion of the transaction takes place at a central cash-wrap counter and in this way differs from self-selection selling.

You will no doubt observe that as one moves from salon selling to self-service merchandising the quality of the sales personnel declines considerably. In many retail lines, independents have found varying degrees of success with each of these types of merchandise presentation. Those to be selected for a particular retail store will depend on the type and nature of the merchandise line, the demands of the target market, and economies of obtaining adequate sales personnel. Whatever choice is made, you must keep in mind that part of your advantage lies in your ability to offer personal service to your customers that is normally not available to them in larger operations.

5

BUYING PRINCIPLES AND PRACTICES

Retail merchandising is frequently referred to as the business activity of having the right merchandise in the right quantity at the right price at the right time and in the right place. To satisfy these five rights, the activities involved in the buying function are primarily concerned with the execution of the first four while the right place has been the responsibility of selecting the location and layout for the store. The discussion which follows regarding the buying function of the retail operation will primarily be concerned with the management principles involved in the determination and implementation of these fundamentals of merchandising.

BUYING-SELLING CYCLE

In an effort to ensure that the five rights have been accomplished, you must realize that there exists an essential interdependent relationship between the buying and selling functions of the retail store. Together these two functions represent a continuous cycle that will ensure that the profitability of the store is properly executed. This execution requires the understanding and feedback of communications among the three elements of the cycle as illustrated in Exhibit 5-1.

As an independent retailer you will generally be responsible for all three of these functions. Estimating customer requirements and making the goods available for sale are part of the buying function of determining what, how much, when, and from where the goods should be purchased. The procedure of motivating the customer to buy falls within the realm of the promotion function of the store and as such includes the activities of selling. While

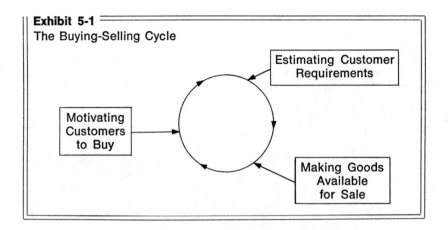

Exhibit 5-1
The Buying-Selling Cycle

- Estimating Customer Requirements
- Motivating Customers to Buy
- Making Goods Available for Sale

pricing is generally perceived to form part of the negotiations of the buying function, it exercises a considerable impact on the promotion or selling function of the store and, as such, becomes part of the motivational procedure of the cycle.

The continuity of the cycle is an important aspect of the relationship between the buying and selling activities of the firm. The independent must realize that the constant provision of feedback from the customers' motivation to buy to the phase of estimating customer requirements gives the retailer that information which is necessary to make adjustments to the inventory assortment. The cycle continues as the assortment is offered to the customers to determine their reaction based on their purchases at the store.

While the task of buying merchandise for the store is much more complex than can be presented in these writings, a summary of the activities that are generally associated with the buying activity are classified in Exhibit 5-2.

In the independent retail operation it should be clear that the owner/manager is generally charged with all or the majority of these duties unless he or she has taken the opportunity of delegating some activities to other store personnel. The larger the organization, the more likely the buyer is to have assistance in the execution of these duties and the more complicated and restricted is the relationship between the buying and selling units of the organization.

Since we are primarily concerned with the retail management function as it applies to the small business operation, our discussions will centre on those principles and techniques that can be effectively used by these independent merchants. As a result, the more sophisticated developments in the application

Exhibit 5-2
The Buying Activity

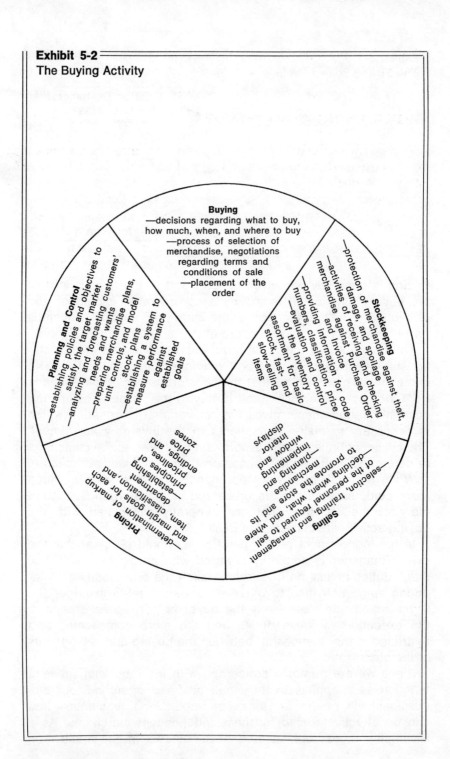

Buying
—decisions regarding what to buy, how much, when, and where to buy
—process of selection of merchandise, negotiations regarding terms and conditions of sale
—placement of the order

Planning and Control
—establishing policies and objectives to satisfy the target market
—analyzing and forecasting customers' needs and wants
—preparing merchandise plans, unit controls, and model stock plans
—establishing a system to measure performance against established goals

Stockkeeping
—protection of merchandise against theft, damage, and spoilage
—activities of receiving and checking merchandise against Purchase Order and Invoice
—providing information for code numbers, classification, price evaluation and control
—of the inventory
—assortment for basic stock, fast- and slow-selling items

Selling
—selection, training, and management of the personnel required to sell
—deciding when, what, and where to promote the store and its merchandise
—implementing and planning window and interior displays

Pricing
—determination of markup and margin goals for each item, classification, and department, establishing of principles of pricelines, endings, and price zones

of scientific principles to the buying function have been omitted to offer you practical solutions to the buying problems.

DETERMINING WHAT TO BUY

The primary task in the buying function is your attempt to estimate what merchandise your customers will want to buy from your store. For many buyers this is also the most difficult task, since customers have, over the past several years, reached greater levels of sophistication, have become more knowledgeable, and as a result tend to be more demanding and discriminating about the merchandise they buy. Therefore, you must establish a process of interpreting your customers' demands in an effort to determine what to buy.

We have witnessed in Chapter 2 that consumer income and populations are changing constantly, with significant impact on the demands of the market. An effective buyer will be concerned with the clues that might signal the emergence of new demands and new trends in the market. Independent merchants, like large-scale retailers, require information that will facilitate their decisions regarding the items that should constitute their assortments.

Before you proceed with the process of assembling and tabulating this information, your store must develop a buying strategy based on the alternative policies available to it. Once you have clearly defined the buying policy for your store, you are ready to meet these policies with the acquisition of merchandise that will satisfy customer demand. Customers shop for merchandise first and secondarily for service; consequently, the inventory should always show distinctive characteristics that customers will come to recognize and appreciate.

In terms of the buying process involved in many merchandise lines, retail stores have generally been classified as one of the following types of operations.

The Depot Store

The depot store represents those retail operations which carry standardized merchandise that is purchased by the consumer primarily because of convenience of location. Since no real selling takes place and the selection problem of buying for the store is relatively simple, such operations merely represent storage places for convenience goods. These types of buying operations are best exemplified by the convenience jug milk stores and the neighbourhood drug stores. Taken to the extreme, the large banks of vending machines found in apartment buildings, office towers, and transportation terminals could be considered depot stores.

The Bargain Store

The bargain store is the retail store which only stocks merchandise items that can be sold in quantity at below-market prices. The buyer for such an operation is constantly seeking out sources of distressed merchandise and job lots which can be bought in quantity. Such a store is not concerned with maintaining a wide or deep assortment but rather with ensuring a sufficient quantity of stock by constantly seeking new sources of supply.

The Selector Store

The selector store represents the largest group of retail stores operating in Canada. In these establishments the buying function is primarily concerned with selecting the right merchandise for its customers and maintaining the proper assortment based on consumer demand. In this buying function, the retail merchant assumes the role of a purchasing agent for the store's customers.

In your determination of what to buy for your customers, the discussion which follows will be essentially concerned with the problems and techniques associated with the largest category of retail stores—selector stores. In this context, the buyer must conform to the store's established policies to ensure the enhancement and preservation of the store's image as perceived by the customer. Some of the choices of buying policies which are available to the independent are listed below.

Breadth and Depth of Assortment Decisions must be made by retail firms regarding the extent to which the store will concentrate its assortment in depth and breadth. Some retail stores opt to carry merchandise in breadth—by carrying a limited assortment of all lines or specialized lines only; other merchants offer the customer depth of assortment—by stocking large quantities of the popular merchandise items only. Still other merchants attempt to carry certain items in both breadth and depth.

Time Utility This merchandising policy, established by some retail stores, represents the time when the merchandise will be introduced to the store's market. Some independent specialty stores attempt to buy the newest styles or the latest novelties with the hope that their stores will be recognized as the fashion leaders in the community. Other retail merchants play the more conservative role by offering the merchandise to their customers only after general acceptance by the public.

Merchandise Quality A visit to any merchandise supplier will reveal that items are available in numerous variations of quality. Depending on the image the store has attempted to create, retailers may select only the best quality the market has to offer, or, alternatively, items which might be designated as serviceable quality in their price-quality relationship. Independent merchants must decide which route to take and ensure that all purchases made for the store fall in line with this policy.

Price Levels As a result of the merchant's desire to maximize the inventory investment, all price levels of merchandise cannot be offered in any one store. The small retailer's decision must be centred on those price ranges which are best suited to the market to which the store's image is projected. In general, the retail buyer will be aware of the relationship that must exist between the price levels and the desired quality ranges in the items bought.

Merchandise Exclusivity Retail merchants have always attempted to acquire merchandise items that would set their stores apart from their competitors. One way this has been achieved is through the acquisition of merchandise on an exclusive basis. In this process, retailers work with manufacturers or other suppliers to obtain the exclusive rights—for one particular line or a total assortment of merchandise—in a geographical area. Some merchants have carried this further, by offering merchandise to their clientele under the store's private label, while other retailers have sought to only carry nationally-advertised items available in all stores. You must seek to establish your own policy with regard to the extent of exclusive items you require for your operation.

Merchandise Ensembles Some retail stores have emphatically stressed to the buying public that their stores are concerned with providing the consumer with a complete look. While this policy has been used primarily for fashion merchandise in both men's and women's apparel, furniture and appliances, and sporting goods, it has also recently been extended to many other areas of retailing. The degree to which buyers will stress the availability of ensembles will essentially depend on their ability to assess the tastes and desires of the store's customers.

It is obvious that retail merchants must select those policies that, when combined, will project a unified image to the customer about the store's merchandise assortment. A retail merchant cannot stress low prices and at the same time the best quality the market has to offer. Nor is it possible for a merchant to project an image of fashion leadership that would be consistent with an image of a deep assortment of popular items. Therefore, to effectively use these policies, you should choose those which you wish to emphasize and rank these in order of importance to your store.

In selecting from these alternatives, you must consider the nature of your merchandise lines and its relationship to the designated target market. In the final analysis the policy choice must be one which is consistent with the character of the store, and one which will effectively emphasize the desired image.

Information Sources: What to Buy

Once the buying policy of the firm has been established, you must attempt to evaluate the various sources of information at your disposal to determine what the needs of your customers are. The following sources of information have been used by retail merchants in their preparation of buying plans for a department or store.

Store's Customers Perhaps the most important source of information for the retailer is the analysis of the data provided by the store's own customers. Such information is available to the merchant through the review of the sales and inventory records by the various selection factors. In this way the merchant can assess the customers' preferences for sizes, prices, brands, colours, styles, fabrics, and other classification differences. Customers tend to exhibit habits in their purchasing patterns and these patterns tend to change relatively slowly in their overall impact on a store's merchandising strategy. Nevertheless, this continuous assessment must be undertaken to familiarize the buyer with the customers' preferences.

Further information about customers' demands can be obtained by an analysis of complaints, merchandise exchanges, and want-slip systems. In each of these areas of merchandise management, retail merchants should take the time and effort to record the reasons given by customers for dissatisfaction. When this information is collected, tabulated, and analyzed merchants can take corrective action in their buying. In this context, successful retailers have discovered that a formalized want-slip system has provided vital information on customer demands. When handled effectively, the want-slip system should record every request for merchandise which was not in stock and should also indicate whether or not a substitute article was sold. Because it is virtually impossible for the store owners or managers to be on the selling floor at all times, such a recording system will allow them to keep abreast of their customers' requests.

Exhibit 5-3
Sample Want Slip

Want Slip

DATE _____

CLERK _____ DEPT. _____
SUPERVISOR'S
SIGNATURE _____

BASIC ITEM OUT OF STOCK:

_____

_____

_____

_____

_____

CORRECTIVE ACTION:

_____

_____

_____

_____

_____

Retailers have also been able to obtain information about the preferences of customers by analyzing customer charge cards. For retail firms restricting themselves to the commercial cards like Visa, Mastercharge, or American Express an analysis may still be undertaken by reviewing the merchant's copy of the transaction.

In some independent retail operations, merchants have attempted to acquire information about customers through the use of consumer surveys. While independents generally do not engage in formal marketing research, brief questionnaires as part of a direct mailing have been effective in soliciting customer response in certain areas. Surveys may provide the merchant with information about the store's services, image, and atmosphere as well as the merchandise assortment of the firm. Of particular importance to retailers of fashion goods are style counts given by observers in the store who designate the style awareness of the store's customers.

In addition to the internal information provided by the store's customers, sales personnel operating in the store also represent a vital link in the determination of the needs and wants of the customers. As well as being in constant contact with the customers on the selling floor, they are consumers in their own right with tastes similar to those who patronize the store. As a result, you should encourage communication and suggestions from your personnel with the hope that such involvement will not only assist the buying function but also the motivation to sell the merchandise once it is in the store.

Therefore, the retailer should note that the internal sources of information provided by the store's customers and personnel provide the most valuable data on the customers' needs and wants for both staple and fashion merchandise.

Competitors   Independent merchants who are unable to afford the more expensive data on market trends and extensive consumer surveys will often shop in competing stores which will provide them with other retailers' interpretations of the needs and wants of customers. Many independent merchants make extensive use of visiting successful retail stores carrying similar merchandise lines in adjacent towns and cities. Further comparisons are usually undertaken on vacations and buying trips at other, more distant, locations. This primary research has proven most valuable to the progressive merchant seeking new and unique ways of meeting the demands of the market.

The comparison of competitive store offerings can provide a

wealth of information about customers, merchandise, services, and general presentation to the individual undertaking a first venture in retail marketing, as well.

Suppliers Probably more than any other external source of information on determining customer demands, the suppliers of merchandise to the independent retailer performs the role of both advisor and salesperson. The vendor's awareness of merchandise which is in demand is usually wide, and is a source of customer research which is otherwise unavailable to the independent merchant.

In assessing each source of supply it is important to differentiate between those firms which sell what they produce and those which produce what they can sell. It is vital to the retailer to accept information and merchandise from those suppliers who have carefully looked at the consumer before offering a line of merchandise. In this need to keep abreast of what various suppliers are offering, merchants have discovered that some firms offer descriptive bulletins on merchandise items while others have attempted to simplify the buying process by offering the merchant an inventory-control system adaptable to automatic reordering.

In general, the proper use of the vendor's salespeople can give the independent merchant the consultative advice needed to keep up-to-date with the demands of the market and the availability of products in the market.

Resident Buyer Some retail merchants have found it advantageous to use the services of a resident buyer. Resident buyers' offices are located in the central markets, and for a fee they will provide member stores with information about new and popular items in that market. They generally represent the eyes and ears of the merchants in the marketplace by watching fashion trends, observing vendor offerings, and checking the promotions of the larger stores. To those independents belonging to such an office, product and customer information is readily available.

Trade Associations and Publications The print medium remains a vital and essential communication link between the store buyer and the marketplace. The information that independents are able to obtain from thoroughly scrutinizing the trade publications for their line of merchandise is extremely economical when the cost of the subscription is considered. The advertisements and feature articles bring independents the assistance required in more accurately assessing their buying function and its implementation. Publications such as *Men's Wear, Style, Hardware Merchandising,* and *Women's Wear Daily* are just some of the trade publications that have, over the past years, demonstrated their usefulness to the independent.

Similarly, some trade associations have been of considerable value to the independent in obtaining information about the market and in providing a range of member services that have been heavily used. These associations are normally responsible for the operation of trade shows and market weeks offered to facilitate the buying function of the merchant and the selling responsibility of the suppliers.

While we have been concerned up to this point with those techniques needed by you to determine what to buy for your store, we must now proceed to an examination of the factors which determine where you will purchase the merchandise for your retail store.

DETERMINING WHERE TO BUY

Since retailers are responsible for implementing the five rights of merchandising to ensure the profitability of their enterprises, they must seek out suppliers who will provide merchandise that will satisfy their target markets. It should be recognized that almost all merchants have many sources from which to choose as well as many decisions that need to be made regarding the prices and terms of sale in the negotiations. It is generally in this process of negotiations that conflicts may develop between the retailer and the supplier. It is the intention of this section to briefly outline those principles and activities required in establishing an effective relationship with the store's vendors.

In general, retailers tend to make their purchases from two types of suppliers—manufacturers and wholesalers. In many merchandise lines, retailers of all sizes tend to buy their assortments directly from the manufacturer either through the company salespeople or representatives. Because of the risks of style obsolescence, manufacturers of fashion apparel have sought to sell directly to the retail trade rather than run the risks associated with storage in wholesale warehouses. In addition, manufacturers have found that a more effective selling effort can be realized from company salespeople in comparison with the many lines carried by the wholesaler and the selling effort given by their personnel. Physical perishability has also made the purchasing of foodstuffs directly from the manufacturer preferable.

Retailers may also choose to purchase part of their merchandise assortment from a wholesaler. Merchants who buy in very small quantities at frequent intervals, as in hand-to-mouth buying, extensively use the wholesale operation. In other cases, retailers may decide to use a wholesaler for fill-in stock or to supplement an existing line. The wholesaler has also played a very important role for the entrepreneur by providing stock quickly when an emergency arises. Since the bulk of most wholesalers' business is concentrated with the independent retailers, these suppliers tend to be very helpful to small merchants. This assistance has generally been provided whether the merchant has chosen to remain independent or become a member of a voluntary chain sponsored by the wholesale organization.

Whether the retailer decides to buy directly from the manufacturer or indirectly through the wholesalers, it is clear that certain characteristics will make one source of supply better than another. The analysis of these attributes provides merchants with the information required to select their key sources of supply. Therefore, in selecting their key resources, retailers must be concerned with the nature of the vendor's line, the overall profitability of the line, the reputation of the supplier in serving the merchant, and the images of the brands of merchandise carried. In addition to these essential characteristics of suppliers, retailers must also be concerned with the financial and promotional assistance some vendors offer their customers.

In appraising all the resources available to your retail store, you should seek answers to the following questions before selecting your key sources of supply:
1. Does the supplier have the type of merchandise suited to my store and market segments?
2. On the basis of my previous experience with the supplier are they dependable in providing my store with the services and merchandise required?
3. Does the supplier show fashion or product leadership in satisfying the requirements of my store?
4. In light of delivery problems encountered by small retailers, can the resource be relied upon to provide on-time delivery of the merchandise in good condition?
5. Will this resource provide me with dealer aids to effectively promote the merchandise line through advertising, display, and personal selling assistance?

6. To what extent can this supplier satisfy my buying requirements in a number of merchandise lines in an effort to reduce the number of suppliers required for my store?
7. Will the supplier provide me with the quantity needed or will the minimum order quantity be uneconomical for my store?
8. As a result of vendor analysis, how successful has my store been with regard to the sales and profitability of this supplier's merchandise lines?

While these questions represent just some of the facts that are required by the independent in the appraisal of the various sources of supply, the factual information can be obtained from the store's records of transactions with the vendor. Information on the markdowns required, the turnover obtained, the availability

---

Exhibit 5-4
Resource Diary

Classification:	Nature of Business:	Source Number:

Name:	Office No.:

Address:	Telephone:

City:	Postal Code:

Factory Address:	Telephone:

Representative:	Telephone:

Terms:	Trade Discount	F.O.B.

Date:	Comments

Resource Diary: Retained in a loose-leaf binder, this form records a continual up-date of the important characteristics of each source of supply.

of repeat items, and the maintained markup on the assortment can provide the retailer with the data needed to designate the store's key sources of supply.

Up to this point in our discussion regarding the selection of suppliers, we have concentrated on the assessment of existing resources. It should also be noted that retailers with the use of computer technology can effect a much more sophisticated process of vendor analysis to the point of determining profitability per item per vendor.

While it is generally advantageous to concentrate your purchases with as few sources as possible, it is to your benefit to constantly look out for new and more effective suppliers. Generally, concentration with a few key suppliers tends to make the small-scale retailer an important customer in terms of overall purchases. However, the constant comparison of other vendors' offerings is essential if the merchant is to keep up-to-date in the marketplace. As a result, retailers increasingly seek out sources of supply rather than depending on vendors to come to their place of business. In their attempts to find new sources, or simply to review existing suppliers, retailers have visited local, central, and even foreign markets.

In the majority of cases, though, independent merchants have made contact with new sources of supply at market weeks and trade shows. At those shows, where a significant number of manufacturers and wholesalers exhibit their lines, attendance by independent retailers seeking to place part of their seasonal budget has been excellent. Amidst all the excitement of a buy-mart, merchants tend to buy more heavily than they had planned to; nevertheless, these shows have played a very important role in satisfying the basic needs of the independent.

As well, various suppliers will constantly be seeking ways of expanding their markets by contacting merchants rather than waiting for their requests for information. This contact can be made through the mailing of catalogues and price lists to potential retail customers. Where it is generally not economical—because of volume—for the manufacturer or wholesaler to provide frequent visits by salespeople, printed solicitation is used.

Perhaps more important than any other means of initiating contact with the merchants throughout the country, is the personal impact made by the salesforce of the supplier. The number of visits that a salesperson makes to a retail store will depend on the merchandise line and the frequency with which the goods are sold. In many cases in which suppliers would value the account of a particular independent, frequent visits will be made to exert some selling and personal pressure.

Independent retailers should make use of the information that the salespeople bring to the store as a result of their constant communication with all levels of the market. Because sales people must be in touch with the likes and dislikes of both large and small merchants—their livelihoods depend on it—they are, although somewhat clouded by their desire to sell their lines, valuable sources of advice.

On the basis of this information, it should be clear to you that a sound business relationship must exist between the store's suppliers and yourself to provide for the desired merchandise assortment. The following list of principles are presented in the hope that both the merchant and the supplier will readily recognize the mutual interdependence for information, sales, and profitability. Obviously, suppliers engage in a process of rating their accounts just as merchants assess their vendors.

Establishing Good Vendor Relations

Concentrated Buying   For each merchandise line and classification, attempt to secure key sources of supply from whom the bulk of your purchases will be made. But in concentrating your purchases with these suppliers, constantly evaluate their assortments and services to ensure they are the best available.

Resource Performance   In the assessment of each source, it is vital to the retail store to evaluate the performance and productivity of the merchandise items selected from its inventory. If it is your decision to drop a source, informing the supplier as to your reasons may offer constructive criticisms that may provide an important buy-sell contract in the future.

Potential Resources   Retail establishments are well advised to see as many sources of supply as time and effort will allow. During trips to the market, or in the confines of the store, vendors' representatives should be encouraged to present their line or discuss merchandising possibilities with the company. It is important to retain an open line of communication with as many vendors as possible for future assessment.

Ethical Practices   Some retail merchants have tended to incur the wrath of their suppliers by engaging in petty and shrewd practices by taking discounts in excess of those agreed upon or after the last discount day. Retailers should also resist such practices as cancelling orders before the delivery date established on the purchase order and excessive rechargeable expenses of co-operative advertising, telephone calls, or physical merchandise defects. Likewise, business ethics require the appropriate handling of merchandise returns to suppliers.

Order Confirmation While independent retailers frequently use the order forms of the supplier in place of those that are designated specifically for their operations, the confirmation of specific elements on either form is essential. In placing the order with the supplier, the retailer should confirm in writing the merchandise selection, the terms and conditions of the purchase, and any special instructions that constitute part of the purchase with this company.

DETERMINING HOW MUCH TO BUY

Once you have determined what to buy for your retail operation, your biggest problem centres on the determination of how much you should purchase. The majority of independent retailers tend to find themselves with merchandising problems as a result of being overstocked or understocked in the merchandise assortment. An overstocked situation results in large markdowns and subsequent reductions in gross profit. On the other hand, the loss of sales due to out-of-stock situations can also seriously affect the profitability of the firm. The ultimate aim of the independent is to maintain a balance in inventory investment that will maximize the store's return on its financial commitment.

The retailer must make a difficult decision; the proliferation of goods available in the variety of selection factors complicates the task immensely. But it is essentially because of these enormous choices available that the merchant must plan purchases before making any inventory commitment. For example, a men's wear retailer who wishes to carry only one shirt in each size, colour, collar style, fabric, cuff style, and price line could conceivably wind up with an investment in this item alone of several thousand dollars.

Exhibit 5-5 illustrates that the store carrying only one shirt in each of the selection factors listed would commit an investment of $28,800, if the average price of the shirt were $10. Once the retailer has sold one of these items, the store is in an out-of-stock position in that combination of selection factors. Obviously, planning is required to create the right inventory balance among the various selection factors.

Exhibit 5-5
Combination Factors—Men's Dress Shirts

Selection Factor	Variations	Number
Neck Size	14½, 15, 15½, 16, 16½, 17	6
Sleeve Lengths	32, 33, 34, 35	4
Colours	white, blue, beige, grey, assorted stripes	5
Collar Style	button-down, spread, long-point, tab	4
Fabric	cotton, polyester blend	2
Cuff Style	convertible, single, french	3
Total Variations:	6 x 4 x 5 x 4 x 2 x 3	2880
Total Investment:	One shirt in each factor at average wholesale price of $10 per shirt	$28,800

In attempting to make these decisions regarding the proper assortment, merchants are required to determine the inventory investment in both breadth and depth as related to the anticipated stock turnover rate. As a result, retailers attempting to make decisions regarding the quantity of items to purchase must balance their assortment on the basis of their dollar investment. The relationship between the breadth and depth factors must be recognized since expanding the variety of items carried will necessarily result in fewer varieties or fewer units of each item in the assortments. Thus, retailers who overlook this important relationship as it applies to inventory dollars generally discover an improper balance in their assortment and their investment.

Some independent retailers have been buying for many years on the basis of intuition or what is sometimes called "a feel for merchandise." There are indeed individuals who are capable of buying in this manner, but in the great majority of cases where retailers have relied on this technique of determining what and how much to buy, financial problems have resulted because of a poor balance in the merchandise assortment.

Today's successful independent has learned to adapt the techniques used by the larger retail organization in reaching decisions on the quantity to purchase. These techniques are discussed in the next chapter, under the heading Merchandise Planning. Essentially, these techniques represent the development of a buying plan before placing orders with the suppliers.

Therefore, the development and understanding of the mechanics of a merchandise plan, a model stock plan, and open-to-buy figures are discussed to simplify the buying decisions to be made by you.

Buying plans tend to motivate the independent to restrict, where possible, the process of memorandum or hand-to-mouth buying. While some merchants find it useful for periodic fill-ins and others use it for the bulk of the store's buying, independents should realize that generally hand-to-mouth buying results in inadequate assortments. This, in turn, leads to lost sales, loss of customer goodwill, as well as higher wholesale costs due to fewer quantity discounts.

At the other extreme, some retailers, anticipating rising prices in inflationary times, engage in speculative buying by committing themselves to large bulk orders. Such a buying practice occurs more frequently with staple merchandise which is not generally subjected to the style perishability of fashion merchandise. Such a buying practice results in top-heavy assortments in some merchandise lines while leaving other areas of the assortment completely relegated to a process of hand-to-mouth buying. Speculative buying has been successful for some merchants, but retailers with limited funds and space must carefully ensure the maximization of their inventory investment and turnover in the total assortment. Caution must therefore be exercised in the practices of both hand-to-mouth and speculative buying.

Decisions regarding the quantity of merchandise to purchase for the store must also be related to the store's financial position and storage facilities, particularly when the store is experiencing acute delivery problems from suppliers.

Perhaps what needs to be emphasized at this point is the fact that buying in large quantities (as does the mass merchandiser) is not necessarily the most economical way to buy. The real way to big profits is through buying small—that is, buying high turnover items in small lots at frequent intervals. It should be recognized that such purchasing should not be so small that it is uneconomical. Therefore, a modified version of hand-to-mouth buying might prove beneficial in some merchandise lines. In this way the retailer tends to take the emphasis off high gross profits and put it on high net profits. This is achieved through selling more, through controlling expenses, through variable pricing, and through turning capital at a faster rate.

6

MERCHANDISE PLANNING FOR RETAIL

Every retailer, whether small or large, has entered the field of retailing with the goal of making a profit. In order to make a profit, the retailer must consider both the qualitative characteristics of the merchandise and the quantitative data regarding the assortment. As a result, planning and control in the buying and operational functions depend on the merchant's ability to use the numerical data to simplify the decision-making process. The planning data which follows should be regarded as a guideline to effective buying rather than as an absolute from which all purchasing must stem.

Since the inventory for the store represents the largest dollar investment in current assets, sound financial planning and control together with sound assortment planning are essential to the profitability of the firm. This chapter is devoted to those techniques that independent merchants must adapt to their operations to ensure effective planning of the elements of the buying-selling cycle. Small independent merchants have been notorious for their difficulties with inventory investments as a result of a general lack of planning before visiting the suppliers and the trade shows.

While the overall plan which is being presented may at first appear rather complex, familiarity with all the terms and techniques will soon become routine. On this basis you should follow each step in the development of the six-month merchandise plan. Following the preparation of the merchandise budget, a discussion of the procedures involved in the development of a model stock plan is presented to further your ability to invest profitably in inventory.

THE MERCHANDISE PLAN

The dollar merchandise plan is the co-ordination of the various merchandising activities for determining the purchases needed by the retail operation to achieve the planned sales. As such, the merchandise plan is a budget in dollars for a certain period of time, which is generally specified as a six-month season. The time frame of February 1 to July 31 is generally designated as the spring-summer season, while the fall-winter period is from August 1 to January 31. These dates are classified as the beginnings and endings of each of the store's seasons since the dates of February 1 and August 1 should be the periods of the store's lowest inventory level.

THE MERCHANDISE PLAN FORMAT

The format of the merchandise plan which is presented here is not the sole design used in the retail trade. Each organization may have minor variances in the plan, but all designs will include the same basic elements to establish the following relationship:

Retail Purchases = Merchandise Needed − Merchandise Available

The essential design of the plan, in order to be useful to the independent, must ensure that the information is provided in a clear and useful manner.

In the merchandise plan which is presented in Exhibit 6-1, the store's control data is placed on the left-hand side of the purchase plan. The right-hand side provides for the calculation of sales, stocks, reductions, and purchases for the season on a monthly basis. The total completion of this plan is required by the merchant to balance the merchandise which is needed for the season with that which is or will be available for sale.

In scrutinizing the plan, note that the merchandise needed for the store is derived by adding the planned sales, the planned reductions, and the planned end-of-month (EOM) stock. Obviously, then, the merchandise which the store has available will be represented by the beginning-of-the-month (BOM) stock on hand in the store. Understanding this basic relationship is fundamental to the techniques and procedures of merchandise planning and control.

Exhibit 6-1
Sample Merchandise Plan

			Spring	Feb.
Six-Month Merchandise Plan		Folio	Fall	Aug.
Department _____	Sales		Last Year	
Department No. _____			Plan	
From _____ 19___			Actual	
To _____ 19___		+	Last Year	
Department Control Data	Retail EOM		Plan	
L.Y. T.Y.			Actual	
% Initial Markup ____ ____		+	Last Year	
% Reductions ____ ____	Reductions			
% Maintained Markup ____ ____			Plan	
% Alteration Expense ____ ____				
% Cash Discount ____ ____			Actual	
% Gross Margin ____ ____				
% Operating Expense ____ ____		−	Last Year	
% Net Profit ____ ____	Retail BOM			
Season Turnover ____ ____			Plan	
Control Period ____ ____				
			Actual	
Planning and Authorization		=	Last Year	
Buyer _____	Retail Purchases		Plan	
Merchandise Controller _____			Actual	
Date Prepared _____	Cost Purchases		Last Year	
Date Authorized _____			Plan	
			Actual	

Source: Albert P. Kneider, *Mathematics of Merchandising,* © 1974, p. 219.

Mar.	Apr.	May	June	July	Total
Sept.	Oct.	Nov.	Dec.	Jan.	

In calculating the merchandise needed for the month of March, as an example, we would add the planned sales anticipated by the store for the month of March to the planned stock the store wants to have available at the end of March to carry on business during the next month. To this total we would then add the planned reductions for the month of March. The sum of these three figures less the stock which the merchant has on hand on March 1 will represent the dollar figure of the purchases the store will need to make for the month of March.

The format of the plan has also been designed to include a place to record the actual results of the months as the season progresses. This data can then be used to continually make adjustments to the plan based on the results as they occur. Such data is also extremely helpful to the merchant in the preparation of the merchandise plan the following year.

Merchandise plans are generally drawn up by independents three to four months in advance of the period to which they refer. The length of the lead time will vary with the store but must be completed before actual buying for the season commences. Remember, the plan is a guide to buying; as such, it should be both specific and flexible in its attempt to forecast sales for the period. Therefore, as the season unfolds, the plan will need to be reviewed and adjusted to meet any changing conditions.

PREPARATION OF THE MERCHANDISE PLAN

The preparation of the merchandise plan follows a relatively simple procedure as outlined by the following steps:

Steps in the Merchandise Plan

1. Planning Seasonal Sales
2. Planning Seasonal Stock Turnover
3. Planning Seasonal Stocks
4. Planning Reductions
5. Planning Purchases
6. Planning Control Data

1. Planning Seasonal Sales

The first step in the preparation of the merchandise plan is the realistic calculation of the forecasted sales for the season.

Once the store is able to determine the planned sales for the six-month season, the estimated sales for each month in the season is based on the previous year's sales distribution. While the dollar figures inserted in the sales columns represent estimates by the merchant, they should also be considered the sales goals for the store for the season.

Retailers generally express their sales goals in dollars and as a percentage increase or decrease in the actual sales as compared with last year's results. In arriving at these sales estimates for the season, and each month, remember that the sales figure is really derived from a relationship between the number of transactions experienced by the store and the average sale of these transactions. Thus, a merchant who seeks to improve the sales picture may do so by attempting to increase the number of transactions while maintaining the same level of the average sale, or vice versa. It is also possible to increase the store's sales by effecting an increase in both the number of transactions and the average sale. Therefore, the merchant's merchandising strategy will affect the relationship between the average sale for the store and the number of transactions anticipated.

Once the seasonal planned sales have been estimated, you can calculate the sales goals for each month based on a predetermined percentage distribution as indicated in the following sample. These percentage figures are normally derived from the trends developed in the firm over the previous years of operation. Monthly sales distribution figures are also available in most cases from trade associations and publications.

Sample Monthly Sales Distribution

Spring-Summer		Fall-Winter	
February	10%	August	10%
March	15%	September	10%
April	15%	October	15%
May	20%	November	20%
June	25%	December	30%
July	15%	January	15%
Total	100%	Total	100%

The monthly sales figures which are forecasted for the store can be affected by variations in the number of selling days in a month, or by such factors as the changing date of Easter. In planning for each month's sales goal, you must also realize that special events in previous years might have seriously affected actual sales and hence may now affect future results. Delivery problems, severe changes in weather conditions, special attractions in the community, or special promotions encountered by competitors can significantly affect the sales results of retail stores. In many cases successful retailers keep a daily store diary in which they list special conditions that have affected sales during the day, week, and month.

Once the monthly sales figures (based on the percentage distribution) have been calculated, the figures are entered on the six-month merchandise plan under last year's figures. These monthly figures are then used in the calculation of the planned-stock figures as we shall see.

For example, a men's apparel store (let's call it Dean's Men's Wear) had actual sales last year of $210,000 and have planned for a 15% increase this year as a result of rising prices and improved merchandising activity. The seasonal distribution of monthly sales is expected to be the same as last year as indicated below.

Seasonal Sales Distribution

Dean's Men's Wear

February	10%
March	15%
April	15%
May	20%
June	25%
July	15%

Since the planned sales this season will increase by 15%, the total spring-summer sales goal will be $241,500 for this year's season. The sales goal for each month will then be based on the sales percentages listed above as the seasonal distribution. As the season progresses, the actual sales figures will be entered on the plan to determine if and where changes are needed.

Exhibit 6-2
Merchandise Plan—Sales in Dollars

Sales in Dollars	Spring	Feb.	Mar.	Apr.	May	June	July	Total
	Last Year	21,000	31,500	31,500	42,000	52,500	31,500	210,000
	Plan	24,150	36,225	36,225	48,300	60,375	36,225	241,500
	Actual							

2. Planning Seasonal Stock Turnover

The rate of stock turnover is perhaps the most commonly quoted figure in the retail trade. However, different individuals have used the term in different ways. While some merchants tend to equate turnover with the gross sales realized by the store, the true meaning of the term is that stock turnover refers to the rate at which the average inventory on hand has been sold and replaced. Simply, the stock turnover is an index of the velocity with which the merchandise moves in and out of the store. Therefore, a hardware store operating with a seasonal stock turnover of 2.5 has sold and replaced its average stock two and one-half times during that season.

While retailers generally calculate the stock turnover for the store as a whole, more meaningful information can be obtained by calculating the turnover rate in the various departments or merchandise lines for the store. In this way, the merchandising efficiency of all sectors of the store can be measured more accurately.

The calculation of the stock turnover rate can be done either by using cost figures or retail figures. Most progressive merchants operate on the retail method of inventory and, as such, maintain their inventory records at retail prices. Using retail figures, the formula for obtaining stock turnover would be as follows:

$$\text{Stock Turnover Rate (at Retail)} = \frac{\text{Dollar Net Sales}}{\text{Dollar Average Inventory at Retail}}$$

Retailers still operating on the cost basis of inventory would calculate their stock turnover rate using the cost figures in the following manner:

$$\text{Stock Turnover Rate (at Cost)} = \frac{\text{Dollar Cost of Goods Sold}}{\text{Dollar Average Inventory at Cost}}$$

It is essentially an understanding of the relationship between the sales figures and the average inventory investment that makes the stock turnover rate such an important figure in the retail trade. If we are able to increase the stock turnover for the store by increasing the sales and maintaining the same average stock, we are in fact being more productive with the same dollar investment in inventory. The essential role of stock turnover is to ensure the proper balance between sales and inventory.

Stock turnover rates are generally quoted by the various trade

Exhibit 6-3

Stock Turnovers for Selected Merchandise Departments

Merchandise Lines	Median	Superior
Women's Dresses	3.7	4.3
Bridal and Formal Wear	2.8	5.3
Separates and Co-ordinates	4.2	4.7
Corsets and Bras	2.1	2.9
Lingerie and Sleepwear	3.1	3.7
Jewellery and Watches	3.7	4.6
Costume Jewellery	3.3	3.8
Hosiery	2.9	3.6
Handbags	4.1	4.8
Women's Footwear	3.8	4.7
Men's Clothing	2.5	3.2
Men's Furnishings	2.4	3.1
Children's Apparel and Accessories	2.7	3.0
Stationery and Office Equipment	2.6	3.8
Cosmetics and Toiletries	2.3	3.6
Hobby, Recreation & Transportation	2.0	2.8
Toys	2.0	4.3
Books, Arts and Photo	2.1	3.1
Home Furnishings	1.8	2.3
Floor Coverings	2.4	3.6
China and Glassware	1.6	1.9
Gifts	1.6	2.0
Housewares	2.3	2.7
Lawn and Garden	2.6	3.3
Linens and Domestics	2.4	2.7
Patterns	.5	1.0
Fabrics	1.4	1.8

Source: National Retail Merchants Association, *Department Store and Specialty Store Merchandising and Operating Results* (New York: 1975).

associations. Exhibit 6-3 indicates the stock turnover of retailers in the various merchandise lines and is generally used by existing retailers as a means of comparing their productivity with other merchants in the same merchandise lines.

For the calculation of the stock turnover rate, the average stock is assumed to be the average of the amount of the inventory on hand during a specific period of time. As such, the average inventory for a month is found by adding the BOM inventory to the EOM inventory amount and dividing this total by two. Therefore, the average inventory for a month with a BOM stock of $43,000 and an EOM stock of $58,000 would be $50,500 ($101,000/2). In a similar manner, the average inventory for the season can be found by finding the average of the sum of the six BOM stocks for each of the months in the season and the EOM stock for the last month and then dividing this figure by seven.

As we shall see in the next step, the planned stock turnover is used by the retailer in the preparation of the beginning-of-the-month stock of the merchandise plan.

3. Planning Seasonal Stocks

Once the merchant has planned the monthly sales for the season and has planned the seasonal stock turnover, the next task is that of determining the amount of stock that will be required in the store to achieve these sales figures. On the merchandise plan two stock figures will be required for budget purposes: the beginning-of-the-month (BOM) stocks, and the end-of-the-month (EOM) stocks. Both of these figures are calculated in retail dollars.

The objective in planning a BOM inventory is to provide a sufficient dollar investment in breadth and depth of assortment to achieve the budgeted sales figures for the month. On the other hand, the planning of the EOM inventory ensures that on the last day of the month sufficient stock will be on hand in the store to achieve the next month's sales goals. Thus, the EOM stock for one month is in fact the BOM stock for the following month. Barring theft or fire, the stock on hand when the store closes on March 31 should be identical to the inventory available at the time the store opens on April 1. However, the retailer's primary concern is in estimating the opening inventory for each month. It is essentially to this problem that this section will be devoted.

There are different mathematical approaches to the planning of stocks; you must select the one which best satisfies your operation. The method selected will depend on the frequency of the stock turnover rate of the merchandise line and the stability of demand for the items in the line. The four methods of planning stocks for each month are the basic stock method, the percentage variation method, the stock-sales ratio method, and the weeks' supply method.

The Basic Stock Method The basic stock method is recommended for use when the stock turnover is three times or less per season and is based on the premise that such a retail store will always have a basic amount of stock on hand regardless of the sales volume. This represents the minimum amount of stock that a retailer will have in the store at any point in time. Once the retailer calculates the basic stock, this amount will be added to the planned sales for that month to determine the BOM for the month in question. By definition, the basic stock is equal to the average stock for the season minus the average monthly sales for the season. In equation form,

$$\text{Basic Stock} = \text{Average Stock} - \text{Average Monthly Sales}$$

$$\text{and BOM Stock} = \text{Basic Stock} + \text{Planned Sales for the Month}$$

For example, let us return to Dean's Men's Wear. Let's say the merchant has planned for a stock turnover of 2.5 for the season, with planned sales of $241,500. With this information, it is now possible to calculate the BOM stock for each month in the spring-summer season. Since the turnover is less than three per season, the basic stock method is recommended for use. With this data,

$$\text{Average Stock} = \frac{\text{Planned Net Sales}}{\text{Planned Stock Turnover}} = \frac{\$241,500}{2.5} = \$96,600$$

$$\text{Average Monthly Sales} = \frac{\text{Planned Net Sales}}{\text{Number of Months}} = \frac{\$241,500}{6} = \$40,250$$

$$\begin{aligned}\text{Basic Stock} &= \text{Average Stock} - \text{Average Monthly Sales}\\ &= \$96,600 - \$40,250\\ &= \$56,350\end{aligned}$$

Therefore, to arrive at the beginning-of-the-month inventory (in dollars), the basic stock of $56,350 is added to the sales for each month in the example illustrated by Exhibit 6-2.

Exhibit 6-4
Merchandise Plan—BOM Stock

BOM	Spring	Feb.	Mar.	Apr.	May	June	July	Total
	Last Year							
	Plan	80,500	92,575	92,575	104,650	116,725	92,575	579,600
	Actual							

Since these figures represent the BOM stock for each month in the season, it is now possible to insert the EOM figures. Since one month's EOM is the following month's BOM, the first five figures can be entered on the plan.

Exhibit 6-5
Merchandise Plan—EOM Stock

	Spring	Feb.	Mar.	Apr.	May	June	July	Total
EOM	Last Year							
	Plan	92,575	92,575	104,650	116,725	92,575		
	Actual							

We are missing the EOM figure for the month of July, since this would be represented by the BOM for August. However, we do know that the total of the six BOM stocks for the season plus the EOM stock for July must equal the average stock for the season. These seven figures represent the average stock, since the season is designated by the time frame from February 1 to July 31. Therefore, this relationship can be expressed as follows:

$$\frac{\text{Average}}{\text{Stock}} = \frac{\text{Sum of 6 BOMs} + \text{July EOM}}{7}$$

But we know the Average Stock is $96,600 $(\frac{\$241,500}{2.5})$

And from the plan the sum of the 6 BOMs = $579,600

Therefore, $96,600 = $\frac{\$579,600 + \text{July EOM}}{7}$

$$\begin{aligned}
\text{July EOM} &= 7 \,(\$96,600) - \$579,600 \\
&= \$676,200 - \$579,600 \\
&= \underline{\$\ 96,600}
\end{aligned}$$

This figure can now be inserted into the merchandise plan
as the EOM for the month of July.

We have now completed the BOM, EOM, and planned sales data in the preparation of the complete merchandise plan. Before proceeding with the compilation of the plan, though, it is necessary to explain the three remaining methods of planning stocks. **The Percentage Variation Method** The percentage variation method of stock planning is used in retail establishments which experience a more rapid rate of stock turnover than do those stores using the basic stock method. Merchants with a stock turnover rate of more than three per season do not require a basic stock on hand at all times but rather tend to vary the amount of stock that will be available for sale.

The amount of this variation to the average stock for the season is one-half the variation that exists between the planned sales for the month in relation to the average monthly sales for the season. While this appears to be relatively complex it simply means that if the planned sales for April, for example, are 30%

greater than the average monthly sales for that season, then the BOM for April would only need to be 15% (½ the variation) greater than the planned average stock for the season. The same variation will apply if the planned sales for the month are less than the average monthly sales for the season.

The calculation of the BOM stock using the percentage variation method is usually expressed by the following formula for easier understanding:

$$\text{BOM Stock} = \text{Average Stock} \times \tfrac{1}{2} \left(1 + \frac{\text{Planned Sales for Month}}{\text{Average Monthly Sales}}\right)$$

Since the example of the men's apparel store that we are using has a planned stock turnover of 2.5, the merchandise plan to be completed for illustration uses the basic stock method of planning.

Stock-Sales Ratio Method   In the example of the men's apparel store that is being used, it is possible to establish a direct relationship between planned sales and the stock that should be on hand to achieve the planned sales goals. Some merchants have attempted to plan their BOM stock solely on the basis of these ratios, since the stock can be planned for a specific period of time rather than being based on the average stock (as is required in the basic stock method).

Such ratios are developed from the store's past experience or from data published by the various trade associations. An example of the stock-sales ratios for selected trades can be seen in Exhibit 6-6.

If the BOM stock-sales ratio for the month of March is planned at 2.8, and the planned sales for the month of March are designated as $30,000 then the BOM stock for that month should be $84,000, or 2.8 times the planned sales of $30,000.

You'll notice that calculation of the amount of stock required in a retail store using the stock-sales ratio is by far the simplest of the three methods of stock planning. For this reason, retailers who are able to establish a direct relationship between stock and sales for their merchandise lines use this method of stock planning extensively.

Weeks' Supply Method   The weeks' supply method of stock planning is generally used for staple merchandise where the rate of sales per week can be relatively accurately determined. In such cases, sales are planned by the week rather than on a monthly basis since the store experiences fairly stable sales volumes with these lines or items. The number of weeks of supplies needed on hand is dependent upon the planned stock

Exhibit 6-6

Monthly Stock-Sales Ratios by Selected Departments

Merchandise Lines	Jan.	Feb.	Mar.	Apr.	May	June	July	Aug.	Sept.	Oct.	Nov.	Dec.
Women's and Misses' Dresses	3.36	3.25	2.94	2.31	1.87	1.69	2.57	2.78	2.21	2.90	2.77	1.46
Women's and Misses' Sportswear	2.71	2.86	2.86	2.75	2.39	2.33	2.74	2.84	1.88	2.65	2.39	1.15
Furs	2.25	4.70	11.23	18.80	28.05	34.03	9.12	6.06	5.78	4.45	3.39	2.12
Infants' and Children's Apparel	3.82	4.46	3.53	3.88	3.79	3.57	4.31	3.66	3.07	3.69	3.10	1.75
Intimate Apparel	4.11	4.28	3.13	3.13	3.17	2.73	3.18	3.51	2.82	4.00	3.68	2.28
Men's Clothing	4.54	5.83	3.57	4.29	4.45	3.56	5.17	6.17	3.94	3.78	3.33	2.06
Men's Furnishings	4.73	5.20	4.45	4.56	4.52	3.06	4.09	4.81	3.96	4.38	2.82	0.93
Boys' Apparel	5.88	6.58	3.82	4.01	4.75	4.24	6.56	3.35	3.35	4.58	3.54	1.76
Photographic Equip. & Supplies	4.48	4.87	4.05	4.73	4.36	2.88	2.79	3.55	3.48	5.45	4.18	1.37
Linens and Domestics	3.32	6.09	5.33	5.35	4.93	4.14	3.38	3.91	2.96	4.46	4.07	2.73
China and Glassware	7.24	8.91	7.32	7.35	7.52	6.71	6.56	7.30	5.67	7.77	4.92	2.13
Furniture	3.45	5.35	4.83	4.99	4.60	3.99	4.04	4.54	3.63	4.42	4.59	5.38
Hardware, Paint, and Wallpaper	5.54	6.34	5.16	3.76	3.88	3.62	4.26	4.94	4.10	4.61	4.55	3.22
Jewellery	7.66	7.49	6.40	6.12	6.14	4.94	5.09	5.67	4.69	6.67	3.86	1.34
Sporting Goods and Luggage	4.08	6.51	6.33	4.66	4.24	3.23	3.53	5.38	5.11	6.33	4.40	1.84
Stationery, Books, Magazines	3.60	3.66	3.77	3.86	4.45	3.74	3.44	3.32	2.55	4.29	2.93	1.07

Source: Statistics Canada, Department Stores Sales and Stocks, June 1977, pp. 16-17.

turnover for the store or merchandise line. Thus, if the turnover is planned at 8 for the six-month season for an item, then the number of weeks' supply required as coverage for the sales would be 3¼ (26 weeks in season/8). If we assume that the item in question sells at the rate of 100 per week, this would indicate that the amount of stock needed on hand to cover 3¼ weeks' supply would be 325 units.

This method of stock planning does not provide for a minimum basic stock no matter how low sales drop, since the stock will vary directly with changes in the sales volume. As a result, it has the disadvantage of bringing about changes in the stock position ahead of anticipated changes in sales. Therefore, it is generally used for the unit control of some staple items.

The retailer should note that the calculation of the stock to be carried will depend on the type and nature of the merchandise and how accurately the relationship between stock and sales can be planned.

4. Planning Reductions

The next step in the preparation of the merchandise plan is to budget the monthly reductions that are anticipated during the season. Since virtually every retailer must recognize the fact that reductions in the retail value of the store's inventory will inevitably result from markdowns, stock shortages, or discounts to employees, planning and control of the amounts are essential.

Markdowns represent reductions in the retail price of a single item or group of items. Mysterious disappearances from inventory through customer shoplifting, employee pilferage or inaccurate stock counts and inventory checking are referred to as stock shortages. Employee discounts represent special discounts offered to employees of the store. The retailer will note that all reductions are in fact the dollar difference between the previously recorded price of merchandise and the price to which the merchandise is being reduced in order to be sold.

Since reductions inevitably occur in all retail stores, they must be considered in planning the purchases required for the store. As such, reductions, in addition to sales and EOM inventory, help determine the merchandise that will be needed by the retail establishment.

The total reduction figure anticipated for the firm is planned as a percentage of each season's sales. Thus, a retailer who has planned for reductions of 11% has arrived at this percentage based on previous experience which may have caused mark-downs of 8%, stock shortages of 2%, and employee discounts of 1%. When this percentage is converted to total dollar reductions, the monthly distribution is calculated based on the store's allocation of when and to what extent the reductions will occur.

As a general principle, it is important to stress that markdowns should be made while there is still sufficient demand for the items, so that the goods can be sold with a minimum of price reductions. Independent retailers tend to find themselves in difficulty by postponing markdowns to clear their stocks until the end of the season. As a result, customer demand may have been satisfied at other outlets, forcing the merchant to take drastic reductions or carry over the inventory for another year. In either case the gross margin is seriously affected.

For example, proceeding further with the merchandise plan for the men's apparel store, we find that the retailer has anticipated that markdowns will represent 8% of sales, while stock shortages and employee discounts together will constitute another 2% of total sales. The seasonal distribution of these reductions is planned to be allocated to each month as follows:

February	15%	May	15%
March	10%	June	20%
April	10%	July	30%
	Total: 100%		

With total reductions equal to 10% of total sales of $241,500, the total reductions will be $24,150. These total dollar reductions are then divided on the merchandise plan according to the percentage distribution figures indicated above. The monthly percentage reduction is a per cent of total reductions, and not a per cent of each month's sales.

Exhibit 6-7

Merchandise Plan—Reductions

Reductions	Spring	Feb.	Mar.	Apr.	May	June	July	Total
	Last Year							
	Plan	3623	2415	2415	3622	4830	7245	24,150
	Actual							

5. Planning Purchases

We have now reached the stage in the preparation of the merchandise plan in which the planned purchases at retail can be calculated. As indicated earlier, for each month we apply the basic premise:

Total Merchandise Needed — Total Merchandise Available = Retail Purchases

In referring to the total merchandise plan in Exhibit 6-8, you'll note the folio column which spells this relationship and allows for easier calculation of the monthly purchases:

Sales + Reductions + Retail EOM — Retail BOM = Retail Purchases

Merchandise Needed — Merchandise Available = Retail Purchases

The completion of the merchandise plan for our men's apparel store is now possible.

The calculation of the purchases at cost for the store will be determined by the store's planned initial markup which is indicated in the control data section of the plan.

In our example, the planned initial markup has been established as 40%. In this case, the cost complement is 60% (100% − 40%). It is this cost percentage—60%—which is applied to the retail purchase figure to determine the cost of merchandise in dollars. Thus, if retail purchases are calculated to be $70,000, the cost of these items would be $42,000 based on a cost complement of 60%.

The completed merchandise plan, with the cost and retail purchases, is shown in Exhibit 6-8 on pages 118 and 119.

6. Planning Control Data

As indicated, the left side of the merchandise plan provides the planning of markup and expense controls that the merchant is anticipating for the season.

Initial Markup Initial markup represents the beginning markup placed on an item or group of items. Each retailer attempts to place an original (initial) markup on an item that will be large enough to cover all expenses and still provide the store with a profit. Therefore, the following components must be considered by the merchant in calculating the initial markup to be placed on the merchandise as it enters the store:
1. Operating expenses
2. Net profit
3. Reductions
4. Alteration expenses
5. Cash discounts

It has been noted above that the initial markup must at least cover the first two components listed, but experience dictates that in most retail stores the remaining elements play a very important part in determining the size of the initial markup as well.

Each retail store encounters difficulty in selling the merchandise at the original retail prices. Whether this results from inefficient buying by the merchant, changes in demand by the customer, or damage to the items, retailers are required to reduce the retail value of these items by means of markdowns in order to induce customers to purchase them. In addition, stock shortages occur in the store as a result of theft by both customers and employees. Consequently, the total retail dollars the store will receive are reduced by these shortages. Further, retail merchants offer employees discounts on merchandise purchased from the store for their own personal use. Whether the retailer offers employees discounts of 10%, 20%, 25% or offers merchandise at cost, these also represent a reduction in the retail dollars received by the store. Therefore, in planning the initial markup for the store, the merchant recognizes that these three elements (markdowns, stock shortages, and employee discounts) will occur in the operation and provides for them through inclusion in the original markup placed on the merchandise. If reductions are composed of markdowns of 7%, stock shortages of 1%, and employee discounts of 2%, then the total of 10% of planned sales must be covered by the initial markup.

In order to determine initial markup per cent, we must establish a fraction to calculate a ratio. The numerator in this fraction will represent the elements of the operation that must be covered by the markup—operating expenses, net profit, and reductions.

The fraction or ratio must also provide for a denominator which will represent the base upon which the ratio is calculated. Since we are attempting to establish the beginning markup that should be placed on the merchandise, the base (denominator) must represent the original retail price. Therefore, the denominator of the fraction must be composed of the sum of the net sales plus the total amount of the reductions. Since net sales represent the final retail price received by the store, and hence the amount rung up on the cash register, and the total reductions represent the decrease in retail value of this merchandise sold by the store, then the sum of these two factors must represent the original retail prices in the store. If a ski jacket carries an original retail price of $75.00 and is reduced to $50.00 as part of a clear-

Exhibit 6-8
Completed Merchandise Plan

		Spring	Feb.
Six-Month Merchandise Plan	Folio	Fall	Aug.
Department _DEAN'S MEN'S_	Sales — Last Year		21,000
Department No. _APPAREL STORE_	Sales — Plan		24,150
From _February 1_ 19 __	Sales — Actual		
To _July 31_ 19 __	+ Retail EOM — Last Year		101,500
	+ Retail EOM — Plan		92,575
Department Control Data	+ Retail EOM — Actual		
	+ Reductions — Last Year		2520
	+ Reductions — Plan		3623
	+ Reductions — Actual		
	− Retail BOM — Last Year		91,000
	− Retail BOM — Plan		80,500
	− Retail BOM — Actual		
	= Retail Purchases — Last Year		34,020
	= Retail Purchases — Plan		39,848
	= Retail Purchases — Actual		
	Cost Purchases — Last Year		20,413
	Cost Purchases — Plan		23,909
	Cost Purchases — Actual		

	L.Y.	T.Y.
% Initial Markup	40.0	40.0
% Reductions	8.0	10.0
% Maintained Markup	35.2	34.0
% Alteration Expense	5.0	6.0
% Cash Discount	1.0	2.0
% Gross Margin	31.2	30.0
% Operating Expense	27.0	26.0
% Net Profit	4.2	4.0
Season Turnover	2.0	2.5
Control Period	—	—

Planning and Authorization

Buyer _____

Merchandise Controller _____

Date Prepared _____

Date Authorized _____

Source: Albert P. Kneider, *Mathematics of Merchandising*, © 1974, p. 219.

Mar.	Apr.	May	June	July	Total
Sept.	Oct.	Nov.	Dec.	Jan.	
500	31,500	42,000	52,500	31,500	210,000
,225	36,225	48,300	60,375	36,225	241,500
,500	112,000	122,500	101,500	105,000	AVERAGE STOCK 105,000
,575	104,650	116,725	92,575	96,600	96,600
80	1680	2520	3360	5040	16,800
115	2415	3622	4830	7245	24,150
500	101,500	112,000	122,500	101,500	630,000
575	92,575	104,650	116,725	92,575	579,600
180	43,680	55,020	34,860	40,040	240,800
640	50,715	63,997	41,055	47,495	281,750
908	26,208	33,012	20,916	24,024	144,480
184	30,429	38,398	24,633	28,497	169,050

ance sale, and then is sold, the $50.00 is recorded in the cash register as the final retail received as the net sale, while the $25.00 reduction is recorded in the markdown register.

To this point in our analysis, the initial markup fraction will now appear as follows:

$$\text{Initial Markup \%} = \frac{\text{Operating Expenses} + \text{Net Profit} + \text{Reductions}}{\text{Net Sales} + \text{Reductions}}$$

As noted, the numerator of this fraction represents expenses that must be covered by the initial markup. Since some retail operations handle alteration expenses or workroom costs separately from operating expenses, such charges must be considered in the calculation of initial markup. While some retailers, such as those selling women's apparel, charge customers for the alterations completed on garments purchased, the expenses of such a service generally exceed any revenue generated. Therefore, this excess of expenses over revenue must be included as part of the numerator of the equation as an element to be covered by the initial markup.

$$\frac{\text{Initial}}{\text{Markup}} = \frac{\text{Operating Expenses} + \text{Net Profit} + \text{Reductions} + \text{Alteration Expenses}}{\text{Net Sales} + \text{Reductions}}$$

The final factor that must be considered is that represented by the planned cash discounts for the store. Cash discounts are premiums allowed by the suppliers off of the invoice price of the merchandise if payment is made within a specified period of time. As such, cash discounts will increase the gross margin and are then viewed by the merchant as income earned. Thus, in the calculation of initial markup, the cash discount planned by the retailer as a per cent of net sales is deducted from the total requirements of the numerator in the equation.

$$\frac{\text{Initial}}{\text{Markup}} = \frac{\text{Operating} \atop \text{Expenses} + \text{Net} \atop \text{Profit} + \text{Reductions} + \text{Alteration} \atop \text{Expenses} - \text{Cash} \atop \text{Discounts}}{\text{Net Sales} + \text{Reductions}}$$

Therefore, the final equation for the calculation of initial markup has now been presented. You should note that this fraction represents a ratio and as such can be expressed in either dollars or per cents providing each component is defined in the same units. Using the figures presented in the merchandise plan shown in Exhibit 6-8 (in the Department Control Data section), the initial markup per cent is calculated as follows:

$$\text{IM \%} = \frac{26\% + 4\% + 10\% + 6\% - 2\%}{100\% + 10\%} = \frac{44}{110} = 40\%$$

Therefore, based on the information planned by the merchant, the initial markup for Dean's Men's Wear for the spring-summer season will need to be 40%.

Maintained Markup Maintained markup is the final markup realized by the retail store. This markup differs from the initial markup by the reductions on the selling price of the merchandise in the store. Thus, the cost of the planned reductions is subtracted from the initial markup per cent to determine the maintained markup per cent.

In our example, initial markup is planned at 40% and the cost portion of this markup is 60%, as we have noted earlier. With the planned reductions of 10% in the men's wear store, we have a cost of reductions figure of 6% (60% of reductions of 10%) and the maintained markup would be 34% as illustrated below.

$$\text{Maintained Markup} = \text{Initial Markup} - \text{Cost of Reductions}$$
$$\text{Maintained Markup} = 40\% - 6\%$$
$$= 34\%$$

Gross Margin Gross margin represents the dollar difference between net sales for the period and the net cost of the merchandise sold during that period. As such, the gross margin (sometimes referred to as gross profit) differs from maintained markup by the effect of the cash discounts and alteration expenses. Since the maintained markup is the final markup realized, it will be the same as the gross margin if the operation has no alteration expenses and plans to take no cash discounts. However, where these items occur, the cash discount will increase the gross margin, while alteration expenses will decrease it. Therefore, we arrive at the following equation:

$$\text{Gross Margin} = \text{Maintained Markup} + \text{Cash Discounts} - \text{Alteration Expenses}$$

You will also note that the gross margin planned by a retail store must be large enough to cover all operating expenses and provide the store with a net profit. The relationship is best illustrated on the store's income and expense statement, so that:

$$\text{Gross Margin} = \text{Operating Expenses} + \text{Net Profit}$$

The merchandise plan has now been completed. You can use the blank merchandise plan shown in Exhibit 6-1 to prepare a merchandise plan for your retail establishment by working through the process which has been illustrated.

OPEN-TO-BUY (OTB) CONTROLS

Retail merchants engaged in the buying function frequently make reference to the term open-to-buy (OTB) before committing their stores to any purchases. The OTB in dollars represents the amount of money available for merchandise purchases in a given period. To be effective, the dollar OTB must be calculated at frequent intervals to ensure that purchases during the period do not exceed those planned for the period.

In the merchandise plan which we prepared in the previous section, the dollar OTB at the beginning of the period will be identical to the planned purchases. But as orders are placed during the period, these commitments must be deducted from the planned purchases to arrive at the OTB figure at any given time. As merchandise orders are placed for delivery within that period, the planned purchases are correspondingly reduced by the retail value of the orders, to adjust the dollar open-to-buy.

To ensure that actual purchasing is done according to plan, retailers maintain what is known as an OTB control. This control represents a system of charging off the committed orders against the buying limits set in the merchandise plan. Orders which the merchant has placed but not received into stock are referred to as outstanding orders which reduce the OTB for the period in which delivery is anticipated.

The OTB control is essential in retail stores which spread their seasonal buying over the six-month period rather than committing total purchases at the beginning of the season. By purchasing throughout the season, the merchant is able to take advantage of new lines or items that are introduced during the season, or of special promotions offered by suppliers as the season progresses. Without such controls, many independent retailers find themselves in overbought situations that ultimately lead to large markdowns, inventory difficulties, and the inability to capitalize on seasonal changes or merchandise promotions.

The unit OTB controls—on one line of merchandise—are calculated from planned purchases in the same manner as OTB controls for a store. Unit OTB controls are generally used with staple merchandise items that exhibit a fairly stable demand. In these cases minimum and maximum stock positions are established for the items so that at any point in time during the season the open-to-buy in units can be calculated.

MODEL STOCK PLANS

The model stock plan has been defined as a plan on paper of a unit assortment of merchandise, kept with dollar control limits, and distributed in such a way as to best satisfy customer demand at the store for a specified period of time. It is essentially a quantitative picture of the assortment for a season. As such, the model stock plan is used primarily for fashion merchandise when certain selection factors remain relatively stable from one year to another. For example, a merchant may discover that only 10% of the store's sales are coming from the small sizes, as indicated by records over the past few years.

In building a model stock, the merchant should note that it is not advisable to keep the stock in direct proportion to the planned sales for the merchandise line. Some items of merchandise will require a larger assortment of stock than others if the planned sales are to be obtained. Generally, a greater percentage of stock is placed in the merchandise classification that accounts for a smaller percentage of the total sales.

If a women's clothing store has planned sales of $200,000 for the year, with only $2000, or 1%, of the sales generated by neck scarves, the store will require more than 1% of its stock to be in this merchandise line in order to achieve these sales. This occurs since only 1% of the stock on hand would provide the customer with a very limited assortment from which to choose. Therefore, if the same store has a planned annual stock turnover of 4, the store would be operating with an average inventory at retail of $50,000 and consequently only $500 (1%) in neck scarves. With the various selection factors available in this item, the choices available to the customer would be much too limited. However, it is not possible to say with certainty the proportion of stock that might be provided for such a classification. Closer observation of the store's clientele and the merchant's past experience might reveal that perhaps 2% should be placed in these items to achieve the planned sales volume of $2000.

Conversely, merchandise classifications or departments which account for a large percentage of the store's total sales may require a smaller proportion of the total store's inventory to be placed in these items. Each merchant must carefully assess the merchandise line, the planned sales, and the characteristics of the target market to determine the extent of the assortment required to achieve the planned figures.

Exhibit 6-9
Sample Model Stock Plan

Department: _____ MEN'S SUITS _____

Dept. No.: _____

Season: Fall-Winter _____ ✓ _____

Spring-Summer _____

Classification	Size	Quantity for Model Stock		PLAINS		
		%	#	%	#	%
2 BUTTON	36	5	1	1/3	—	1/3
	38	10	3	1/4	1	1/2
% 30%	40	30	8	1/3	3	1/3
	42	30	8	1/3	2	1/3
# 27	44	20	6	1/2	3	1/4
	46	5	1	1/2	1	1/4
Total		100	27		10	
3 BUTTON	36	5	3	1/3	1	1/3
	38	10	5	1/3	1	1/3
% 50%	40	30	13	1/4	3	1/2
	42	30	13	2/5	5	2/5
# 45	44	20	9	1/3	3	1/3
	46	5	2	2/5	1	2/5
Total		100	45		14	
DOUBLE-BREASTED	36	10	2	1/5	—	2/5
	38	15	3	1/3	1	1/3
% 20%	40	30	5	1/5	1	2/5
	42	30	5	1/3	1	1/3
# 18	44	10	2	1/3	1	1/3
	46	5	1	2/5	1	2/5
Total		100	18		5	
Planned Grand Total			90		29	

Source: Albert P. Kneider, Mathematics of Merchandising, © 1974, p. 254.

Item: TWO-PIECE SUITS

Retail Price: $200.00

Buyer: _____

Colour Selections

EDS	CHECKS			%	#	%	#	%	#
#	%	#	%	#	%	#	%	#	
—	1/3	1							
2	1/4	—							
2	1/3	3							
3	1/3	3							
1	1/4	2							
—	1/4	—							
8		9							
1	1/3	1							
2	1/3	2							
6	1/4	4							
5	1/5	3							
3	1/3	3							
1	1/5	—							
18		13							
1	2/5	1							
1	1/3	1							
2	2/5	2							
2	1/3	2							
1	1/3	—							
—	1/5	—							
7		6							
33		28							

The actual planning of a model stock involves deciding on the optimum quantities to have on hand on a specific date in each of the major selection factors that is offered in the merchandise line. The quantities in each factor are determined by evaluating and applying previous year's statistical sales and stock information.

Model stock planning has been used successfully by retailers planning assortments by selection factors in draperies, gifts, lamps, linens, men's and women's apparel, and furniture. These and many other types of shopping goods are generally purchased by retail stores after a model stock plan has been prepared to achieve the proper balance between the selection factors and customer demand.

As an example of model stock planning, let's return once more to Dean's Men's Wear. In our merchandise plan we assumed a planned sales volume of $241,500 for the season. The model stock plan which follows has been prepared for the store's suit line on the basis of these planned sales and data:

1. The model stock plan is being prepared for the store's two-piece men's suits which retail at $200.
2. The store has indicated that 30% of the season's sales will come from the suit department.
3. It is also anticipated from previous years that 50% of the suit sales will be generated by the two-piece suit line in the $200 range.
4. The distribution by style, colour, and size is indicated on the model stock plan in Exhibit 6-9.

Doing the calculations, we find:

Men's suit volume: 30% of $241,500 = $72,450
Two-piece, $200 suits: 50% of $72,450 = $36,225
In units, two-piece, $200 suits = $36,225/$200 = 181 suits

This represents six-months' sales, and assuming the store wishes to maintain three-months' supply because of delivery and assortment, the model will be a 90-suit assortment. This assortment must be divided on the basis of the percentages indicated on the model stock plan. Remember, this is only a guide, and adjustments will need to be made on the plan and in the purchasing.

In contrast to model stock planning, merchants experiencing a great degree of stability in the selection factors of the merchandise they sell make use of basic stock lists. In this type of assort-

Exhibit 6-10
Sample Reorder Form

PERIODIC REORDER FORM

Department: MEN'S FURNISHINGS
Department No.:
Buyer:

Line: UNDERWEAR
Item: REGULAR BRIEF – WHITE
Price: $2.00 **Unit:**

Size	Maximum Stock	Date OCT. 6			Date OCT.13			Date OCT.20			Date OCT. 27		
		OH	OO	S	OH	OO	S	OH	OO	S	OH	OO	S
SMALL	24	8	16	6	18	6	8	16	8	7	17	7	8
MEDIUM	30	9	21	6	24	6	7	23	7	7	23	7	7
LARGE	40	12	28	10	30	10	12	28	12	10	30	10	12
X-LARGE	20	10	10	5	15	5	6	14	6	8	12	8	6

Source: Albert P. Kneider, *Mathematics of Merchandising*, © 1974, p. 248. Reprinted by permission of Prentice-Hall, Inc., Englewood Cliffs, New Jersey.

ment planning, retailers tend to periodically fill the inventory to ensure a proper balance of the breadth and depth of the selection factors offered. Hardware, hosiery, notions, housewares, sporting goods, luggage, and confectionery are some of the items which are planned on the basis of a basic stock list.

Exhibit 6-10 illustrates a periodic reorder form. It is completed for a four-week period to indicate the sales (S), the merchandise on order (OO), and the stock on hand (OH) figures for men's underwear in our men's wear store.

You will note that a maximum stock is established for each size based on the delivery period, the reorder period, and a safety, or reserve factor. Once the maximum has been determined, the stock on hand and on order must equal this amount. Therefore, based on the nature of the merchandise as a staple item, the retailer will constantly build the assortment to the maximum stock level.

For a more detailed explanation of many topics covered in this chapter, you can refer to *Mathematics of Merchandising* (Albert P. Kneider, Prentice-Hall, Inc., 1974).

7
RETAIL MERCHANDISE CONTROL

Controls in any business are designed to direct the operation toward its predetermined objectives. At the very least, the control function should monitor the firm's ability to adapt its business strategy to its target market. Merchandise control attempts to accomplish these objectives by protecting the physical inventory against the various forms of loss associated with stock shortages. Simultaneously, a merchandise-control system must also be able to provide the retailer with information that will assist the store in maintaining the optimum level of inventory investment in both dollars and units. It is essential that the store attempt to balance the merchandise assortment to customer demand in order to maximize the overall inventory investment. Too much inventory results in lost markup through heavy markdowns, while too little inventory results in additional lost markup through lost sales. Therefore, various tools and techniques are used by retail stores to establish merchandise-control systems that will provide the merchant with the necessary information.

BASIC ELEMENTS IN MERCHANDISE CONTROL

Stock-Sales Relationship The basis of any merchandise-control system is to ensure that adequate records are kept to assist the merchant in balancing the assortment to customer demand. In the previous chapter, the merchandise plan was used to balance purchases to anticipated sales. In addition, an effective merchandise-control system attempts to provide the proper assortment of stock each day throughout the month, season, and year in contrast to just the BOM and EOM stock figures which appear on the six-month merchandise plan. Simply, the system is further refined.

To be effective, the relationship of the amount of stock on hand to the anticipated sales should be established for each department or classification in the store. To this end, the BOM stock-sales ratios which were discussed in the previous chapter and illustrated in Exhibit 6-6 outline the relationship that does exist between the BOM stock and the planned monthly sales for various merchandise lines.

For example, if the planned sales in a photographic equipment store have been established at $20,000 for the month of February, and the BOM stock-sales ratio for the month is 4.87 (Exhibit 6-6), then the planned stock required for beginning the month would be $97,400. While this represents the opening inventory for February, it will be necessary to balance the inventory through the month by using an inventory-control system.

Stock Shortages   While retail merchants tend to budget a specified percentage of their planned sales for stock shortages, the effective control of this shrinkage can significantly affect the profitability of the store. Stock shortages occur in retail stores as a result of theft by customers (shoplifting) and by employees (pilferage). Stock shortages also occur in a merchandising operation through errors by employees in recording the merchandise facts. Whatever form it takes, unless controls are established to record this information, the firm's profitability is in jeopardy.

Supermarket operators are generally required to work at a net-profit figure of approximately 2% of net sales. In the event that a customer shoplifts a tin of shrimp which is priced at $2.00, it is necessary for the merchant to sell $100.00 worth of merchandise at retail to recover the loss if the store is operating at a 2% profit margin.

As a result of the popularity of self-service retailing and the subsequent rise of shoplifting, independent retailers are well advised to adopt effective controls that will locate and minimize the amount and incidence of shortages in the store.

You'll note in the discussion of inventory valuation later in this chapter what effect a decrease in stock shortages can have on the overall profitability of the firm. A commitment is needed by the independent to actively seek to control this risk of the retail operation.

Control of Markdowns   Since an important aspect of merchandise control is to ensure the proper balance between stock and sales, independents must establish controls that will signal when the inventory is in excess of what is required. Such a system seeks to expose those items that need to be reduced in price to clear at an early stage. The later the problem of excessive merchandise is discovered, the greater the markdowns required to move the stock. The effect that this will have on the maintained markup and gross margin has already been explained in the previous chapter. Consequently, an accurate recording and control of all markdowns will be essential to improve profits in the retail operation.

Departmental Control   To ensure that all departments and merchandise classifications are contributing to the store's overhead, independent retailers are advised to establish merchandise controls for their operation that will seek to identify the weak departments or classifications. Consequently, it will be necessary for the merchant to organize the operation by departments prior to establishing the control system.

For example, a sporting goods store should be categorized into departments on the basis of the designated sports and service areas provided for the customers. It is then possible, with effective controls, to determine whether the repair department, for example, is contributing its share to the store's overhead.

These four areas represent certain aspects of the retail operation that signify the importance of merchandise control for the independent. The system of establishing and maintaining such controls will vary with respect to the size of the business and the type of merchandise handled. The controls required for the chain organization operating 50 stores across Canada are much more complex and sophisticated than those needed for the independent operation with one store in the local community. Further, it should be noted that the merchandise-control system for big-ticket merchandise like electric lawnmowers will be much different than those required for small plumbing supplies found in the local hardware store. Therefore, different controls may be required in the same store for different merchandise lines.

The discussion which follows in this chapter will need to be reviewed by each independent to determine which concepts and controls will most effectively provide the information required in operating a successful retail establishment.

In general, the need for a merchandise-control system in a retail store becomes especially apparent at the time the buying plans need to be made. To effectively prepare the six-month merchandise plan illustrated in the previous chapter, merchandise information and records must be available to indicate the past experience of the store. Adjustments can be made to this plan on the basis of the anticipated sales and purchases, when the actual figures are recorded on the plan on a monthly basis.

At the beginning of this section, it was noted that an effective merchandise-control system must be designed to protect the physical inventory and to determine the appropriate level of inventory investment. To achieve these objectives, merchandise control is generally accomplished on the basis of either a dollar-control system or a unit-control system. The unit-control system is generally used to supplement and refine the dollar-control system established and already explained by the merchandise plan. Effective merchandise control therefore requires that the retail purchases of $39,848 for the month of February in Exhibit 6-8 be further broken down by units on the basis of the various selection factors. To avoid both overbuying and out-of-stock situations, such unit planning is essential.

MERCHANDISE-CONTROL SYSTEMS

Dollar-Control System

Before a dollar-control system can be established, it is necessary to organize the various merchandise lines into departments. The larger the store becomes, the more numerous will be the merchandising divisions. As a result, a large retail operation may group the merchandise assortment in the store on the basis of divisions which are then subdivided into departments and then into classifications. For example:

> Division: Women's Ready-to-Wear Apparel
> Department: Coats
> Classification: All-weather Coats

It is possible to carry this merchandise grouping into a finer division on the basis of size or the importance of the various classifications. Therefore, in the above example a subclassification might be hooded, all-weather coats, or petite all-weather coats. The larger the role of the computer or automatic processing system in tabulating and analyzing the information of the store, the more likely the grouping is to be carried from superdivisions to many subclassifications. Generally, the factors of sales volume, markup, turnover, and customer buying habits determine their importance to the store and their designation as a division, department, or classification.

Regardless of the degree to which the retail store extends its merchandise control, the same system of control can be employed by both departments and classifications. You'll note throughout this chapter that the dollar-control system is used in the merchandise plan, the dollar open-to-buy, and the inventory-management controls for each division, department, and classification.

Unit Control

While dollar control of the merchandise is essential to the operation of the independent store, it may be necessary to implement a system of unit controls to supplement this information. Unit control is a system designed to determine, analyze, and control the sales and inventories in units. Each independent must do some planning in terms of units as well as dollars. To efficiently and profitably execute the function of buying and selling merchandise items for the store, unit information will be required in varying degrees of detail.

A men's furnishings' store which buys casual shirts may only have to establish a requirement for 12 dozen long-sleeve sport shirts in assorted colours. On the other hand, the same store may wish to carry dress shirts, in which case much more detail in planning the unit information for the shirts—by neck size, sleeve length, collar type, colour, fabric, and cuff choice—is necessary.

In an independent retail operation, dollar control is first established by the store, then by the department, and then by classification. The further the system of dollar control is extended, the greater the need for the information provided by a unit-control system. Merchants are required to purchase items for the store and therefore need information on the quantitative aspects of the merchandise as well as the dollar value. Any merchant responsible for purchasing an assortment of women's or men's footwear and the many, many selection factors available, will extensively use the information provided by the unit-control system.

A unit-control system is employed to control the relationship between the inventory available for sale and the planned sales in units for the period. This information is used by the buyers in planning their merchandise assortment. Retailers responsible for the selling function in the store also require unit information to establish the store's on-hand position with each item and the item's rate of sale in an effort to ensure effective promotion of the total inventory.

Regardless of the complexities of the various unit-control systems, every application involves the following steps:

1. Deciding on the system for the store, the division, the department, and the classification
2. The daily or periodic recording of unit information
3. The analysis of the daily, weekly, or monthly summaries
4. Effective interpretation of the information for control and decision making.

While there are variations in the methods and techniques of merchandise-control systems that can be used by the independent, it should be remembered that the primary purpose of the system is to provide information that can be effectively applied in the store. Such information is of very little value if the retailer simply collects and assembles such data without making use of it for merchandising decisions. Functionally, the control system should assist the retailer:

1. In planning the merchandise assortment in dollars and units
2. In planning purchases by price lines and selection factors in each classification
3. In planning the anticipated sales in dollars and units
4. In planning the purchase of special promotional items
5. In planning for the disposal of "sleepers" or slow-selling merchandise.

Therefore, the merchandise-control system for each independent must be planned to provide the store with useful, practical information. Throughout this chapter, the emphasis is to be placed on the importance of a control system rather than on all of the techniques of implementing such a system. In summary, the primary purpose of the merchandise-control system instituted by the independent must be an attempt to maximize sales from the dollars invested in inventory.

With this objective in mind, retailers will require some means of recording the dollar and unit investments in inventory. In simpler terms, the merchant must be able to measure, control, and analyze the quantitative data about the stock carried in the store. To this end, retailers use either a perpetual or periodic inventory system. The method used will depend on the capabilities of the store and the type and nature of the merchandise assortment.

Perpetual Inventory Control

The perpetual inventory record consists of detailed records of the dollar or unit investment of the merchandise on hand, showing daily changes in the stock received and the merchandise sold. Thus, as the name implies, the inventory record is updated with daily purchases received into stock and daily sales.

Consequently, to determine the inventory on hand by using a dollar control and a perpetual system, the retail value of the purchases is added to the retail value of the opening inventory to determine the total merchandise available for sale in retail dollars. When sales and reductions are subtracted from this total, the dollar inventory on hand at retail at any point in time can be calculated. Let's refer back to the completed merchandise plan in Exhibit 6-8. The relationship established for the month of February can be illustrated using a perpetual inventory control system at retail dollars:

BOM Inventory, February 1, at Retail		$ 80,500
Planned Purchases, February 1-28, at Retail		39,848
Total Merchandise Available at Retail, February		$120,348
Less:		
Planned Sales, February 1-28	$24,150	
Planned Reductions, February 1-28	3,623	27,773
EOM Inventory, February 28, at Retail		$ 92,575

While we have used the above example to explain the relationship of the factors on a monthly basis to tie in with the merchandise plan, the same application will result when recording purchases, sales, and reductions on a daily basis.

The implementation of a perpetual inventory system is as easily applied to retail stores and merchandise lines which use a unit-control system of inventory management. Exhibit 7-1 illustrates a type of unit-control record that might be employed by a retail store seeking to maintain a perpetual record of a line or item of merchandise. You'll note that the form seeks to record information on a daily basis in units using the perpetual inventory relationship:

Exhibit 7-1
Unit Stock Control Record

Stock No.					Description					Mfg. Name				
Cost					**Retail**					**Mfg. No.**				
Date	On Hand	Rec'd	Sold	On Order	Date	On Hand	Rec'd	Sold	On Order	Date	On Hand	Rec'd	Sold	On Order

Department | **Classification**

Inventory On Hand	(On Hand)
+ Purchases Received	(Received)
= Merchandise Available	
− Sales	(Sold)
= Inventory On Hand	(On Hand − Next Period)

Thus, you'll note that a perpetual inventory control, whether in dollars or units, will provide for a rapid calculation of the inventory on hand at a specific point in time without taking a physical count. The information can be derived from the sales receipts and records, purchase journals, and markdown registers rather than from the onerous task of physically counting the stock on hand. However, it will be necessary at some point during the fiscal year to reconcile the stock on hand at book value with a count of the physical inventory to determine the amount of stock shortages or overages.

The use of the perpetual inventory system simplifies the adoption of the retail method of inventory valuation that will be discussed later in this chapter. Therefore, when the perpetual system is extended to the retail method of accounting, the independent merchant is not only able to maintain a continuous record of stock-on-hand but also the daily computation of initial markup and gross margin realized in each classification.

Periodic Inventory Control

Many independent merchants have not adopted the technique of updating their inventory accounts each time a purchase or sale is made. Such merchants use the periodic inventory method which requires that a physical inventory be taken at the end of each accounting period to determine the stock on hand.

Stock taking in retail stores has always been considered a major operation by the independent and consequently is generally relegated to completion on an annual basis only. A periodic inventory control system requires the physical stock taking of items to balance the stock on hand with the purchases and sales figures during the period.

While the periodic system can be implemented as an inventory management tool in both dollars and units, the relationship of the elements in its application will remain the same.

For example, purchases at retail are added to the opening inventory at retail for the period to determine the merchandise that was available for sale. On the basis of a dollar-control system, the physical inventory is then taken in retail dollars and subtracted from the total merchandise handled to determine the sales and reductions that were achieved during the period.

Continuing with the example of the merchandise plan in Exhibit 6-8, and using the same figures, the relationship of a periodic system is as follows:

Opening Inventory, February 1	$ 80,500
+ Purchases Received, February 1-28	39,848
= Merchandise Available, February 1-28	$120,348
− Physical Inventory, February 28, EOM	92,575
= Derived Sales and Reductions	$ 27,773

For purposes of this calculation only, we are assuming that the physical inventory is the same as the planned EOM. In actual fact, the coincidence of this happening in a retail store would be rare. What is important here is the relationship rather than the accuracy of the numbers presented.

Thus, the periodic system of inventory control requires the tabulation of a physical inventory in dollars and/or units to determine sales, reductions, and shortages.

In selecting whether to employ a periodic or perpetual inventory system, you must examine the costs of each system as well as the extent of the information required to make decisions. With new developments in cash register systems, and the subsequent applications of the computer to information retrieval, the arduous task of a perpetual system has been significantly simplified. As a result, many more retailers (including a growing number of independents) have chosen a perpetual inventory system made possible by point-of-sale recording of information.

THE INVENTORY COUNT

Whether a periodic or perpetual inventory system is used by the independent, a physical count of the inventory on hand is mandatory at some time during the accounting period. It is only through a careful and accurate count of the physical inventory that the stock on hand can be compared to the book inventory to determine the amount and degree of stock shortages being experienced by the store.

As noted earlier, this task is a time-consuming one for the merchant and, as a result, is only taken on an annual basis by many independents. However, the information that can be provided by this activity may induce the merchant to take physical inventory at least for each turnover period. The physical counting and listing of the stock on hand at a particular time serves the following purposes for the merchant:

1. By establishing the appropriate value of the inventory a more accurate statement of profit is possible.
2. It establishes the rate of sale of various classifications of merchandise noted in the dollar- and unit-control systems.
3. It designates and suggests adoption of a strategy for the merchandising of slow-selling merchandise.
4. It determines the amount and sources of stock shortages in the store.

Since most independents take inventory at their year end, the policy established is to physically count all items in the store as soon after this date as possible. Some merchants use the end of the calendar year, December 31, while others use a low-inventory period like January 31. The store's accountant will play a large role in advising you on the most appropriate date to use for the store's fiscal year end.

However, it should be noted that stores selling high-unit value items such as expensive cameras or jewellery, or large-bulk items like furniture or automobiles have opted to physically count the merchandise on a much more frequent basis and are consequently more likely to use a perpetual inventory system.

In taking the physical inventory, you are advised to plan in advance the system to be used to ensure that an accurate count is taken. Decisions on taking the count in dollars and/or units, at cost or at retail prices, and by the different geographical areas in the store layout, must be made and clearly defined before the physical activity commences. While each retail store will attempt to establish its own method of recording the information, Exhibit 7-2 illustrates a physical inventory columnar sheet that is used by some merchants. An attempt should be made to keep the form to be used as simple as possible for the recording of the necessary data.

Book Inventory and Physical Inventory

After the physical count of the inventory has been completed, tabulated, and applied to the data available in the store, you must

Exhibit 7-2
Physical Inventory Sheet

INVENTORY SHEET

Dept. No. _____ Department _____ Date _____

Called by: _____ Written by: _____ Sheet No. ___

Stock No.	Merchandise Description	Quantity	Unit Price	Extension
		TOTAL		

compare this figure with what the records show should be available in the store's inventory. In situations where the physical count of the inventory on hand in the store is less than the inventory which should be available, this discrepancy is called a stock shortage. Where the count exceeds the amount that should be available in the store according to the purchases and sales records, the difference is referred to as a stock overage. In either case, you will note that a discrepancy exists between the physical inventory for the store and its book inventory.

As we noted in our discussions of initial markup, retailers recognize that it is virtually impossible to totally eliminate these shortages from retail operations and, as a result, plan a small percentage of their planned sales to be allocated to this element. These shortages are generally attributed to employee and customer theft. Minor variances in inventory figures, whether shortages or overages, result most frequently from inaccurate physical counts or incorrect pricing of merchandise items which are placed into stock.

Recapping

To this point in the chapter we have established that the function of merchandise control is that process of accounting for the investment in inventory in both dollars and units. Such a process implies either a periodic or perpetual inventory control system, both of which require that a physical count of the inventory be taken at some point during the fiscal year. Once the count has been taken, and the system established, a means of valuing the inventory at cost dollars or retail dollars will need to be determined. The remainder of this chapter seeks to explore the concepts relating to the methods of inventory valuation.

INVENTORY VALUATION

The anatomy of any profit and loss statement for a retail store will reveal that the valuation of the beginning and ending inventories is essential to the calculation of the store's cost of merchandise sold. By reviewing this relationship, it will become evident that the valuation of the cost of goods sold will play an important part in stating an accurate value of the net operating profit of the store.

$$
\begin{array}{l}
\text{Net Sales} \\
- \text{ Cost of Goods Sold} \\
\hline
= \text{ Gross Margin} \\
- \text{ Operating Expenses} \\
\hline
= \text{ Net Operating Profit}
\end{array}
$$

As noted, it is the cost of goods sold section of this relationship that is affected by the valuation of the inventory of the store. From the fundamental components listed above, it will be obvious that an incorrect valuation of the inventory may tend to overstate or understate the store's profit and subsequently affect the taxes to be paid by the store. Care must be taken in deciding on the method and techniques to be employed in establishing a value for the inventory on hand.

To determine the cost of goods sold, the following procedure had been noted previously:

> Inventory, Beginning of the Period
> + Purchases, During the Period
> + Freight on These Purchases
> _____
> = Total Merchandise Handled During the Period
> − Sales and Reductions During the Period
> − Inventory on Hand, End of the Period
> _____
> = Cost of Goods Sold During the Period

Although there are different methods of evaluating the inventory and consequently the cost of goods sold, all are concerned with the proper flow of cost records from one period to another. Generally, retailers are confronted with two basic methods—namely, the cost method of inventory valuation and the retail method of inventory valuation. We will look at each method.

The Cost Method of Inventory Valuation

The cost method of inventory valuation requires that the beginning inventory be taken at cost, that purchases be recorded at cost from the invoices received, and that all sales be calculated through a coding system on the price tickets to determine costs. Therefore, in establishing the value of the inventory, each item and its quantities are listed, the cost price code on the ticket is then translated into dollars, and the extension of units multiplied by cost dollars per unit is recorded on the inventory sheet. When this has been completed for all items on hand, the total cost of the merchandise on hand is determined, and represents the inventory on hand at the end of the period.

Since such a system requires a price-coding system, a common method of indicating the cost of an item is through the use of a ten-letter word or expression with non-repeating letters corresponding to the numerals to be used. It should be noted at this time that it is also extremely useful and essential to the profitability of the store that you attempt to build a date code into the system being employed to determine the age of the items in inventory. The following word code may be used to represent the cost designation of an item on the price ticket so that the customer will not be able to determine its cost.

RETAIL SHOP
1 2 3 4 5 6 7 8 9 0

A retailer using such a code could indicate the cost of $3.67 for an item (which, perhaps, retails at $6.95) as TLS with each letter representing the number indicated. The date code used to signify that the item was brought into stock in June of 1979 may be indicated on the coded price ticket as 6TLS9, showing the sixth month of the ninth year (June 1979). Other retailers have opted to use a numerical code to indicate the cost and date of the item. Consequently, a code to show the same information indicated above at a cost of $3.67 and brought into stock in June 1979 might be indicated as follows:

637967

In this code, the first, third, and fourth digits signify the date of June 1979, while the remaining numbers represent the cost of the item. Merchants using the cost method of inventory valuation must develop codes which can easily be used by their operations.

While the cost method of inventory valuation is used by many independents, it generally should be restricted to merchants selling high-unit value items, where transactions are few, and where the number of items in stock are limited. An additional criterion might be that the items be staple in nature with limited style or physical perishability. In other words, the merchandise value of the inventory at the time of valuation should be approximately the same as the original cost indicated on the invoice or cost code. Therefore, the cost method might be applied efficiently in furniture, furs, jewellery, and china.

In addition to determining the inventory valuation on the basis of costs, accountants have also sought to establish the value of the inventory to assist in the reduction of taxes. To this end, first-in, first-out (FIFO), and last-in, first-out (LIFO) methods have been used. Further analysis of these methods can be found in a basic accounting reader or in discussions with the store's accountant to determine the impact on the store's taxes.

Further, many stores selling general merchandise have adjusted the cost method to record the original cost of the items when the cost is lower than the current wholesale price. The current cost is recorded if it is in fact lower than the original purchase price. This method of valuing the inventory is referred to as the cost-or-market, whichever is lower. Thus, the original cost price and the current replacement price of each item in the inventory is determined and recorded. That price which is lower per unit is multiplied by the quantity on hand to determine the current cost value of the inventory. This method is intended to give the merchant a conservative valuation of the stock on hand.

In calculating the store's gross margin and net profit using the cost method, the following information and procedure would apply.

	At Cost	At Retail
Opening Inventory	$ 60,000	
Purchases Received	20,000	
Total Merchandise Handled	80,000	
Net Sales for Period		$ 75,000
Ending Inventory	40,000	
Cost of Goods Sold	40,000	
Gross Margin		35,000
Operating Expenses	26,000	
Net Operating Profit		$ 9,000

You'll note from this example of random figures that the gross margin and net operating profit figures will depend on your ability to accurately determine the value of the opening and closing inventories for the store. While we have omitted the effect of markdowns, shortages, and transportation charges in this illustration, you should remember that these will affect the cost of goods sold by adjusting the closing inventory and the purchases received.

It is very important to recognize, then, that the true market value of the inventory must be established by you. Consequently, retailers are required to make adjustments for depreciation in the existing inventory by bringing its value in line with current market conditions. This process of adjusting the existing inventory may be undertaken by one of the three following methods when the cost method of inventory valuation is used.

Quotation Method This method implies that the merchant will compare the initial cost prices with those of the supplier's current catalogues and price lists. Because of the time-consuming nature of this task, it is generally restricted to high-volume, staple items which are handled in large quantities.

Markdown Method Such a system demands that the original selling price, the reduced selling price, and the cost price code are recorded on the price ticket. In this way the initial markup is applied to the markdown to determine the depreciation in the cost value of the inventory. You'll remember the calculation of the cost of the reductions in our explanation of maintained markup. Again, this method requires a large number of calculations to convert the existing inventory to market value.

Aging Method This method represents an alternative to establishing the market value of the inventory by determining the length of time the merchandise has been in stock and then depreciating the value of the items on this basis. The merchant may opt for determining the market value of the merchandise by depreciating the cost value at predetermined rates as indicated by one retailer's schedule in Exhibit 7-3 below.

Exhibit 7-3
Inventory Depreciation Rates

Age of Stock	Depreciation Rate
Less than 3 months old	0%
3- 6 months old	25%
6-12 months old	50%
12-24 months old	75%
More than 2 years old	100%

These rates must only act as a guide, since each retailer will differ from others in the field. There are even variations within the same store's departments or classifications. It could be argued that some merchandise increases in value over a two-year period rather than depreciating at the 100% rate.

To value and control merchandise inventory on the basis of cost, you have to adopt a means of converting this merchandise to current market value. The fact that the cost method is a direct and simple means of valuing the inventory has caused many small retailers to continue to favour this method of inventory valuation.

Retail Method of Inventory Valuation

Most successful retail merchants have adopted the system of valuing and controlling inventory on the basis of the retail method of inventory management. While we noted the simplicity of the cost method, it in fact requires the physical counting and evaluation of the merchandise on hand before a reading on the operating results of the store can be obtained through the gross margin realized. The retail method makes it possible to calculate the gross margin much more frequently with a minimum amount of effort.

This method simply implies that the physical inventory can be taken at retail prices indicated on the tickets and then, by applying the calculated markup achieved on the total merchandise handled, the cost value can be obtained. The task of interpreting cost codes, establishing cost records, and the determination of market value can be eliminated by the retail method. But the retail method will require the maintenance and control of adequate record systems to ensure the accurate reporting of the store's gross margin. Some of these records will be explained in this section.

By itself, the retail method is not a complete bookkeeping system; it merely provides the means of maintaining a perpetual inventory at the retail value of the merchandise, by adjusting the purchases and sales journals and introducing a price change record. An inventory record is used to combine the totals of these journals in such a way that the cost value of the inventory can be determined at any time without the necessity of taking a physical count. These records can all be used in conjunction with the store's existing cash register, established forms, and its general bookkeeping system.

The retail method will give you a closing inventory proportional to the retail value rather than a figure of what was actually paid for the merchandise at the time it was received into stock. This proportional cost figure will be based on the store's cumulative markup as items are received into stock.

Instituting this system will require two additional phases in record keeping; first, a continuous perpetual inventory of the retail value of the merchandise in a purchase or receiving journal, and second, maintenance of a careful record of the relationship between the original cost and retail values of the stock. In this way, the cost value of the inventory can be determined at any time during the period by applying the cost complement of the cumulative markup to the perpetual inventory. A physical inventory will still need to be taken at least once per year to check the accuracy of the records and the degree of stock shortages. But, unlike the cost method, a physical count is not required to determine the gross margin from operations during the period.

The perpetual inventory is maintained by adding all increases in the stock at retail value and subtracting any decreases. To determine the value of the total merchandise handled by the store, the increases in inventory will consist of the retail value of the merchandise received and any subsequent increases over the original retail value through additional markups taken. In addition, the effect that transfers into the store or department may have in increasing or decreasing the merchandise available for sale must be considered. The total cost value of the merchandise available for sale is then found by adding the invoice cost of the net merchandise purchases to the beginning retail value of the inventory, additional markups, and net transfers into the store.

The example which follows will become the basis for explaining the retail method of inventory throughout the remainder of this chapter. To explain the procedure for calculating the value of the total merchandise available for sale at both cost and retail under the retail method, the following illustration is provided:

	Cost	Retail	Markup $	Markup %
Opening Inventory	$247,500	$450,000		
Net Purchases	272,700	505,000		
Transportation Charges	5,500			
Net Transfers-In	4,200	7,000		
Net Additional Markups		2,000		
Total Merchandise Available	$529,900	$964,000	$434,100	45%

The calculation of the markup difference between the cost and retail value of the merchandise available for sale is referred to as the cumulative markup. In the above example this is represented as $434,100 or 45%. Since the markup and rates of sale vary greatly among the various departments in a store, the retail method requires that each group of merchandise be controlled separately.

This example also illustrates additional terms that may need further explanation to understand their impact on the calculation of the value of the inventory through the retail method.

Transportation Charges The transportation costs involved in receiving merchandise from suppliers into the store are recorded by the merchant and added to the purchases to determine the cost of the merchandise received by the store. By increasing the cost of the merchandise in relation to its retail price, the initial markup will be reduced if the list price is predetermined. Under the retail method it is important for you to keep an accurate record of the transportation charges.

Transfers-In and Transfers-Out When merchandise is transferred from one store of a chain to another, or from one department to another, it must be recorded at both cost and retail. To effectively control this merchandise inventory it is also necessary that this information be recorded as incoming merchandise by the receiving department and outgoing merchandise by the shipping department. The net transfer figure is determined by deducting the transfers-out of the department from the transfers-in. The resultant figure will represent the net addition to stock of the merchandise that has been received by this method. It must be recognized here that if the transfers-out exceed the amount of the transfers-in, the resultant figure will signify a decrease in the total merchandise available for sale. Stores engaging in the practice of transferring items throughout the store or chain maintain merchandise transfer forms similar to that illustrated in Exhibit 7-4.

Additional Markups On occasion, merchandise already in stock may be subjected to an increase in the retail price without a corresponding increase in the cost. As a result, the initial markup will be increased and the additional markup dollars need to be recorded to ensure the proper reporting of gross margin obtained. The increase in retail generally results from inflationary pressures causing increases in the replacement value of the items already in stock at the store or by incorrect pricing of the store personnel. It must be observed that additional markups do not refer to items where markdowns have been removed, placing the merchandise back to its original retail. Such changes are referred to as markdown cancellations. Let's look, for example, at the dinnerware merchant who receives a notice from the supplier indicating that the retail prices of dinner sets will increase by 15% effective February 1. By increasing the prices on the existing sets of china in the store, the merchant is obtaining additional markups on these items. Since other merchants are likely to institute the same procedure, the price increases result in additional markups for all merchants selling the line.

Exhibit 7-4
Sample Transfer Form

MERCHANDISE TRANSFER FORM

Transfer Number

To:

Store: *Seneca Mall*	No. 3	**Authorization:**	**Date:**
Dept. *Swimwear*	No. 37	*a. DiThorne*	*3/16*

Stock No.	Description	Units	Unit Retail	Retail Extension	Cost Extension
F172	2 Piece Sea-Queen – Asst. Colours	12	$40.00	480.00	288.00
F137	2 Piece Bikini Catalina – Asst. Colours	18	$23.00	552.00	330.00
	Totals	36		$1,032.00	$618.00

From:

Store: *Garden Mall*	No. 1	**Ship Via:**	**Date:**	**Authorization**
Dept. *Swimwear*	No. 17	*P.C.*	*3/16*	*a. DiThorne*

This form is used by retail stores to control the movement of merchandise between stores or departments. Depending on the size of the organization, the form may be prepared in duplicate or triplicate. While the retail inventory method also requires that this information be recorded at cost as well as retail, the cost portion of the transfer will be allocated to each form in the accounting department or office of the independent store.

The Ending Inventory Once the total merchandise available for sale has been determined, it is necessary to find the decreases that occurred in this stock in order to establish the amount of the ending inventory and the gross margin.

The available merchandise in the store has been reduced by the sales during the period, and the markdowns and employee discounts that were allowed during the period. The total of these items represents the reduction in the retail value of the merchandise that was available for sale. The resultant figure therefore represents the closing book inventory at retail.

We have already noted that it will be necessary at some point during the fiscal year or season to undertake a physical inventory of the merchandise in the store. The difference between the closing book inventory figure established and that determined by the physical count is the stock shortage or overage experienced by the store for the period under study.

The previous example is now expanded to include the calculations that become necessary to determine the closing inventory using the retail method of inventory valuation.

	Cost	Retail	Markup $	Markup %
Opening Inventory	$247,500	$450,000		
Gross Purchases	278,100	515,000		
Purchase Returns	5,400	10,000		
Net Purchases	272,700	505,000		
Transportation Charges	5,500			
Net Transfers-In	4,200	7,000		
Net Additional Markups		2,000		
Total Merchandise Available	$529,900	$964,000	$434,100	45%
Less: Net Sales		500,000		
Net Markdowns		40,000		
Employee Discounts		10,000		
Total Retail Deductions		550,000		
Ending Inventory, Book Value		414,000		
Ending Inventory, Physical	225,500	410,000		
Stock Shortages		4,000		

In this example notice that the ending book inventory is found by subtracting the total retail deductions from the total merchandise available for sale at retail ($964,000 − $550,000). The physical count of the inventory revealed a figure of $410,000 at retail indicating a stock shortage of $4000. The cost of this physical inventory is determined by using the complement of the cumulative markup of 45%: to determine the cost of the physical inventory of $410,000 at retail, this figure is multiplied by 55% (100 − 45) with the resultant cost figure of $225,500.

Our next step in this procedure is to determine the effect that these elements will have on the store's gross margin and net operating profit. In order to establish this relationship, it is necessary to calculate the cost of goods sold for the period. That is, we need to determine what it cost the store for the merchandise to achieve the sales of $500,000 that are indicated. This figure can now be determined by deducting the closing physical inventory at cost of $225,500 from the total merchandise handled at cost, $529,900, which leaves a gross cost of goods sold at $304,400. We can now proceed, in Exhibit 7-5, to complete our example with the inclusion of all figures necessary to determine our net operating profit.

Exhibit 7-5
Retail Method of Inventory—Net Operating Profit

	Cost	Retail	Markup $	Markup %
Opening Inventory	$247,500	$450,000		
Gross Purchases	278,100	515,000		
Purchase Returns	5,400	10,000		
Net Purchases	272,700	505,000		
Transportation Charges	5,500			
Net Transfers-In	4,200	7,000		
Net Additional Markups		2,000		
Total Merchandise Available	529,900	964,000	434,100	45.0%
Less: Net Sales		500,000		
Net Markdowns		40,000		
Employee Discounts		10,000		
Total Retail Deductions		550,000		
Ending Inventory, Book Value		414,000		
Ending Inventory, Physical	225,500	410,000		
Stock Shortages		4,000		
Cost of Goods Sold	304,400			
Gross Margin			195,600	
Operating Expenses	162,000			
Net Operating Profit			33,600	6.7%

Please refer to the records which follow in this section to see how the figures are arrived at in the calculation of the gross margin by determining the cost of goods sold. These figures represent those experienced by the store on an annual basis.

The Mechanics of the Retail Method

It has not been the intention of this book to outline the detailed mechanics associated with the operation of the independent retail store. Our goal has been to establish a management awareness helpful to the successful operation of the retail enterprise.

In the previous section we outlined the basic philosophy of the retail method of inventory. It was noted that accurate records of the activity of the retail store would need to be kept if the retail method is to function efficiently. Information on purchases, price changes, and inventory levels will offer you the means to calculate the store's gross margin on a more frequent basis and to make adjustments to the merchandising strategy of the operation as the need arises.

To this end, the remainder of this chapter is devoted to offering illustrations of the type of records that are needed when the retail method of inventory valuation is adopted.

The Purchase Journal This is a record of the net purchases at both cost and retail for the store or the department. Each time merchandise is received into the store, the shipment is checked against the invoice and purchase order, and a copy of the freight bill is attached to the invoice. The retail value of the goods is established by the manager or buyer after the transportation charges have been considered. The transportation charges may be prorated per item or may be distributed throughout the store via a transportation clearing account established at the end of the month.

The sample purchase journal or receiving record in Exhibit 7-6 allows you to maintain a continuous record of the markup being obtained on each shipment of merchandise received by the store.

The monthly total figures, tabulated with the remaining months in the season, establish the net purchase figure which is found in Exhibit 7-5.

Markdown Book This record collects adjustments that are made to the retail prices on the merchandise in the form of net markdowns. While some adjustments may result in additional markups as indicated earlier, these price changes may in fact be recorded in the purchases journal and separately recorded, as noted in Exhibit 7-5.

The more frequent price changes found in the retail store will be in the form of markdowns—reductions in the retail selling

Exhibit 7-6
Purchase Journal

PURCHASE JOURNAL

Date	Invoice No.	Particulars	Cost	Additional Freight	Retail	Markup %
Mar. 3	4263F	Sito's Designs	$475.50	21.40	$895.00	44.5%
" 4	1369	Michelle Fashions	230.00		475.00	51.6%
" 5	KB146	Tricia Sportswear Ltd.	197.60		350.00	43.5%
" 5	A2622	Cher Susan Ltd.	175.00		300.00	41.7%
" 5	AK708	Katherine's Ltd.	365.00		675.00	45.9%
" 5		Christopher's Transport		12.00		
" 7	C34	Maura's Sportswear - Credit Note	(27.90)			
" 10	16778	Jean's Designs Ltd.	187.50		350.00	46.4%
	Total		$25,175	375.00	$47,500	47.0%

price of the merchandise. Markdowns become necessary if the merchant seeks to liquidate some of the stock by making it more attractive to customers in terms of price.

In some cases, items which have been marked down are later returned to their original retail prices when they remain unsold. This move back to the original retail price is recorded in the markdown book in red and designated as a markdown cancellation. This must not be considered as an additional markup but rather as a return to the original retail selling price. To obtain the net markdown figure of $40,000 noted in Exhibit 7-5, markdown cancellations for the period have been deducted from the gross markdowns taken.

A sample page of a markdown book is illustrated in Exhibit 7-7 to note those areas of the markdowns that must be recorded for effective control. Careful and faithful record keeping in this journal is essential to the success of the retail method of inventory valuation.

Monthly Inventory Summary The third important record that will need to be maintained by the merchant adopting the retail method is designed to combine purchases, markdowns, and sales information to find the cost value of the inventory on a monthly basis. Because of the information contained in this record, you can calculate stock turnover, average inventories, and monthly sales and markdown distribution.

The record is divided on the basis of the retail and cost information, with a monthly running total of the store's inventory position. Depending on the information needed by the store, additional columns can be added to summarize such items as stock shortages, alteration expenses, or cash discounts.

By calculating the inventory at cost and at retail in this summary, it is also possible to continually scrutinize the cumulative markup per cent being realized.

The procedure for completing the monthly inventory summary as illustrated in Exhibit 7-8 is relatively easy once the basic concepts are understood. The fundamental requirement of determining the ending inventory that is recorded by this summary is explained by the following relationship:

> Opening Inventory at Retail
> + Net Purchases at Retail
> ---
> = Total Available at Retail
> − Net Markdowns + Net Sales
> ---
> = Ending Inventory at Retail

Exhibit 7-7
Markdown Record

Date	Particulars	Old Price	New Price	Change Each	Quantity	Amount	Reason
Mar. 4	Wool Cardigans - B2625	$35.00	$26.00	$9.00	16	$144.00	odd sizes + colours
Mar. 7	Boucle Shells B2176	15.00	9.97	5.03	24	120.72	limited assortment
Mar. 10	V-Neck Pullover - B2771	24.00	17.77	6.23	11	68.23	end of line
Mar. 13	L/s Pullovers B2711	30.00	36.00	(6.00)	5	(30.00)	cancel markdown
Mar. 13	Sleeveless B6114	17.95	11.77	6.18	36	222.48	slow-movers
Mar. 14	s/s Cardigan B2615	27.95	19.97	7.98	14	111.72	odd sizes
Month March	Total					$5,600.00	

Note: Enter all Markdown Cancellations in Red

Retail Merchandise Control   155

Once the information has been obtained at retail value, then it is possible, under the retail method of inventory management, to proceed to a calculation of the cost portion of this statement. The following procedure for completing this section of the summary has been illustrated in Exhibit 7-8.

Opening Inventory at Cost
+ Net Purchases at Cost
_____
= Total Available at Cost

You'll note that to this point the net purchases figures at both cost and retail are derived from those tabulated in the Purchase Journal illustrated in Exhibit 7-6. The information on net markdowns has been transferred from the Markdown Book in Exhibit 7-7.

However, in order to determine the cost of sales for the month, it will be necessary to determine the inventory value at cost at the end of the month. With the information given in Exhibit 7-8 to this point, the cost of sales will be determined in the following manner:

Total Available at Retail
− Total Available at Cost
_____
= Cumulative Markup on Goods Available

The cumulative markup which has now been calculated in dollars must now be converted to a per cent. This is accomplished by expressing the cumulative markup dollars as a per cent of the value of the goods available at retail. The complement of this cumulative markup per cent will then represent the cost portion of the ending inventory at retail. Therefore, to determine the closing inventory at cost, the following calculation will be required:

Ending Inventory at Retail × Cost Complement of Cumulative Markup
or
Ending Inventory at Retail × (100% − Cumulative Markup Per Cent)

The resultant figure represents the closing inventory at cost. We have now reached the position where it is possible to determine the cost of sales. The cost of goods sold during the month is then determined by subtracting the closing inventory at cost from the total goods which were available at cost.

Total Goods Available at Cost
− Ending Inventory at Cost
_____
= Cost of Goods Sold

Exhibit 7-8
Monthly Inventory Summary for the Year

Retail — Inventory at JANUARY 1 $450,000
Cost — Inventory at JANUARY 1 $247,500

Month	Retail										Cost						
	Net Purchases	Net Transfers-In	Net Additional Markups	Total Goods Available	Net Markdowns	Employee Discounts	Net Sales	Ending Book Inventory	Ending Physical Inventory	Stock Shortages	Net Purchases	Transportation Charges	Net Transfers-In	Total Goods Available	Cost of Sales	Ending Inventory	Cumulative Markup Per Cent
Jan.	$38,000	—	—	488,000	5000	1000	40,000	442,000	—	—	22,000	200	—	269,700	25,774	244,724	44.7%
Feb.	42,000	1000	200	485,200	3500	500	52,000	429,200	—	-	24,350	250	600	269,626	31,001	238,625	44.4%
Mar.	47,500	600	180	477,480	5600	1000	60,000	410,880	—	—	25,175	375	300	264,475	36,847	227,628	44.6%
Apr.	53,600	500	200	465,180	4200	700	72,000	388,280	—	—	27,100	300	275	255,303	42,137	213,166	45.1%
May																	
June																	
July																	
Aug.																	
Sept.																	
Oct.																	
Nov.																	
Dec.																	
Total	505,000	7000	2000	944,000	40,000	10,000	500,000	414,000	410,000	4000	272,700	5500	4200	529,900	304,400	225,500	45.%

The calculation of the cost of goods sold permits the determination of the gross margin for the store for the period without the onerous task of completing a physical inventory. Since net sales less the cost of goods sold will represent the gross margin obtained by the store, you can maintain a more effective control over your operation.

The Gross Margin Summary This record represents the month-to-month and year-to-date results of the store's operations. In the monthly inventory summary explained in Exhibit 7-8, you determine the cost of goods sold; then this information is applied in the following manner to determine the gross margin on operations:

$$
\begin{array}{l}
\text{Net Sales} \\
\underline{-\text{ Cost of Goods Sold}} \\
=\text{ Gross Margin}
\end{array}
$$

Since the retail method of inventory management has been employed, you can summarize the store's records into this report to determine the success of your operation on a monthly or annual basis.

By adding each month's activity to the previous results in the year-to-date section of the summary, a continuous record of the resulting gross margin from the operations is maintained. Without this kind of control record, you wouldn't be able to determine what aspects of the store's merchandising strategy need to be improved. Using it, you can rectify any operational problems that might be occurring and subsequently you can increase the store's profitability.

The maintenance of a gross margin summary permits you to control the number of sales events the store might have in order to clear merchandise. It also allows you to promote the higher markup items, to reduce the number of markdowns taken, to reduce the amount of shrinkage taking place, and to more effectively control the buying of merchandise for the store.

Summary of the Retail Method of Inventory Management

This section of the chapter on merchandise control has sought to explain the fundamental concepts inherent in the adoption of the retail method of inventory management. For most independent retailers the advantages of this system far outweigh the

Exhibit 7-9
Gross Margin Summary—Retail Method of Inventory

Month	CURRENT MONTH				YEAR-TO-DATE				
	Net Sales	Cost of Sales	Gross Margin $	Gross Margin %	Net Sales	Cost of Sales	Gross Margin $	Gross Margin %	% Change
Jan.	$40,000	25,274	14,726	36.8	40,000	25,274	14,726	36.8%	—
Feb.	52,000	31,001	20,999	40.4	92,000	56,275	35,725	38.8%	+2.0%
Mar.	60,000	36,847	23,153	38.6	152,000	93,122	58,878	38.7%	− .1%
Apr.	72,000	42,137	29,863	41.5%	224,000	135,259	88,741	39.6%	+ .9%
May									
June									
July									
Aug.									
Sept.									
Oct.									
Nov.									
Dec.					$500,000	304,400	195,600	39.6%	
Total	$500,000	$304,400	$195,600	39.6%					

benefits that one might anticipate under the cost method of inventory management. For this reason, you should seriously consider the adoption of this technique as a means of establishing a more effective control system for your store.

The establishment of records that will control purchases received, price changes, inventory balances, and gross margin figures will also supply independents with the information needed to execute the retail method of inventory management.

8

PRICING POLICIES AND PRACTICES

Of primary importance to the profitable operation of a retail store is the development and implementation of an effective pricing strategy. While it is common in some merchandise lines for independent retailers to accept the selling prices set or recommended by suppliers, control of the overall pricing policy must rest in the hands of the merchant. The selection of the price for the item or group of items in the store will affect both the sales volume and the profitability of the store. Charging too high a price for an item will deter sales, while too low a price reduces the markup to unprofitable levels. Therefore, the selection and control of pricing policies and strategies is an essential ingredient of the merchandising mix.

The cost of the merchandise, the operating expenses, the desired net profit, and the anticipated reductions must all be carefully considered in planning the prices to be placed on the merchandise assortment. While this quantitative data is vital to the execution of the pricing function, the qualitative aspects of the environment in which you operate also plays a significant role in the adoption of a pricing policy.

It is conceivable that two articles cost the same from the supplier but that their values in the eyes of the consumer are drastically different. Therefore, by carefully analyzing the items from the customer's point of view, higher markups on certain selection factors may be possible. It has been discovered that customers purchasing items that are not highly standardized generally evaluate the merchandise on a relationship between price and quality. Thus, merchandise which is priced below expectations (as a result of a special buy, for example) may generate less customer activity than anticipated, based on lack of confidence in the price-quality relationship.

Retailers also recognize that their ability to obtain exclusive merchandise lines for the store will provide their operation with more freedom in its pricing strategy. In the designated geographical area, customers will be unable to compare the exclusive items with competing stores, since only substitute items will be available. However, where stores handle similar merchandise, competition must be considered before final decisions on pricing can be employed. The extent to which competitors' prices must be considered will depend on the image of the store, the type and nature of the merchandise, and the degree of rivalry among the stores.

Both large and small merchants undergo the process of comparing their merchandise and prices with competing stores in an effort to retaliate to maintain market share. If the merchant decides to match competition with lower prices, additional markup or volume will have to be achieved on other items to yield the overall profit objective.

Over the years, and as a result of frequent purchasing, the customer may have developed preconceived ideas of the retail value of specific items. Standard convenience goods which customers tend to purchase on the basis of habit or custom will restrict the pricing decisions made by the store. While the price of these items do change over a period of time, the price tends to be standardized in most stores at any specific period. As a result, such items as cigarettes, gasoline, magazines, or candy bars are priced at points that have become habitual to the customer.

We have noted that the type and nature of the merchandise carried will have a direct bearing on the retail prices to be charged by the store. Merchandise that suffers from physical or style perishability must be priced to accommodate anticipated reductions and still provide for a suitable profit margin for the store.

These points have been included to establish a framework for discussing the pricing policies and practices of retail firms. A basic theory of modern retailing states that ideal prices are those that will move the largest amount of goods in the shortest time at a reasonable profit to the store. In general, merchandise turnover of the sale of a large number of items is to be preferred to large profits obtained from the sale of a few items. Thus, a men's clothing store with a wide range of apparel is safer than a store which specializes in tailor-made suits only.

THE PROFIT AND LOSS STATEMENT

All entrepreneurs tend to rely on the information provided in the profit and loss statement to determine the results of their firm's operations. Also known as the income and expense statement, the information provided is a summary of the income earned by the store for a specified period of time and the expenses resulting from generating this revenue. The deduction of the expenses from the income determines the profit earned or loss suffered for the designated time period.

Therefore, in order for the independent merchant to develop an effective pricing strategy for the store, it is essential that the components of this profit and loss statement be understood. In addition, the prices charged for this merchandise must be viewed in light of the effect this strategy will have on the overall profit of the store. The profit and loss statement is therefore the score card of the store in determining whether the merchant is winning or losing. But it is not the figures alone which have meaning for the operation of the store, but rather the interpretation of this data that results in implementing an effective merchandising strategy.

The financial statements (such as the profit and loss) are generally prepared by the store's accountant at the end of the year. From the retailer's point of view, it is unfortunate that the preparation of interim statements at more frequent intervals during the year is not requested by the merchant. Information provided after the end of the fiscal year tends to become historical data, rather than operational results that can affect current decision making. It is, therefore, advisable to obtain at least quarterly statements, with monthly operating data providing even more useful information. However, this data is of very little value to those merchants whose only concern is the bottom line or net profit earned. A thorough analysis and understanding of the elements of the statement is required if the data is to provide for more effective merchandising decisions.

You will observe from the profit and loss statement which is included in Exhibit 8-1 that the data provided outlines the operational results of the store for a period of time on the basis

Exhibit 8-1

THE GIFT SHOPPE
Statement of Income and Expense
as at December 31, 1979

Gross Sales		$240,000	
Sales Returns and Allowances		3,000	
Net Sales			$237,000
Cost of Goods Sold:			
Inventory, December 31, 1978		75,000	
Purchases	160,000		
Purchase Returns & Allowances	2,500		
Net Purchases	157,500		
Transportation-In	3,000	160,500	
Cost of Goods Available for Sale		235,500	
Inventory, December 31, 1979		110,000	
Total Cost of Goods Sold			125,500
Gross Margin on Sales			111,500
Operating Expenses:			
Accounting		1,800	
Bad Debt Expense		600	
Bank Charges		800	
Buying Expense		1,275	
Canada Pension Plan		500	
Communication—Telephone, Postage		1,800	
Credit Collection Expense		3,600	
Depreciation Expense—Office		500	
Depreciation Expense—Store		3,000	
Employee Benefits		1,100	
Insurance		2,100	
Interest		4,100	
Occupancy—Rent, Utilities		24,000	
Promotion		8,600	
Supplies—Office		1,400	
Supplies—Store		3,300	
Taxes—Business		600	
Travel		1,100	
Unemployment Insurance		600	
Wages—Office		5,000	
Wages—Store		31,000	
Total Operating Expenses			96,775
Net Operating Profit			14,725
Net Other Income			2,300
Net Profit Before Income Tax			$ 17,025

of sales and expenses. The essential components of the statement are represented by the following relationship:

$$
\begin{array}{l}
\text{Net Sales} \\
- \text{ Cost of Goods Sold} \\
\hline
= \text{Gross Margin} \\
- \text{ Operating Expenses} \\
\hline
= \text{Net Profit}
\end{array}
$$

Sales

The gross sales figure which appears on the store's operating statement is derived from the sum of the daily sales of merchandise purchased by customers. This figure represents the final retail prices charged to customers and recorded by means of the cash register or charge accounts. As such, the gross sales figure will include the retail prices of items which have been discounted as a result of employee discounts or merchandise markdowns.

The derivation of the net sales is simply the deletion of the customers' sales returns from the gross sales figure. Since most retailers allow for customer exchanges of merchandise, with more and more also offering refund privileges, adjustments to the sales figure for the period are required. By subtracting the total sales returns from the gross sales, you can determine the total retail value of the merchandise sold. It is this net sales figure that is used as the basis for comparison of the remaining operating data on the statement. From the net sales base of 100%, all other items are calculated in percentage terms.

Cost of Goods Sold

The cost of goods sold referred to in the store's operating statement is the delivered dollar cost of the goods which have been sold during the period under review. It is essentially the total of the prices the merchant must pay the suppliers for the items which have been sold during the period. Understanding the concept of the cost of goods sold is relatively simple, but the inclusion of various elements tends to complicate its calculation. You will note in Exhibit 8-2 that the derivation of the total cost of goods sold will be affected by the purchases made, the transportation of these purchases, the opening and closing inventories, and the alteration expenses and cash discounts.

Exhibit 8-2
Calculation of Total Cost of Goods Sold

Inventory, Beginning of the Period		$ 75,000
Gross Purchases	$160,000	
Purchase Returns and Allowances	2,500	
Net Purchases	157,500	
Transportation-In	3,000	160,500
Cost of Goods Available for Sale		235,500
Inventory, End of Period		110,000
Gross Cost of Merchandise Sold		125,500
Cash Discounts Earned		500
Net Cost of Merchandise Sold		125,000
Net Alteration Expenses		500
Total Cost of Goods Sold		$125,500

The calculation of the cost of goods sold indicated in Exhibit 8-2 is based on employing the retail method of inventory which we explained in Chapter 7. The opening inventory for the period represents the value of the merchandise on hand as the season or month opens. To this merchandise is added the net purchases of the retail store, eliminating any items which have been returned to the suppliers or for which special allowances have been made. In addition, the charges incurred in transporting the merchandise to the store must be considered as part of the cost of the goods rather than an operating expense. The sum of these components represents the total merchandise handled in the store and is reduced by the amount of the merchandise still on hand at the end of the period. The resulting figure represents the store's gross cost of goods sold.

However, since some merchants take advantage of cash discounts negotiated with their suppliers, the amount earned will reduce the gross cost of the goods sold to provide us with the net cost. Finally, retailers who offer customers alterations without sufficient workroom revenue to offset these expenses will increase the cost of goods they sell by the net amount of these expenses. Note the differences among the gross, net, and total cost of goods sold figures used in the store's operating statement.

Gross Margin

The gross margin in the profit and loss statement simply represents the difference between the dollar figure of the store's sales and the total cost of the merchandise sold. In some business establishments, this term is also known as the gross profit, but in the retail sector the bulk of this figure is taken up with operating expenses and is therefore referred to as margin rather than profit.

It is the gross margin figure that is affected by the pricing strategy of the firm. Obviously, the higher the gross margin, the higher the net profit before taxes, assuming operating expenses are held under control. As indicated earlier, the initial markup is the original markup placed on an item, while the maintained markup represents the final markup received—after all reductions, when the items have been sold. Since the maintained markup and the gross margin differ only by the impact of the cash discounts and alteration costs, the gross margin is a direct result of the prices charged for the merchandise.

Operating Expenses

As can be seen in Exhibit 8-1 the bulk of the gross margin earned by independent retailers is absorbed by the expenses incurred in operating the store. These expenses include payroll, occupancy, communications, promotions, professional, and other costs essential in the operation of the business. These expenses are distinct from those which constitute the costs of goods sold, as described earlier.

Selected Operating Expenses

Accounting	Insurance
Bad Debt Expense	Interest
Bank Charges	Occupancy
Buying Expense	Promotion
Canada Pension Plan	Supplies—Office
Credit Collection Expense	Supplies—Store
Communication Expense	Taxes—Business
Delivery Expense	Taxes—Real Estate
Depreciation Expense (Delivery Equipment)	Travel
Depreciation Expense (Office Equipment)	Unemployment Insurance
Depreciation Expense (Store Fixtures)	Wages—Office
Employee Benefits	Wages—Store

Net Operating Profit

Net operating profit represents the difference between the gross margin and the store's total operating expenses, and is generally looked upon by the merchant as the means of measuring the degree of success the firm has experienced for the reported period. It is referred to as the net operating profit since it results from the operation of the business as distinct from the net profit which may also include earned income from sources other than the retail operation.

Therefore, while the profit and loss statement is required by law to calculate the tax liability of the store, it becomes the essential statement for merchants to evaluate their merchandising performance with respect to their objectives and goals. By converting the information provided to percentage figures based on net sales, it becomes possible to compare the store's operating results with others in the industry—a most useful technique for the entrepreneur.

PRICING MECHANICS

While some merchandise received by the store has already been prepriced by the supplier, other items must be priced at the store. If the supplier does not provide the store with suggested selling prices, it becomes the retailer's responsibility to calculate the prices at which the items will be sold to the customer. Regardless of the situation, you will find that the planning of the prices of the merchandise assortment, whether prepriced or not, must be undertaken and analyzed to ensure a profitable operation.

Markup

The markup is the difference between the amount that is paid for the merchandise and the price for which the goods are sold. In essence, it is the difference between the retail (selling price) and the cost (price to the store). In planning the markup for the store, the markup earned must be large enough to cover the operating expenses of the store and still provide a net profit.

At this point it should be noted that retailers are required to plan markups for individual items or for a group of items using the same basic principle:

$$\text{Cost} + \text{Markup} = \text{Retail}$$

$$\text{Retail} - \text{Cost} = \text{Markup}$$

Markup for a retail store is generally expressed as a percentage rather than as a dollar amount. Although it is important to know the dollar markup, the percentage figure greatly simplifies the planning process. In addition, the dollar markup obtains its true meaning only in its relationship to the retail selling price.

For example, if a sporting goods operation is able to realize a $12 markup on a baseball glove retailing at $32, this represents a 37.5% markup on the retail price ($12/$32 × 100). If the same store achieves a markup of $12 on a pair of water skis that retail at $60, then this same dollar markup only represents 20% of the retail price ($12/$60 × 100). Therefore, assuming a similar turnover rate, the profitability of the baseball glove is almost twice that of the water skis, with the same dollar markup.

Markup Based on Retail The previous examples of the baseball glove and the water skis had their percentage markup expressed as a percentage of the retail selling price. Thus, a 20% markup on the water skis represents 20% of the selling price of $60, or a markup of $12.

While many existing independents have for years calculated markup as a percentage of their costs, the progressive merchants are basing calculations on the selling price of the items. Not only is a standard base required when comparing results among other firms in your trade, but merchants have realized that markup is not achieved until the item is sold and thus must be based on the selling price. Since the cost price of the item is fixed as per invoice, the retail price may change as a result of reductions and subsequently affect the markup obtained. In addition, more and more retail firms have adopted the retail method of inventory with the resultant need for the expression of markup on a retail base.

In calculating the markup on retail, the selling price of the item must become the base figure of 100%. Therefore, the cost and markup figures are expressed maintaining the same relationship:

$$
\begin{array}{ll}
\text{Cost} & C \\
\underline{+\ \text{Markup}} & \underline{+\ M} \\
=\ \text{Retail} & =\ R
\end{array}
$$

For example, a store purchases a line of cardigan sweaters at a cost of $15 each with a suggested selling price of $25. In order to calculate the markup per cent on retail for the sweater, we substitute in the basic formula:

$$
\begin{array}{llll}
\text{Cost} & = & \$15.00 & = \\
+ \text{ Markup} & = & & = \\ \hline
= \text{Retail} & = & \$25.00 & = 100\%
\end{array}
$$

Since retail is the base, it will be represented by 100%, and the cost will be expressed as a per cent of this figure, just as markup is. Since the sweater cost $15, this will be 60% of retail ($15/$25 × 100%). The markup is $10 ($25 − $15); expressed as a percentage of the retail base it will be 40% ($10/$25 × 100%). Thus, the equation can be completed to express the relationship:

$$
\begin{array}{llll}
\text{Cost} & = & \$15.00 & = & 60\% \\
+ \text{ Markup} & = & 10.00 & = & 40\% \\ \hline
= \text{Retail} & = & \$25.00 & = & 100\%
\end{array}
$$

Markup Based on Cost As indicated, most progressive merchants are now basing their markup on retail, but many independent merchants continue to use the merchandise cost as the base. In using cost to calculate markup, the exact cost of the merchandise must be determined—including the invoice cost plus any transportation charges incurred in receiving these items. Retailers should realize that the cash discounts received from suppliers are not deducted from the invoice to arrive at the cost. There is no certainty that the discount will be taken or will continue to be offered by the supplier. As a result, cash discounts are considered as a separate element in the calculation of initial markup and gross margin.

It should be obvious that the markup using cost as a base will be greater than when the retail figure is used. Since the cost figure provides a smaller denominator in the fraction, the resulting markup percentage will be greater. A comparison of the equivalent markup per cents of cost and retail is provided in Exhibit 8-3 to facilitate your understanding of the two bases.

In the previous example with markup based on retail, we noted the calculation of a markup of 40% with an item cost of $15 and a selling price of $25. Assuming that another merchant has purchased the same line of sweaters but is accustomed to calculating markup on cost, we would find the following relationship with the cost representing 100%:

$$\begin{array}{lllll}
\text{Cost} & = & \$15.00 & = & 100\% \\
+ \text{ Markup} & = & \underline{10.00} & = & \underline{} \\
= \text{Retail} & = & \$25.00 & = &
\end{array}$$

Since the basic equation still applies, the dollar markup will remain at $10, but expressed as a per cent of cost, we will then have 66⅔% ($10/$15 × 100%). The retail price of $25 must also be expressed on the basis of the cost of 100% and will therefore be 166⅔% ($25/$15 × 100%). Therefore, the equation can now be completed:

$$\begin{array}{lllll}
\text{Cost} & = & \$15.00 & = & 100\% \\
+ \text{ Markup} & = & \underline{10.00} & = & \underline{66\tfrac{2}{3}\%} \\
= \text{Retail} & = & \$25.00 & = & 166\tfrac{2}{3}\%
\end{array}$$

You'll note from these two examples that a markup of 40% on retail is equivalent to a markup of 66⅔% on cost.

Exhibit 8-3

Markup Conversion Table: Selected Per Cents

MU% of Cost	5.0	5.3	6.4	7.5	8.7	10.0	11.1	12.0	12.4
MU% of Retail	4.8	5.0	6.0	7.0	8.0	9.0	10.0	10.7	11.0
MU% of Cost	12.5	13.6	15.0	16.3	17.7	19.1	20.5	22.0	22.7
MU% of Retail	11.1	12.0	13.0	14.0	15.0	16.0	17.0	18.0	18.5
MU% of Cost	23.5	25.0	26.6	28.2	29.0	29.9	30.0	31.6	33.3
MU% of Retail	19.0	20.0	21.0	22.0	22.5	23.0	23.1	24.0	25.0
MU% of Cost	35.0	37.0	37.5	39.0	40.0	40.9	42.9	45.0	50.0
MU% of Retail	26.0	27.0	27.3	28.0	28.5	29.0	30.0	31.0	33.3
MU% of Cost	53.9	55.0	56.3	58.8	60.0	61.3	64.0	66.7	70.0
MU% of Retail	35.0	35.5	36.0	37.0	37.5	38.0	39.0	40.0	41.0
MU% of Cost	72.4	75.0	80.0	85.0	90.0	95.0	100.0	150.0	300.0
MU% of Retail	42.0	42.8	44.4	46.1	47.5	48.7	50.0	60.0	75.0

Source: Albert P. Kneider, *Mathematics of Merchandising*, © 1974, p. 37. Reprinted by permission of Prentice-Hall, Inc., Englewood Cliffs, New Jersey.

The calculation of markup has been greatly simplified by the sliding markup chart as illustrated in Exhibit 8-4. However, while this and other similar devices are valuable tools for quick reference, being able to determine markup mathematically is needed in planning markup variations.

Up to this point we have explored the process of calculating the markup on cost and retail. What is important for the merchant

Exhibit 8-4
Markup Calculator
Sliding Markup Chart

3.00	3.36	.28	.37	.40	.42		.43	.45	.47	.51
3.9%	9.64	9.0	.40	.43	.46		.47	.49	.51	.55
				.47	.49					
				.50	.52					

MARK UP CHART

COST ┌─Mark up percent on Selling Price─┐

PER DOZ	+ 12%	EACH	25	30	33½	35	37½	40	45
6.00	6.72	.66	.74	.80	.84	.86	.89	.94	1.02
PER DOZ	+ 12%	EACH	33½	43	50	54	60	66½	82

└─── Mark up percent on Cost ───┘

**FOR CONTROLLED PROFITS AND
COMPLETE CUSTOMER SATISFACTION
THE YEAR ROUND — STOCK**

TURNBULL
HANES

MANUFACTURERS OF FAMOUS

CEETEE, *Triples*, *Tru-Eze*, FIG LEAF
UNDERWEAR
MERRICHILD, *Rest-Eze*, SLEEPWEAR
AND SMARTLY STYLED
Sportswear

ALL GARMENTS ARE SIZE STANDARD APPROVED

C. TURNBULL LIMITED
GALT   ONT
ESTABLISHED 1859

29.00	32.48	2.71	3.60	3.86	4.06	4.18	4.32	4.52	4.93
90.00	99.80	9.82	3.72	3.99	4.90	4.97	4.47	4.88	5.10
			* 84	4.12	4				
				4.20					

MARK UP CHART

COST ┌─Mark up percent on Selling Price─┐

PER DOZ	+ 12%	EACH	25	30	33½	35	37½	40	45
41.00	45.92	3.83	5.08	5.45	5.74	5.90	6.11	6.40	6.97
PER DOZ	+ 12%	EACH	33½	43	50	54	60	66½	82

└─── Mark up percent on Cost ───┘

**THIS WILL HELP YOU
CHECK YOUR PROFITS**

For Example: If you buy an item at $12.00
per dozen and wish to know the retail price
per garment at a mark up of 33 1/3% on the
Selling price pull the card up or down in the
envelope until $12.00 appears under the
column heading "Cost per doz." and you will
find your answer, $1.68, under the column
heading 33 1/3% (printed above the slot). If
you figure your mark up on your cost
instead of selling price, use the lower row
of column headings printed below the slot.
Please note: all calculations allow for 10%
sales tax and 2% for freight.

TURNBULL
HANES

THE BEST IS ALWAYS THE MOST SATISFACTORY

Source: Albert P. Kneider, *Mathematics of Merchandising*, © 1974, p. 40. Reprinted
by permission of Prentice-Hall, Inc., Englewood Cliffs, New Jersey.

in the calculation of these markup per cents is the ability to plan the percentage to be applied to the dollar figures.

Initial Markup As we pointed out earlier, the initial markup placed on an item by a merchant represents the original markup used in setting the retail price. In order for you to determine how large the initial markup per cent needs to be, you will need to plan your expenses, profit, sales, and reductions. Since you're in business to make money, the markup to be placed on the items must be large enough to cover the store's expenses and still provide you with a profit.

To calculate the initial markup required for a store, let's again look at the formula for initial markup per cent.

$$\text{Initial Markup Per Cent} = \frac{\text{Operating Expenses} + \text{Net Profit} + \text{Reductions} + \text{Alteration Expenses} - \text{Cash Discount}}{\text{Net Sales} + \text{Reductions}}$$

If we assume a store has calculated its initial markup to be 45%, then the retailer will ideally initially place this markup on items entering the store. Merchandise which costs the store $33 will be retailed at $60 to obtain the store's initial markup of 45% based on retail:

Cost	=	$33.00	=	55%
+ Markup	=	27.00	=	45%
= Retail	=	$60.00	=	100%

The merchant who sets retail prices on the basis of a planned initial markup has established the store's profit objective with due consideration to the various elements that will affect markup. In this way, the retailer is also able to obtain information feedback that can be compared to the planned objectives.

Obviously, the same markup percentage cannot be used for every item in the store, since goods having the same cost may differ greatly in customer appeal and will permit or require very different markups.

Maintained Markup A retailer's pricing strategy would be greatly simplified if all merchandise in the store could be sold at original retail prices. The initial markup would then represent the actual markup received by the store. However, the final markup obtained by the firm is known as the maintained markup and differs from the original markup by the effect of the reductions taken.

We pointed out earlier that the reductions found in retail operations are usually composed of the sum of markdowns, stock shortages, and employee discounts. In all cases, these three elements represent reductions in the retail value of the merchandise taken from inventory.

In the process of planning a pricing strategy for the store, the merchant must set budgetary guidelines for these three elements. Experience shows that markdowns, shortages, and employee discounts are inevitable in the operation of a store.

Since the amount and percentage of the reductions will be planned by the merchant in the determination of the initial markup, these same figures will be used in the calculation of the maintained markup. In observing this relationship it will be evident that the difference between the initial and maintained markup is determined by the cost value of the planned reductions:

Maintained Markup = Initial Markup − Cost of Reductions

For example, assume the initial markup has been planned at 45%, as in the previous example, with markdowns of 7%, stock shortages of 2%, and employee discounts of 1%. The maintained markup would be calculated as follows:

Markdowns	7%
Stock Shortages	2%
Employee Discounts	1%
Total Reductions	10%

This 10% represents the *retail* value of the reductions as a per cent of the net sales. With planned net sales of $250,000, the total reductions would then be planned at $25,000 at retail (10% of $250,000). With an initial markup of 45%, the cost value would be 55% (100% − 45%).

The cost value of the reductions is based on the same relationship established between cost and retail in the initial markup. Thus, to find the *cost* value of the reductions we employ the same basic equation:

Cost	=		= 55%
+ Markup	=		= 45%
= Retail	=	10%	= 100%

The cost of the reductions is determined by taking 55% of the retail value of 10%. The cost of the reductions in this example is, then, established at 5.5% (55% of 10%). Substituting in the maintained markup equation:

Maintained Markup $=$ Initial Markup $-$ Cost of Reductions
$\qquad\qquad\qquad\ \ =$ 45% $-$ 5.5%
$\qquad\qquad\qquad\ \ =$ 39.5%
<hr>

In retail operations where reductions are a significant factor, careful planning and control of its components are essential to the profitability of the store. Since markdowns generally represent the largest portion of the reductions budget, a brief analysis is presented here to determine its impact on pricing strategy.

Markdowns

There is nothing absolute about the prices retailers establish for their merchandise. Customers of the store are concerned with the prices they pay rather than whether the store operates at a profit. Thus, if the merchant finds the merchandise is not selling at the price intended it will be marked down to a level that will induce customer buying.

Markdowns occur in retail operations for a number of reasons, some of which are indicated by the following:

1. *Improper Pricing.* Establishing too large an initial markup resulting in too high a price, or establishing an initial markup at a level above competitors will inevitably result in markdowns.

2. *Buying Errors.* In general, many independent merchants encounter markdown difficulties as a result of buying errors. Overbuying may result from large initial orders being placed or by failing to control the store's open-to-buy figures. Buying difficulties of poor planning of the various selection factors in relation to customer demand have also resulted in large markdowns for many retailers. Independent retailers often find themselves with excessive markdowns as a result of ordering merchandise too late in the selling season to capitalize on customer interest. Knowing the peaks of the selling season is vital to determining the interest of the customer in the merchandise at regular prices.

3. *Selling Problems.* Merchandising problems associated with the selling function can lead to unnecessary markdowns in retail stores. Poorly trained sales personnel, inadequate merchandise presentation, and poor inventory protection have resulted in independent merchants taking markdowns that could be significantly reduced through proper management.

4. *Miscellaneous Factors.* There are a number of environmental factors which tend to cause markdowns on the part of the store's merchandise assortment. New developments in products on the basis of style or function can render existing products obsolete, demanding dramatic and quick markdown action to move the existing inventory. Merchandise which is excessively dependent on the weather may require large markdowns to move the inventory, if the conditions are not those generally experienced in the area. An extremely mild winter could seriously affect the markdown rate of a store's overshoe sales, for example.

When to Mark Down Independent retailers have, on many occasions, carried merchandise over to the same selling season of the next year rather than placing markdowns on existing stock. By reasoning that goods will bring a higher price at the beginning of the same season the following year, the stock is carried over.

This retention of inventory needs to be carefully weighed against the funds that are tied up in inventory which will not be released for a full year. Experience has also shown that merchandise which is carried over for another year tends to take on a shop-worn look as well as damaging the image of the store in the eyes of the customers who recognize the goods as last year's stock.

Therefore, the timing of markdowns is essential for retail stores. But there is no uniform agreement as to whether a retail store should take markdowns on some items early in the season, or delay all markdowns to an inventory clearance closer to the end of the selling season. Arguments have been presented for both phases of the timing of markdowns. You should establish your own policy regarding the timing of the markdowns based on the breadth and depth of the assortment, the nature of the merchandise, the actions of your competitors, and the buying mood of your customers.

While each store must make its own decision regarding markdowns, it is generally believed that markdowns should be taken early to reduce the size of the markdowns and at the same time provide a steady flow of new merchandise to the store.

The Size of the Markdown The markdown is represented by the difference between the original selling price and the new reduced selling price. Therefore, a power saw which has been reduced from $45.00 to $33.00 is recorded as a markdown of $12.00 or 26⅔% of the original retail price.

Independent retailers generally find it difficult to establish the amount by which the items should be reduced. Since the purpose of the markdown is to move the merchandise, the amount of the reduction must be large enough to induce customer buying. Customarily, markdowns taken early in the season can be marked down further if they do not sell, and as a result are generally smaller than the reductions taken later in the season.

Obviously, reducing a $25.00 item to $22.97 is not likely to generate a great deal of buying enthusiasm. A price reduction in excess of 20% is generally considered necessary as the first markdown employed to move goods in the store. The more markdowns that are taken successively to move the inventory, the less the likelihood of selling the items. When this occurs,

Exhibit 8-5

Markdowns as a Per Cent of Net Sales, Selected Departments

Merchandise Lines	Median	Superior
Women's Dresses	20.0	15.0
Separates and Co-ordinates	15.6	11.7
Corsets and Bras	4.3	2.6
Lingerie and Sleepwear	7.2	5.0
Jewellery and Watches	4.3	2.6
Costume Jewellery	4.4	3.1
Hosiery	4.5	3.2
Handbags	6.3	4.4
Men's Clothing	13.6	8.8
Men's Furnishings	9.7	7.5
Children's Apparel and Accessories	11.7	8.9
Stationery and Office Equipment	5.1	3.0
Cosmetics and Toiletries	1.8	1.0
Hobby, Recreation, Transportation	7.6	4.6
Toys	7.8	3.9
Books, Arts, Photography	3.0	1.0
Home Furnishings	8.1	4.8
Floor Coverings	6.4	2.7
China and Glassware	8.2	4.7
Gifts	7.6	4.8
Housewares	5.3	2.9
Lawn and Garden Equipment	16.1	5.1
Linens and Domestics	9.3	5.2
Sewing Notions	5.1	4.5
Fabrics	25.4	14.0

Source: National Retail Merchants Association, Department Store and Specialty Store Merchandising and Operating Results (New York: 1975).

the merchant is well advised to consider the merchandise dead stock and donate it to a charitable organization rather than retaining the items as part of the inventory and possibly damaging the image of the store.

PRICING POLICIES

Up to this point, we have been concerned with the interpretation and mechanics of implementing a pricing strategy for the independent merchant. While the calculation of markup for an item will tell the store what the price will be, it does not in fact indicate what the price should be. Just as buying, layout, promotion, and other merchandising decisions are made on the basis of store policies, so too must pricing policies be established to guide pricing of the store's merchandise.

It should be clear that retailers can compete for customers either on the basis of low-price appeal or on the basis of non-price competitive devices. For the majority of merchandise lines, independent retailers are generally forced to compete on the basis of the non-price elements. Therefore, rather than feature a low-price policy, independent merchants will attempt to establish pricing policies that will be consistent with the overall image of the store.

The basic decisions of pricing the merchandise in relation to the market level of prices must be made by the retailer. Based on the competitive pressures, customer awareness, and the type and nature of the merchandise, the retailer will select from the following choices:

Above the Market

While independent retailers have frequently been charged with having higher prices than their larger counterparts, the practice of pricing above market levels may in fact be justified. By offering more services, wider merchandise selections, more exclusivity, or more expensive-looking environments, specialty stores have been able to obtain a satisfactory volume of sales at prices above the market level. Similarly, corner stores and jug milk shops have also been able to sell at slightly higher prices as a result of their convenient locations and extended business hours.

At the Market

By and large the majority of independent retailers tend to price their merchandise lines at the market level. Such a policy is implemented when the items are very similar and can be compared closely by the consumer. On this basis, the small retail operator accepting the market prices established by suppliers and competitors must seek other means of non-price competition to induce customers to patronize the store.

Below the Market

Retail establishments which stress the price as the distinctive characteristic of the firm generally price the merchandise below market levels. As a result, customer services may be reduced, assortments may be smaller, and markups may be lower. Discount stores and some mass-merchandise operations tend to run the store on the premise that large volumes can be achieved by selling at lower prices with less frills.

COMPONENTS OF THE PRICING STRATEGY

Demand Considerations All retailers must be concerned about the increases or decreases in merchandise they will sell as the price of the item fluctuates. This principle of changes in quantities sold in relation to changes in the price is referred to as the elasticity of demand. A large change in the demand for sandpaper is not likely to occur if the price increases or decreases; as a result, the demand is said to be inelastic. However, a similar increase or decrease of 25% in the price of an electric sander in the same store could result in significant changes in the sales of the item; subsequently, the sander can be classified as having an elastic demand. It is to your advantage to assess the price-quantity relationship for your merchandise line in terms of its elasticity, as well as the elasticity of demand for your store in comparison to others serving the same market.

Competition No retail firm operates in a vacuum with a monopoly position. As a result, merchants must be aware of the competitive considerations in pricing, especially for items which have a wide distribution, are easily compared, and are characterized by high-purchase frequency. Generally, both convenience goods and shopping goods sold under a national brand label are highly influenced by competitive pricing.

Resale Price Maintenance   The passing of federal legislation in 1951 under the Combines Investigation Act, Section 38, prohibits the practice of resale price maintenance in Canada. It is therefore unlawful for the manufacturer or supplier to dictate the price at which the merchant must sell the items. Suppliers who put prices on merchandise and provide stores with retail price lists are careful to designate these as "suggested list prices" and "recommended retail prices."

While resale price maintenance is illegal in Canada, suppliers who wish to retain price control of their merchandise have attempted to do so with little interference from the merchants or the attorney general's office. However, because of the administrative problems and the possible legal implications, suppliers tend to prefer to be more flexible with pricing at the retail level by offering suggestions only.

Leader Pricing   This pricing practice is designed to offer merchandise to the consumer that will not yield the maximum dollar profit return. This less profitable price is used by retail firms to attract customers to the store and to consequently induce the purchase of the other, more profitable, items in the store. When these promotional items are sold at a loss, that is below cost, they are referred to as loss leader items.

To be effective as a leader item, the merchandise should have wide consumer appeal, should be recognized by the consumer as good value, and the price reduction must be large enough to induce the customer to make a special effort to visit the store. The large supermarket chains have been notorious in the past few years for offering leader items in their advertised weekly specials.

Price Lining   The retail practice of establishing predetermined price points at which merchandise will be offered for sale to the customers is referred to as price lining. The merchant then attempts to purchase items for the store that will fit into these price lines. The principle of establishing these price lines is to simplify the buying decisions of both the retailer and the customer. Each price line may consist of items which have different costs and subsequently different markups. Retailers then attempt to select a limited number of popular price lines into which all items in the merchandise line will fit.

Price Endings   While retailers are constantly attempting to determine the price endings of the items they sell, the use of odd or even prices seems to receive much debate. Generally, merchants tend to price regular merchandise with price endings similar to $10.95, $11.98, and $14.00. With the implication of the provincial retail sales taxes, the practice of pricing at the even dollar seems to be more prevalent.

Odd price endings like 77¢, 88¢, and 49¢ are generally used by retailers to signify clearance and specially priced merchandise. As a result, customers purchasing general merchandise items have associated these price endings with special price reductions.

Multiple-Unit Pricing Selecting a pricing policy of specific lines of merchandise that will give the customer a better value by purchasing more than one item is referred to as multiple-unit pricing. The practice of offering the customer an item at 2 for $11.75 or 4 for $21.00 increases the units sold and also increases the size of the average sale. Depending on the reduction in the multiple pricing strategy, the overall markup on the line can be significantly affected.

Anticipated Reductions Merchandise items which are subject to style or physical perishability require higher prices in terms of the initial markup, since markdowns will have to be taken to sell some of the inventory. For this reason, the reduction percentage of markdowns, stock shortages, and employee discounts must be planned to ensure an adequate maintained markup after these reductions have been taken.

RETAIL PRICING POLICIES

The general pricing policies that a retailer adopts will be determined by the store's target market, the desired image, and the nature and extent of the competition. While the pricing policies established by the retail store will offer the merchant the guidelines needed to provide the framework for these decisions, intuition and sound business judgement continue to offer some merchants an advantage in their pricing practices.

Based on the desired image, retail stores will select from the following pricing policies in determining the philosophy to be used in offering the merchandise for sale.

One Price Policy Most Canadian retail stores operate under the policy that the price the store is asking for the item is visibly marked on the merchandise and sold to all customers at that price. If this price is to be changed, then all similar items are reduced to the new designated price through a markdown. Such a policy assures equal treatment to all customers and simplifies the selling function as well as encouraging self-service retailing.

Variable Price Policy Some retail merchants, like car showroom and craft store owners, have indicated the price in code so that the salespeople can determine the retail price with each customer. If sales resistence is met, the price can be lowered, offering the shrewd buyer a better deal than the traditional customer. Such a pricing policy obviously requires more time to sell, as it virtually eliminates self-service retailing.

Trade-In Variations In merchandise lines where trade-in items are accepted as part of a trading-up process, each will have a variable value. As such, the trade-in becomes the lever in the hands of the customer to obtain a lower price on the new item.

Non-Price Policy Some retail establishments which have taken strong measures to develop a quality image prefer not to engage in any type of price competition. While special sales may be offered at these stores, they consider their customer market to be more interested in the image of the store, the services provided, the exclusivity of the merchandise, and the atmosphere of the store rather than the price the store charges.

Competitive Price Policy Some retail firms will not initiate low prices but have a policy of meeting any prices of competing stores on identical merchandise. Department stores opting to meet the competition of the discounter promote their policy that they will not knowingly be undersold.

Low Price Policy Retail stores which have observed that price may be the primary motivating factor in the purchase of some items, have sought to establish low price, discount selling practices. Such stores obviously rely on nationally branded merchandise that can be easily compared by the consumer.

Product-Quality Policies Retail firms which have opted to carry only first quality merchandise have established a different policy from those stores which also stock seconds in their assortment.

Premium Merchandising For many years retail pricing policies have been characterized by premium pricing through the use of coupons, trading stamps, games, and other gimmicks. While these policies have been used to attract and hold new customers, it is usually the first store in the area to offer these that shows an immediate increase in business. As competitors retaliate, the initial advantage is lost and the retailer finds this to be a costly means of price promotion.

Since the pricing policy is a guide for decision making, a general plan of action that directs the merchant in the conduct of the store's operation, this policy of the retail establishment must ensure the attainment of the store's objectives. It should be stressed that these policies must be selected and implemented in relation to the other elements of the store's merchandising strategy to ensure the projection of a unified image to the customers of the store.

9
RETAIL PROMOTIONAL PRINCIPLES

Promotion in the retail industry is much broader than advertising; subsequently, it includes many areas that merchants do not normally consider as part of their promotional budget. If an independent agrees to redeem parking fees at an adjacent lot and consequently attracts customers to the store, then this strategy can be considered as much a part of promotion as an effective newspaper advertisement. Promotion is generally considered to be any communicative activity designed to move a product or service through the retailers' channel of distribution. Through promotion the merchant attempts to influence the sale of merchandise by increasing the quantity of items sold. In an economic sense, it is the task of promotion to shift the entire demand curve for the product or service by increasing the merchandise turnover by any factor other than price.

To truly understand the impact of a promotional strategy for a retail firm, it is important to be familiar with the various components that make up the promotional mix. It is also essential to understand that promotion is one of the four fundamental factors in the overall retail strategy of the store. Exhibit 9-1 is included to assist you in visualizing the relationships among the major areas of promotion and promotion's position in the overall merchandising strategy.

The mixtures and combinations of these four promotional activities are used to increase sales and to meet the established objectives. Therefore, the breakdown of each of these elements offers the merchant the alternatives available in blending the components of the store's promotional mix.

While the objective of the promotional campaign is primarily to increase sales, each plan may be designed to attain this

Exhibit 9-1
Retail Strategy and the Element of Promotion

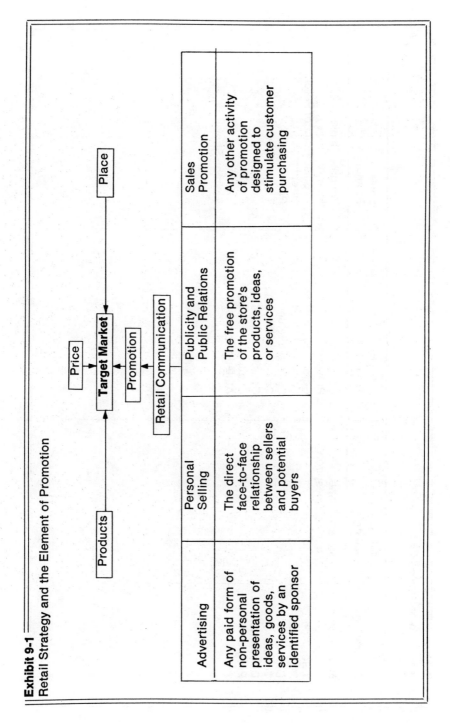

Advertising	Personal Selling	Publicity and Public Relations	Sales Promotion
Any paid form of non-personal presentation of ideas, goods, services by an identified sponsor	The direct face-to-face relationship between sellers and potential buyers	The free promotion of the store's products, ideas, or services	Any other activity of promotion designed to stimulate customer purchasing

Products → Target Market ← Price
Promotion
Place
Retail Communication

Exhibit 9-2
Classification of Promotion

Advertising	Personal Selling	Publicity and Public Relations	Sales Promotion
Newspapers	Store Salespeople	Openings	Window Displays
Radio	Outside Salespeople	Previews	Interior Display
Television		Community Events	Impulse Point of Purchase
Magazines		Community Participation	Direct Mail
Outdoor		Special Events	Premiums
Transit		Consumer Boards	Trading Stamps
Directories		Consumer Relations	Coupons
Programs		Employee Relations	Contests
		Athletic Teams	Exhibits
			Fashion Shows

task by seeking:
1. To generate customer traffic
2. To foster the habit of visiting the store regularly and often
3. To promote the sale of specific items directly
4. To generate talk about the store
5. To obtain press publicity in the various media which serve the store's customers
6. To implant in the customer's mind that the store is a community centre in which many educational and entertaining events are taking place.

In observing the communication function of promotion, it should be noted that promotion is a facilitating function of the marketing process which is designed to assist in the stimulation of the store's sales. The whole promotional effort must be considered as one impetus—all channels of communication with customers are important, all attempt to inform the public and influence it to prefer one retail store over another.

RETAIL ADVERTISING

While promotion includes more elements than just advertising, it should be evident that advertising is usually the most important form of non-personal promotion in the communications mix of the store. As a result of the constant barrage of advertising messages that are seen by each individual each day, it hardly seems necessary to define the meaning or the importance of advertising to the independent merchant.

Advertising is defined as "any paid form of non-personal presentation and promotion of ideas, goods or services by an identified sponsor." (Ralph S. Alexander, Chairman of Committee on Definitions, *Marketing Definitions* [Chicago: American Marketing Association, 1960], p. 9.) To distinguish this element of promotion from the others available to the merchant, let's look at the component parts of the definition.

The phrase *paid form* has been included as part of the definition to distinguish advertising from publicity, which is generally provided free to the store by the designated media. Further, advertising is the *non-personal presentation* when compared to the face-to-face contact of personal selling in the store. Together, these two elements provide the fundamental promotional effort for the store. In addition, retailers do not concern themselves solely with the promotion of *tangible goods*, but may also seek an advantage by advertising the *services* they are prepared to offer their customers. Finally, the definition of advertising requires that the sponsor of the advertisement be *identified* to the receiver of the message to distinguish this element from that commonly referred to as propaganda. All of these facets make advertising a basic tool of the store's promotional strategy.

While the above definition seeks to explain advertising generally, it should be noted that local advertising is that employed by retail stores, while national advertising represents product or service advertising undertaken by manufacturers and suppliers. The distinction is made since retail merchants seek to attract patrons to their stores through their advertising strategies while national advertising is designed to sell a product or service regardless of the retail firm in which the product or service is located. Essentially, manufacturers are concerned with stimulating the sales of their product or service, while retailers are seeking to ensure that this demand is satisfied at their locations rather than at competitors' outlets which may offer the same or similar products.

The advertising strategy for the retail establishment interested in increasing the merchandise turnover must initially define the objectives hoped to be achieved. Prior to establishing these objectives, you must carefully assess the image your store wishes to communicate to its target market and in this assessment clearly outline the type of business you assume yourself to be in. Does the store sell furniture or is it in the home decoration business? Does the store sell sporting goods or is it in the recreation-leisure field? You must know what your store is, and what you wish it to be, before you can communicate this to your potential market.

The primary purposes of retail advertising for independent merchants must first and foremost be to build a reputation for the store by expressing to the market the image and individuality of the firm. As a means of increasing the merchandise turnover of the store, independents also outline as their advertising objective the need to increase customer traffic and subsequently the sales volume. Successfully accomplishing these two objectives will assist merchants in achieving the predetermined profit objectives they have established for their stores.

The task of advertising in the communication mix is explained by the principles listed below.

1. Advertising should continually repeat the advantages of the store in such a believable fashion that it will convince the

customers to develop a shopping pattern that will automatically include its location.

2. Advertising should attempt to sell the store before it sells the merchandise, by giving customers the required buying motives to patronize the store.

3. Advertising explains to prospective customers the advantages of owning merchandise or purchasing a service and thus influences them to come to the advertised store to buy the goods.

4. By attracting increased traffic to the store, advertising will stimulate the sale of both the advertised and unadvertised items. In this context, the power of advertising to attract customers to the store is thought to be more important to the merchant than the specific sales of the advertised items.

5. To attract the largest number of people to the store, the advertising should be executed to promote high-turnover items that are in great demand.

6. Advertising should be designed to attract the store's existing customers first and subsequently to draw new patrons to the operation.

7. Advertising should emphasize the importance of suggestion selling by inducing customers to purchase items they want rather than just those they need.

8. Advertising should be designed and implemented to provide a more continuous flow of sales by keeping customers informed and aware of the merchandising attributes of the store.

9. To be successful in meeting its objectives, advertising must be used on a continuous basis rather than intermittently.

10. Advertising should be used by the merchant to stimulate demand for items the customers want to buy and for which they have the ability to pay. Items which the customers classify as undesirable cannot be sold, even with extensive advertising.

11. Advertising should be employed to inform viewers and readers of the availability of the merchandise in the store and to point out its features, advantages, benefits, and uses.

12. Advertising must continually communicate with the store's target market.

Types of Retail Advertising

We have noted on a number of occasions that the image the store wishes to project to its potential market will significantly affect its total merchandising strategy. While there are numerous media for projecting the image, all retail advertising is either promotional or institutional advertising.

Promotional advertising seeks to build customers traffic to the store through the presentation of specific merchandise for sale during a designated time period. The primary purpose of promotional advertising is to solicit immediate sales from customers on the basis of regular price-line advertising, special sale items, or general clearance advertising.

Institutional advertising is designed to communicate the image of the store as a reputable retail operation which will satisfy the needs and wants of its customers in the merchandise lines presented. Institutional advertising is primarily used to build confidence in the store's merchandise and to emphasize the services and prestige available to the patrons. As such, institutional advertising is designed to produce sales and profit in the long-run as opposed to the immediate impact of promotional advertising.

Each of these two types of retail advertising has its place in the store's promotional mix. Independent merchants are likely to find that their limited funds and expertise will demand the more frequent use of promotional advertising. As a result, independents are advised to carefully consider the employment of the three types of promotional advertising.

1. **Regular price-line advertising** Regular price-line advertising is designed to inform the customers of the merchandise assortment available at the store. This tends to be the most profitable type of advertising done by the independent since it features regular markup items, new merchandise brought into stock, and an overall image that the store has complete and current assortments.

2. **Special sale advertising** Special sale advertising is used by independents to produce immediate sales for a specific period of time. While special sale advertising fulfills the task of disposing of the designated items, it also provides the store with large numbers of customers who may purchase other items or who are visiting the store for the first time. Therefore, a well-planned and executed special sale advertisement outlining the values and desirability of the merchandise plays a large role in validating the reputation of the store as a reliable merchandise source.

3. **Clearance advertising** Clearance advertising serves the primary purpose of disposing of slow selling merchandise at

frequent intervals or at the end of each of the seasons. This type of advertising most often is used as a store's semi-annual sale. While clearance advertising is costly in relation to the markup being obtained on the reduced items, it is nevertheless necessary if the merchant is to clear the stock, replenish the inventory with new items carrying full markup, and free funds that may eventually end up in dead stock. Many independent retailers tend to restrict the frequency of clearance advertising campaigns to avoid establishing an image of a store that is continually dumping stock as a result of poor merchandising.

PLANNING THE ADVERTISING

One of the most frequent problems confronting the independent merchant operating in an extremely competitive environment is deciding upon the amount of money to appropriate for the advertising program. While we propose to look generally at the advertising budget, it is important for you to realize that the planning of a total promotion figure precedes the establishment of the advertising allowance. Once the total promotion budget has been prepared, funds are then allocated to each of its components—advertising, display and other sales promotional techniques, publicity and public relations.

Since most independent merchants allocate the greatest part of these funds to advertising, let's, at this point, review the techniques employed in establishing the budget figure.

The most commonly used method is that which allocates a percentage of the store's net sales to the promotional activities and subsequently a percentage of this figure to advertising. The advertising figure is then generally expressed also as a percentage of the net sales figure. This method establishes a relationship between net sales of the past and the percentage of funds spent on promotion and advertising. Thus, if sales are planned at $300,000 and promotion is planned at 4%, the amount of funds available for the total promotion will be $12,000. Since it is generally assumed that approximately 75% of the promotional budget will be used by the independent as the advertising appropriation, $9000, or 3%, of sales will be available for advertising.

This method of allocating funds to promotion can be easily used by existing merchants. The potential retailer will be required to rely on the statistics available from trade associations and

Exhibit 9-3
Sample Institutional Advertisement

Source: Advertisement in *The Globe and Mail*, p. 12, August 30, 1977. Reprinted by permission of The Trend Shoppe, C. Gaines and Assoc., Agency.

Exhibit 9-4
Sample Special Sale Advertising

The Best Reason to Buy A $250.00 Dinner Set: $89.

For the next two weeks our beautiful Denby fine china dinner sets will be reduced from $250.00 to $89. This high style collection is open stock and dishwasher safe. Eight new designs in both traditional and contemporary styles in varying colour schemes to give your home a new look for spring.

So if you think $89. is a good excuse to buy a dinnerware set of this fine quality, pay us a visit soon. After all, you might wait a long time to find an excuse this good again.

40-Pce. Set
● 8 Cups ● 8 Saucers ● 8 Side Plates ● 8 Soups ● 8 Dinners

87 Bloor St. W.
Mail and Phone Orders Filled
Chargex & Mastercharge accepted

925-4454
Free Delivery Toronto area
orders over $30.00

OPEN THURSDAY TILL 9:00 p.m.

Source: Advertisement in *Toronto Star*, p. E2, October 4, 1977. Reprinted by permission of William Ashley.

trade publications. In actuality, these statistics may also act as a useful guide to existing merchants who wish to compare their appropriations with others in the industry.

The second approach that is used by some retailers in their efforts to plan promotional expenditures is known as the objective and task method. As the name implies, the procedure is to establish an approachable sales goal and then determine the amount of promotional effort that will be required to attain this objective. As a planning technique, this approach forces the retailer to carefully consider many elements before a promotional strategy is implemented. While this method is preferred, independent merchants have tended to choose the simplicity of the percentage-of-sales approach.

While the quantitative analysis of the percentage-of-sales and objective and task methods are effective in allocating dollar amounts to a promotion budget, certain qualitative factors must be considered before the expenditures are finalized.

Competition Obviously the extent and degree of competition that a firm faces will seriously affect the retaliation anticipated in the advertising and promotional expenditures by a store.

Type of Business Retail stores that are classified as generative businesses will tend to spend larger amounts on advertising than those designated as recipient businesses.

Location In relation to the type of business above, recipient firms which seek the prime 100% location need to spend a smaller proportion of their rent-advertising budget on advertising. At the other end of the scale, retailers choosing locations away from the major shopping area will be required to spend larger sums on promotion to attract traffic to the store.

Age and Reputation Retail stores that have been in business in the community for a number of years and which have consequently established a reputation among the residents need to spend much less than the new store which is attempting to establish itself in the market.

Trading Area Retail stores operating in small communities with limited media available are better able to direct their advertising messages with less circulation waste. In larger communities with many forms of communications to the market, the cost of using the media capable of reaching the specific market is much higher. The merchant must then determine how closely the advertising medium selected corresponds with the store's trading area to determine the extent of the wasted advertising coverage.

Store Image Retail firms which seek to project an image of a discounter or highly promotional store will be required to budget greater amounts for advertising expenditures. Their need is to obtain a large volume of sales based on a lower markup and a higher turnover. Similarly, fashion stores obtaining a higher markup may also justify a larger advertising expenditure in their efforts to increase merchandise turnover and to avoid excessive markdowns at the end of the season.

MONTHLY DISTRIBUTION OF ADVERTISING BUDGET

The distribution of the advertising appropriation throughout the year or season begins with an analysis of the anticipated sales volume for each of the months. The more sophistication desired in the allocation, the more likely is the merchant to further break the sales and promotional budgets down into a weekly basis.

It is generally preferred to vary the percentage of advertising expenditures in each month from the planned sales. In a month similar to December, which may account for as much as 25% of the season's sales, it is not, for example, advisable to spend one-quarter of the season's advertising appropriation. Conversely, in a month with low sales, a greater percentage of the budget may be required to stimulate sufficient interest to reach these lower figures.

For example, Seven Seas Gift Shop plans its advertising budget on the basis of 4% of the store's anticipated sales, with the monthly distribution of sales and promotion as indicated below.

Month	Planned Sales %	Planned Sales $	Planned Promotion %	Planned Promotion $
Feb.	5.2	$ 15,600	6.5	$ 780.00
Mar.	6.4	19,200	7.2	864.00
Apr.	6.0	18,000	7.2	864.00
May	6.4	19,200	7.0	840.00
June	7.0	21,000	7.5	900.00
July	6.2	18,600	7.0	840.00
Aug.	7.4	22,200	8.0	960.00
Sept.	5.8	17,400	6.5	780.00
Oct.	9.0	27,000	9.0	1,080.00
Nov.	11.6	34,800	10.0	1,200.00
Dec.	23.9	71,700	18.0	2,160.00
Jan.	5.1	15,300	6.1	732.00
	100.0	$300,000	100.0	$12,000.00

With planned sales of $300,000, the total promotional budget for the year will then be $12,000.

ALLOCATION TO MEDIA

Once the advertising budget has been distributed among the months in the season or year, it is necessary to appropriate the budgeted funds to the various media that will be used. Advertising is by far the largest expenditure in the independent retailer's promotional budget and for this reason the following discussion is offered on the advertising generally available to the small retailer.

Newspapers

The bulk of the retailer's advertising budget is usually concentrated on the use of newspapers serving the store's market. Probably as much as 80% of the independent's media expenditure is allocated to newspaper advertising. Since this medium provides a broad market coverage with all family members reading the newspaper, the cost of reaching each reader is relatively small. However, merchants operating in the neighbourhood of a large city would find an advertisement placed in a large daily of the city to be essentially wasted dollars. Many communities capitalize on this problem by offering special inserts in the large dailies, providing neighbourhood weeklies, or distributing shopper news bulletins to residents of the various neighbourhoods.

Since many independent retailers generally lack the expertise of preparing effective advertising copy or layout, the retail advertising service of most newspapers offer assistance in advertising production that is very beneficial to the merchant.

Radio

Generally acting as an effective supplementary advertising medium, radio offers the independent retailer another means of getting a message to store customers. Like newspapers, radio reaches large numbers of people at a relatively low cost. Its advantage lies in its ability to distribute a live message that can be made to stimulate action and response on the part of the listener. By selecting an appropriate program, the retailer can

Exhibit 9-5
Advertising-Sales Relationship

If you want well-timed advertising to sell more merchandise at lower unit cost, you want a sales and advertising pattern which month by month looks—

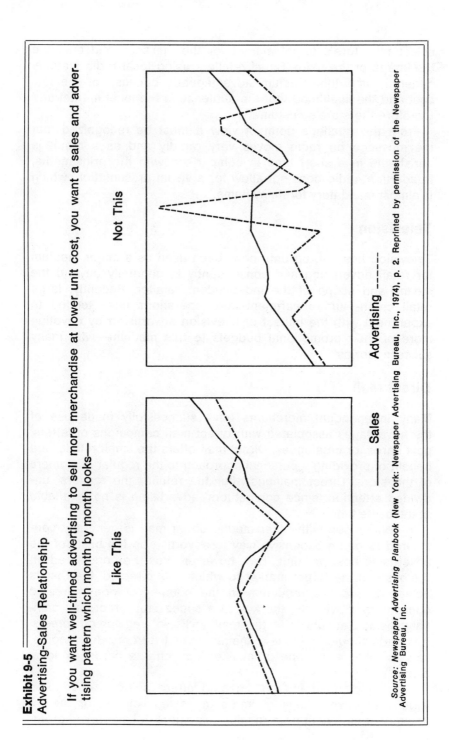

Like This

Not This

—— Sales   Advertising - - - - -

Source: Newspaper Advertising Planbook (New York: Newspaper Advertising Bureau, Inc., 1974), p. 2. Reprinted by permission of the Newspaper Advertising Bureau, Inc.

select the store's target market for the message and enhance the image of the store. Small retailers using local radio stations generally find this medium advantageous because of the low cost and the likelihood that the audience is the local market and therefore the store's customers.

From the retailer's point of view it must be recognized that the message on radio moves very rapidly and as a result is perishable in a short time in comparison with the print media. In addition, radio does not allow for a visual presentation, which is almost mandatory for many items.

Television

Television has not, up until now, been used as a major medium for retail advertising and consequently is generally beyond the means and scope of the independent retailer. Recently, large retail chain- and department-store operations have tended to experiment with the impact of television advertising by devoting more of their promotional budgets to this medium—with many success stories.

Direct Mail

Many independent merchants have successfully made use of the advantages associated with direct mail campaigns of letters, post cards, or catalogues. Direct mail offers the small retailer the benefit of providing a personal approach to the regular customers of the store. Direct mailings offer the retailer the readers' undivided attention, since competitors' advertising is not available at the same time.

In comparison with other media, direct mail is generally considered to be an expensive way to advertise on the basis of the advertising cost per unit. This, however, must be considered on the basis of the target market to which it is directed, the results achieved, and the reduction in the number of non-interested consumers. Obviously, the key to a successful direct-mail campaign is the accuracy of the mailing list of regular customers. All efforts should be made to maintain this list from sales records, service calls, telephone or mail orders, charge cards, or local clubs.

Properly planned and implemented, direct mail can prove to be a very effective means of improving sales volume for the independent merchant from regular customers. It has proved profitable in informing regular patrons of an advance clearance sale before general notification to the public is made, and in letting the regulars know of new arrivals of merchandise for best selection.

Handbills and Inserts

Handbills and inserts are promotional pieces that are used by the merchant as a package insert or handbill which is distributed to the residents in the neighbourhood. Independent retailers operating with a limited trading area have found the use of handbills to be an effective means of communicating with the store's potential market. They have been successfully employed in informing potential customers of sales events, new arrivals, and special presentations. The key to an effective handbill program rests in the supervision of the distribution to ensure that the advertisements reach the audience for which they are intended.

Package inserts, or stuffers, can be selectively distributed in the store with the anticipation that the customer will read the information at leisure at home.

Billboards

For the independent retailer, the cost of leasing billboard space and maintaining its appearance may be prohibitive. However, in smaller communities where outdoor signs tend to be much more reasonable in price, merchants have capitalized on this means of attracting customers. Generally, billboards offer large circulation at a low cost per reader, with the added advantage of visual impact. While such advertisements must be read quickly, outdoor signs generally serve the purpose of keeping the store's name in front of the consuming public. Their impact is especially great when placed beside a major traffic artery in the community in which the store is located.

Transit Cards

Posters placed on buses, street cars, subway trains, or other public transit facilities offer the merchant large circulation with the express purpose of maintaining the customer's awareness of the store. Their drawing power and appeal, for small merchants, is limited, and they are not normally recommended for small retailers operating with a limited budget.

Magazines

On the basis of the wide geographic market required for the distribution of magazines, this medium of advertising is almost non-existent as far as the independent retailer is concerned. However, the merchant's ability to capitalize on the national advertising done by his suppliers in this medium will offer significant results in increasing the products' volume.

Programs

Retailers are constantly asked to make donations by taking advertisements in the various programs of charitable organizations, school activities, athletic events, and other community groups. While these advertisements do not normally generate much traffic to the store, failure to take space in these programs may seriously damage the image and goodwill of the store within the community. You are well advised to allocate a specific amount of dollars for this part of your advertising budget, and you should indicate to the various groups when the budget has been spent. As in all areas of merchandising, control is important with this budget.

THE ADVERTISING PLAN

Every successful retail store requires a plan to ensure the most efficient use of its advertising dollars. The advertising plan of the independent retail store is an attempt to forecast the advertising and promotion that the store intends to use for the six-month season. Since advertising is part of the overall promotional plan, the advertising plan must be considered in light of the activities planned in the other aspects of promotion. All of these activities must be co-ordinated to gain maximum impact from the budget. Because of size, the independent retailer tends to combine promotion and advertising plans on a promotional calendar similar to that illustrated in Exhibit 9-6.

You'll note that the planning calendar worksheets which are provided in Exhibits 9-6 and 9-7 require you to budget and plan your advertising expenditures on a monthly basis. In this manner, you can avoid the common mistake of most independents in preparing last-minute advertisement for the local newspapers. In

Exhibit 9-6
Sample Promotion Calendar

MARCH 19___

SUNDAY	MONDAY	TUESDAY	WEDNESDAY	THURSDAY	FRIDAY	SATURDAY
				Community Midnight Madness Sale 1	2	3
4	5	6	7	8	9	10
11	12	13	14	15	16	St. Patrick's Day 17
18	19	Spring Arrives 20	21	22	23	School Break Begins 24
25	26	27	28	29	30	31

	This Year	Last Year
Selling Days:	27	27
Saturdays:	5	4

	This Year	Last Year
Net Sales:	$	$
Promotion Budget:	$	$

Exhibit 9-7
Sample Promotion Calendar

MARCH

Week	Date	Media	Theme/Features	Budget	Comments
1					
2	5 7 7	INTERIOR DISPLAY INTERIOR DISPLAY WINDOW DISPLAY	SPRING COLOURS - "FRESHEN UP" "LUCK OF IRISH" PROMOTION FOR SCHOOL BREAK - going South	$ 35 $ 10 $ 40	
3	17	WINDOW DISPLAY	"LUCK OF THE IRISH"	$ 15	
4	20 24	NEWSPAPER	SPRING IN BLOOM" - NEW ARRIVALS "THE WINTER BREAK"	$ 140	
5					

Traditional Merchandising
Events and Promotions

addition, the calendar suggests the control of advertising expenditures in relation to the anticipated sales. But perhaps the most important element of the advertising plan is its ability to induce you to co-ordinate all aspects of promotion to strengthen the impact of the merchandising strategy. By recording actual holidays and special events in the community on the calendar you're forced to do some advance planning for activities designed to capitalize on the special day.

It is important to note at this point that the preparation of these plans does not have to be complicated. It should be designed by you to provide your store with the guidelines required in the expenditure of the advertising and promotional dollars you have allocated.

While we have attempted to explore the various planning processes that are required in the management of the advertising function, no attempt has been made to discuss the technical aspects of implementing the advertising strategy. The expertise required in the preparation of effective copy, layout, and typographic style can best be obtained by using the services of the advertising media you select to advertise your store. Many small retailers have gained exceptional knowledge and creativity by carefully observing the advertisements placed in wide-circulation daily newspapers by large retail stores which either employ advertising departments or professional advertising agencies. There is a wealth of information available, as well, from manufacturers, trade associations, libraries, and the various media on the technical aspects of advertising production.

PUBLICITY AND PUBLIC RELATIONS

Publicity and public relations play important roles in identifying the store's policies and attitudes with respect to the community it serves. As such, you must recognize that you are in business to make a profit, but only if you are able to serve the needs and wants of your market will you be able to realize this goal. Therefore, an effective public relations program must be developed and implemented over a period of time to earn the confidence, respect, and goodwill of your customers.

In a similar fashion, publicity represents news or information about the store, its merchandise, or its service which is published on a gratuitous basis for the retailer. Therefore, store activities that have news or information value will generally attract the attention of the community media and as such require their approval before being circulated to the public. Publicity keeps the retailer in the public eye; the effect of good or bad publicity on the store's profitability should be obvious.

Ideally you should always be on the lookout for favourable publicity opportunities using the store, the merchandise, the services, the employees, the customers, or any other elements that may provide a news story of interest to the media and the public at large.

SALES PROMOTION

As defined by the American Marketing Association, sales promotion includes "those activities other than personal selling, advertising, and publicity, that stimulate consumer purchasing. . . ." (Ralph S. Alexander, Chairman of Committee on Definitions, *Marketing Definitions* [Chicago: American Marketing Association, 1960], p. 20.) While the component parts of sales promotion are listed in the promotion chart described earlier, it will be obvious that the independent's most effective means of assisting advertising, personal selling, and publicity is through the dramatic implementation of productive window and interior displays. Only this element of sales promotion will be discussed here, leaving you to research the other techniques listed if applicable to your retail strategy.

Display

The primary purpose of display is to sell merchandise; thus, the greater the number of people attracted to a display, the greater the volume of sales. To attract these people, stimulating displays must be arranged both inside the store and in the window treatments, since statistics indicate that the merchant has virtually only five seconds to stop the customer and start the sale.

It is unfortunate that many more merchants do not realize the importance of visual merchandising or display. A visit to many independent retail stores quickly reveals the ineffectiveness of both interior and window displays in enticing the customer to enter and purchase in the store. It is not sufficient to prepare and install an effective window treatment that will attract customers into the store if the same atmosphere is not created in the interior.

While display is regarded as a very efficient silent sales device for the store, by communicating the message at the point of sale, it is generally discovered that less than 15% of the promotional budget is allocated to this type of sales promotion. However, more merchants will continue to realize the value of display as a source of their most important means of publicity. As such, displays that stress the merchandise itself are gradually giving way to arrangements that simultaneously satisfy the functions of sales, publicity, and prestige. Therefore, the display must inform, educate, and serve the customer.

In observing the impact of effective display on the sales volumes of retail stores it is assumed that good display will:

1. Balance the requirements of the business with those of creativity in presentation
2. Publicize the merchandise and the store
3. Build prestige and goodwill for the store
4. Establish the respect and confidence the store needs to communicate to its customers
5. Support and demonstrate the current trends in style
6. Educate and inform the public about the store, the merchandise, and the image.

While display must satisfy many functions, its primary requirement is to sell merchandise. As such, it is generally impossible to outline formulas and techniques which will guarantee the success of the display. Nevertheless, display specialists operate within a five-point program to achieve effective window and interior selling displays.

1. Attract Attention This step represents the primary aspect of any sales presentation or advertisement. And since the display has a very brief moment in which to gain and hold the attention of the passerby, this aspect of the display must be well planned. Retailers use colour, lighting, form, lettering, sound, and motion to attract the attention of customers.

2. Arouse Interest Once the spectator stops to look at a display, the objective then becomes one of directing the eye movement to all phases of the arrangement. Ideally, the display will direct the customer's eye from the focal point to the merchandise to the information card and, finally, to the price. This means of influencing the eye movement may be accomplished, for example, by the positioning of the mannequin's face and hands; by lines leading from the focal point to the merchandise, such as the rays of the sun; or by colour or light intensification. The goal must be one of making the merchandise irresistible through an effective presentation in both window and interior displays.

3. Create Desire By presenting the merchandise in a manner which demonstrates the properties and qualities of the products, the merchant is in fact creating desire among the spectators of the display. This can generally be achieved by planning the presentation in terms of the theme that will be used for the display, the limitation of competing elements and styles in the display, and the effective use of display props and materials that bear some relationship to the items being exhibited.

4. Win Confidence Essentially, the display which acts as a silent sales person must convince the consumer that the store is reliable and current and that the purchase of the item represents safe and economical buying. Fashion merchants who effectively present a co-ordinated look in the display are in fact establishing confidence with the consumer in the store's ability to assemble a modern look.

5. Cause Action Assuming the previous four steps in the display process have been conscientiously and dramatically applied, then a positive action is likely to result in which the display causes a buying decision.

It should be evident that effective display will require the satisfaction of the five basic principles just outlined. In addition, independent merchants must determine the change schedule that should be implemented, especially for window displays. The frequency with which these should be changed will depend upon the number of the same people passing the store on a daily basis and on the type and nature of the merchandise. For the majority of independent merchants it is highly recommended that the window arrangements be changed at least every two or three weeks to generate excitement among the potential customers who pass by the store.

Similarly, controversy tends to arise over whether price cards or signs should be included with the merchandise in the window displays. With very few exceptions, retail stores should observe the practice of pricing the items which are placed in the window and this policy should be executed on a continuous basis with the changing of each window. While retail stores will vary in their emphasis of the size and style of the lettering on the price cards, their use as an informative element to the customer cannot be overemphasized. Generally, if the item is too expensive to be priced in the window, then (with minor exceptions) it probably should not have been purchased for the store's customers.

In planning the retail operation, merchants are also required to determine whether the window displays should feature a closed background where the customer cannot see into the store, or an open-background window where the whole store in fact becomes the window display. Retailers who wish to create a dramatic and exciting display are more inclined to use a closed-background window. With such a treatment, the viewer's eye concentrates on the merchandise displayed in the window rather than wandering to other merchandise in the store that can be seen from outside the store. Retail stores such as department stores, with different merchandise on the selling floor directly behind the window display from that which is exhibited in the window, are compelled to use closed-background windows. As a general rule, stores selling fashion apparel, furniture, home furnishings, sporting goods, and jewellery have found it advantageous to use this type of window display.

Retailers of staple merchandise, on the other hand, have tended to discount the importance of the window display and as such have opted to make the entire store the display. Therefore, customers standing outside the store are able not only to view the items placed in the window, but also to evaluate the total store. Supermarkets, drug stores, variety stores, and similar merchants have opted for open-back windows on the assumption that the window display would be used better as interior selling space. Others wish to allow the customer to window shop as well as to see into the store from the exterior.

Finally, some retail merchants have sought to capitalize on the advantages of both of these types of backgrounds and have subsequently used a semi-closed window display. By employing partial barriers as backgrounds, on a vertical or horizontal plane, merchandise can be featured and customers are still capable of seeing into the store from the outside. Merchants selling hardware, shoes, gifts, and textiles have sought to use the semi-closed window to project the image of the store and subsequently to sell its merchandise.

Types of Window Display

The major types of window display which are listed below indicate the primary appeals that you can use in presenting your merchandise and services to the customer.

Selling Display This type of presentation is designed to produce immediate sales. Consequently, the primary appeal in building this display must be price.

Prestige Display On occasion, retailers attempt to create window treatments that will enhance the image of the store rather than produce immediate sales. Such window treatments are similar to the impact generated by institutional advertising.

Serial Displays When more than one window of the store is employed to display related merchandise as a means of indicating to the customer the completeness of the store's assortment, a serial display is said to be created. Apparel stores that demonstrate their capabilities in merchandising wedding apparel may use a number of windows to show wedding gowns and accessories during a particular period of time.

Ensemble Display When related merchandise is placed in one window to offer the consumer a completely co-ordinated and assembled look, an ensemble display is being exhibited. Such displays have been very effective in many lines of merchandise such as apparel, sporting goods, furniture, home furnishings, and similar shopping goods. Ideally, the presentation is made to induce the customer to purchase the total look demonstrated in the display.

Campaign Displays These are utilized by featuring the same merchandise during a continuous period of time with the hope that repetition will create buying on the part of the spectator. This type of display is most frequently found in fashion stores which are attempting to generate interest and excitement in a new look or new style.

Single Promotion Display These displays are used by independent merchants to feature a special event in all windows of the store. When special promotions, events, or clearance sales are held in the retail store, the same promotion in all windows has a tendency to attract traffic and emphasize the importance of the promotional event being featured.

Types of Interior Displays

Once you have planned and created effective window displays which draw customers off the street and into the store, it is extremely important for the displays inside the store to direct the customers once they have entered. In essence, the interior displays should be co-ordinated not only with the window displays but also with the total promotional plan. Why spend money on advertising an item in the newspaper if such items are not featured or visible in the interior of the store? The interior display should project the current season.

Open Displays The growing tendency in the retail industry is to extensively use the facilities of open display by offering the customer the convenience of self-service merchandising. As a result, all merchandise on display is in open view to the customer and consequently can be self-evaluated without the service of sales personnel.

Closed Displays Retail stores which avoid the presentation of open displays have opted to protect their merchandise behind glass. Merchandise which is subject to physical damage by excessive handling is generally treated in this manner. In addition, small items of high unit value that can be easily shoplifted are displayed behind glass. This method of display is frequently used in the more exclusive and better-quality retail operations in some sections of the store.

Top-of-the-Counter Displays This type of display represents a type of open display which generally is placed on the top of the selling counter. While it tends to increase impulse buying, it may also generate additional problems if not properly controlled. The merchandise in the counter below is frequently hidden from view and, as a result, sales of these items may be reduced. In addition, unless effectively placed, such displays tend to create blind spots between the customer and the store employee and consequently provide an opportunity for a shoplifter. Therefore, strict control of the numbers and placement of these units should be exercised by the independent.

Architectural Displays Such a display arrangement is represented when a section of the store has been set aside to provide an exact setting for the merchandise being displayed. Such displays are designed to induce the customer to buy the complete group as a result of indicating the total look. A ski chalet in a sporting goods store, room setting in furniture stores, or a workshop in a home improvement centre have been especially effective in generating increased sales through the use of architectural displays.

Ledge Displays Placement of merchandise items on shelves behind the selling counters is referred to as a ledge display. While these displays have little attention value, they have been successfully used to maximize the space available and at the same time to protect items from constant handling by customers.

Wall Space In many retail stores wall space should provide additional selling and display space. More effective use needs to be made by independent retailers of the blank wall space that generally exists above the wall fixtures in the store. Dramatic and exciting arrangements even at this high eye level can stimulate sales and enhance the atmosphere of the store.

A display is a life-size, full-colour, three-dimensional advertisement doing a day-and-night selling job and sitting right on the store's doorstep at the point of sale. Display makes it possible for shoppers to identify a store and to respond to any unique look or selling approach it seeks to employ. Effective interior and window displays represent important promotional elements in projecting a pleasing store personality.

10
PERSONAL SELLING IN RETAIL

PERSONAL SELLING

In the previous chapter, the promotional elements of advertising, publicity, and display were discussed to outline the means of non-personal presentations that are available to independent merchants seeking to induce customers to patronize their stores. At the other end of the promotional scale is the personal face-to-face relationship that exists between sellers and potential buyers in the form of personal selling. Since personal selling represents a very distinct advantage for independent retailers over their large-scale competitors, this promotional tool has been allocated a chapter of its own.

One of the most important developments in retailing is the increasing knowledge and sophistication on the part of consumers. As a result, stores taking an active part in this consumer movement must ensure that their sales personnel are better informed than ever before. If today's retail sales personnel are to keep pace with current developments and trends in retail selling, then they must acquire a great deal of information about the customers, the merchandise, and the selling process.

The degree of importance of personal selling in a retail operation will be affected by the merchandise-presentation policies the store has elected to use in its arrangement. Retail stores which decide to emphasize the purchase of the goods through self service will require very little personal selling, since the main selling effort in self-service stores is usually accomplished through display, advertising, and descriptive signs. At the other extreme, independent merchants using salon selling as a means of merchandising items will require a high degree of personal selling, both in numbers and expertise. Most retail operations fall between these two extremes, with some portions of the store demanding personal selling while other sections can be economically presented on a self-service basis.

Since most communities in this country are being saturated with excessive numbers of retail establishments carrying similar merchandise, the importance of personal selling becomes paramount. In addition, many retail firms are engaging in scramble merchandising—by carrying items outside of their major line—and consequently increasing the competitive facilities available to the customer. It therefore becomes the function of the retail sales force to effectively present the merchandise at the point of sale in such a personal manner that the customer will view it as better than the same item at other stores.

We have already noted that in retailing the most important person is the customer. But what we need to recall on a continual basis is that next in importance is the retail sales person. It is frequently said that nothing happens in a retail store until a sale is made. Consequently, if large sums of money are spent preparing effective advertising, creating exciting displays, and establishing an opulent shopping environment in the store, all is lost if the sales person on the selling floor is unable to make the presentation that will complete the sale. Yet, it is not uncommon to hear disgruntled customers or to find poorly trained and uninterested sales personnel.

With all of the various elements that the independent retailer has available to project the image so desired for the store, none perhaps is more important than that which is identified with the store personnel. On a one-on-one, face-to-face basis, the retail sales person can significantly affect the sales performance and profitability of the operation.

In addition to the major role that personal selling plays in most small retail operations, the proportion of the total operating expenses allocated to this essential element is generally much larger than the others. Consequently, with personal selling expenses accounting for approximately 15% of the planned sales of most stores, productive use must be ensured for this investment.

It is not the intention of this chapter to offer you a complete outline of the techniques of successful selling, since much literature is already available on this subject. What is intended is that you will be motivated, through the various concepts, to realize the vital importance of personal selling to your business.

STEPS IN PERSONAL SELLING

The steps in a retail sales situation are perfectly natural and easy to follow and consequently become the fundamentals of an effective selling presentation. However, it should be remembered that these basic steps are common to all selling situations. To be effective they shouldn't be followed methodically and mechanically, but rather with intelligent application for each selling situation. As a basis, the sales person is required to follow these steps by showing interest, concern, and courtesy to every customer to be served.

Just as the preparation of an effective display uses the principles of attention, interest, desire, confidence, and action (AIDCA), so too must the professional selling presentation. Therefore, in applying the selling steps listed here, the professional sales person will attempt to get the customer's attention, generate interest and desire toward the merchandise or service, establish confidence in the items and the store, and finally cause buying action on the part of the shopper.

Step One: The Approach

The first actual step in the personal selling function of the retail store is meeting the customer upon entering the store or approaching the merchandise. At this point, the customer, if new to the store, is assessing the sales person and the store's environment. Therefore, it is important to both the new and repeat customer that the appearance of the store and the sales person create a favourable impression.

The Merchandise Approach When the customer stops to examine an item on display in the store, the sales person who makes a comment about the particular appeal of the item is using the merchandise approach. Since this technique features the merchandise in the store, and demonstrates the interest and knowledge of the sales person, this approach should be used whenever possible. Experience teaches the sales person how to assess customers and select the best selling points of the merchandise that will appeal to each one.

The Greeting Approach In situations where customers have entered the store but have not concentrated on any specific items, it is advantageous to offer a warm, friendly, and business-like greeting. It is always beneficial to greet the customer by name if it is known. Consequently, the successful retail sales person attempts to establish loyalty with customers by getting to know them as much as possible on a business basis.

The Service Approach This is perhaps the most common, yet least effective, approach found in the retail industry, as a result of the overworked expression, "May I help you?" While this approach is certainly much better than waiting for the customer to approach the sales person to ask for help, it loses its impact when it becomes a mechanical and habitual expression. The retail sales representative must be shown the value and the need to employ the merchandise approach whenever possible.

Whatever approach is used, the sales person should demonstrate through voice, facial expressions, and mannerisms an interest in helping each customer who enters. It is essentially this personal contact and presentation that offers independents their most unique advantage.

Step Two: Determining Customer Needs

Once friendly contact has been made with the customer, the next step becomes one of determining the needs and wants of the shopper. As a result of the large proliferation of goods available in the market, this decision on the part of the customer becomes more and more difficult. However, by studying a customer, listening to what is said, and by asking questions, the successful sales person is better able to present the proper merchandise.

In attempting to determine the wants or needs of the customer at a particular time, the sales representative must recognize that on this shopping expedition the customer may be just looking, may know exactly what to buy or may just have a general idea of what to look for. Analyzing the dormant and conscious motives of customers in their purchasing patterns will assist in the selling presentation.

The effective sales person, through practice and study, learns the art of questioning customers intelligently to determine their needs. Sales representatives should ask as few questions as possible and only those which are necessary. It is generally not necessary to ask questions about price or quality since this will evolve from the conversation in the presentation. In addition, sales representatives who can assess their customer's size do much to establish rapport and confidence in demonstrating their knowledge of the merchandise and customer.

As soon as the sales person has a general idea of what the customer has in mind, she will show him the merchandise which she believes will best suit his needs. By watching the customer's expressions and actions and by listening to what he says, information will be transmitted with regard to what items should be removed from his selection process.

It is therefore the function of the retail sales person to help the customer define his needs and to assist him in the selection of items that will be what he needs and wants, and that will give him satisfaction and service. If the task is handled effectively, customer satisfaction will lead to an established clientele and a significant reduction in the amount of customer exchanges and returns that seem to plague many retail operations.

Step Three: Presenting the Merchandise

Merchandise which is well presented will almost sell itself in much the same way that effective display becomes a silent sales force. When the needs or wants of the customer have been determined, the sales person should begin the sale by promptly presenting the goods he thinks the customer will want. In this way, he will demonstrate his willingness to show and talk about the items the store has available that will be of interest to the customer.

The merchandise should always be handled carefully in the presentation to indicate to the customer that the sales person values and appreciates the items. In a similar fashion, the professional sales representative continually strives to develop a sales presentation that will appeal to as many of the five senses as possible. By appealing to touch, taste, smell, sound, and sight, the customer becomes dramatically aware of the benefits of possessing the item.

The selling points that are made in the presentation of the merchandise will need to be varied on the basis of the customer's needs, wants, and interests. In this context it is always essential that the sales person speak with confidence and enthusiasm about the merchandise to favourably impress the customer. While it is always difficult to determine how much merchandise to show a customer, the guiding principle must be to present enough items to allow her to make a satisfactory selection but at the same time avoid confusing her decisions with too many articles.

Therefore, it is important to carefully choose the items to be presented and to remove those which she has already rejected from the ones which are shown.

The effective sales person continually works to improve his sales presentation both in the way he displays each item and also in what he says about it. With practice and good judgement, he can improve his presentation and increase his sales.

Step Four: Overcoming Objections

Customers frequently raise questions or objections about the merchandise as it is presented. The sales representative must simply regard these as the customer's way of inquiring about the item rather than a means of destroying the sales presentation, as some sales people believe. These objections should present the professional with the opportunity to courteously and satisfactorily tell the customer what the sales person knows about the merchandise as it relates to his needs.

The objections raised by customers can normally be classified as one of the three following types. First, the unimportant, trivial objections are really excuses that customers give to avoid buying or becoming too interested in the merchandise. As such the sales person attempts to direct the customer's attention to some feature of the merchandise that will meet his needs.

Secondly, the important, sincere objections are those raised by the customer after the sales person has presented the merchandise. Such objections could refer to the colour, style, fabric, price, or any of the other selection factors available to the customer. The sales person must attempt to answer these objections fully and truthfully.

Finally, the hidden or false objections are questions asked by a customer to hide or obscure his reason for not buying. This objection commonly occurs when the customer attempts to conceal the fact that the item may be out of his price range but feels embarrassed to indicate this. As a result, statements that "It's the wrong colour" or "It's not exactly what I'm looking for" are offered as objections. In such situations the sales person should attempt to determine the real objection by repeating the best-selling points about the merchandise. If the real objection still appears to be concealed, then the use of tactful questioning may reveal the problem.

In handling objections, the professional sales representative attempts to adopt the following philosophies:

1. Respect every objection
2. Welcome objections
3. Anticipate objections and answer them before they are made
4. Avoid arguing with the customer
5. Discover the real objection
6. Give sincere, honest, and direct answers
7. Move quickly from objection to selling point
8. Do not fear or disregard objections, they are natural in the selling process.

Sales representatives have developed many techniques for answering objections. For example, the sales representative can make a direct denial of the objection—but only if she has convincing facts. Such a technique must be employed with a great deal of tact and with absolutely no indication of superiority. Secondly, the sales person can accept the objection of the customer, but with reservation. In this technique, the sales person agrees with the customer but then presents some other idea that will counteract the objection, with a phrase like "Yes, but . . ." Another technique is to make the objection a selling point. This becomes the process of turning the objection into a reason for buying. Or the sales person can sidestep the objection. By doing this, she indirectly accepts the objection as applying to the item but then points out values that outweigh the inferior point. Another way of handling objections is to refuse the objection by asking a question. This technique is often used by asking the customer to explain the objection. Often the customer will explain away the original objection he had. This is especially evident where the objection is not based on any facts.

Step Five: Closing the Sale

The closing of the sale is the final decision which the customer makes to buy or not buy the merchandise that is being presented. Depending upon the buying pattern and the type of merchandise, the close will come almost immediately after the approach, or only after much time has elapsed. In some cases where customers go away to think about the item, the closing may even come in a couple of days or weeks, as when a customer chooses to purchase an automobile.

The professional sales person is constantly on the alert for closing signals given by the customers. Such clues as facial expressions, actions, or questions may indicate to the sales person that the customer has decided to buy. At this point the

representative stops showing merchandise and narrows the customer's choice by removing articles that she has indicated will
not suit her needs.

A sales person should be aware of the signals given by the
customer, since many sales have been lost by overselling. Sales
people should not attempt to force the customer into a buying
decision; rather, the decision to close should come naturally in
the presentation.

Many customers depend upon the sales representative to help
them decide which item to buy. As a result, there are various
ways in which the sales person can help the customer reach a
buying decision. The effective use of questions can lead to a
customer decision. But it should be remembered that the pressure selling of the past is not acceptable as a selling technique
by progressive retail stores.

It is important to caution the retail sales person to hide any
disappointment that may be felt as a result of a lost sale. These
customers must also be shown courtesy and respect to provide
the type of environment to which they will return when a purchase
is required. By building goodwill for the store, a loyal clientele is
established.

THE POWER OF SUGGESTION SELLING

The skillful and professional sales person constantly engages in
the practice of suggestion selling as a means of assisting the
customer and at the same time increasing the average sale of
the store. As a result of the power and importance that suggestion
selling exercises in the profitability of the store, many operations
have planned merchandise displays and store layouts to induce
increased impulse buying.

Suggestion selling must not be regarded as a form of pressure
selling but rather as a means of helping the customer buy a better
value or some additional article. The following types of suggestions have been beneficial to both customers and retail stores.
Related Merchandise By far the bulk of suggestion selling
undertaken by sales personnel is that which suggests additional merchandise which is related to the first items sold. No
matter what type of merchandise is being sold, sales representatives should be aware of what the store has to offer that will relate
to the items. Shoe trees should be suggested to all customers

buying shoes. Shirts and ties have been powerful suggestion items in the merchandising of men's suits.

Substitute Merchandise In most cases, customers appreciate the suggestion of similar merchandise if that merchandise will serve the purpose as well as the item they originally planned to buy. To successfully engage in this form of suggestion selling, the sales person must not only be able to accurately determine the needs and wants of the customer, but also know the characteristics of the merchandise available in the store that will act as a substitute item.

Value Suggestions When the customer is able to realize a saving in time and money by purchasing a larger quantity, it is the sales person's responsibility to make the suggestion to the customer on the basis of better value. A special multiple-unit price should offer additional savings to the customer.

Trading Up A situation in which the customer can save money eventually, as well as gain greater satisfaction, is through the purchase of an article of better quality. The process of attempting to trade the customer up to better quality merchandise has become an effective means of suggestion selling in many retail establishments.

New Arrivals Most customers are very interested in new items of merchandise and they are generally pleased to have that new merchandise called to their attention when shopping in the store. Thus, a skillful sales person will suggest with excitement the new items which have arrived and been placed in the inventory.

Specials The sales person who is knowledgeable about the store's merchandise and special promotions available is better able to serve the needs of the customers through suggestion selling. By calling the customer's attention to an advertised or in-store special, the power of suggestion selling becomes evident.

New Uses By offering the customer ideas that signify new applications for a product, the average sale of the store can be expected to increase. Many household products have enjoyed expanded markets as a result of suggestions made on the basis of new uses for existing products.

In making suggestions, the sales person should concentrate on those items that will help and interest the customer. But in order to be effective, the sales representative must establish with the customer the rapport and confidence that comes from knowing the available merchandise and making an effective sales presentation.

CUSTOMER TYPES: THE CHALLENGE OF SELLING

Every time the door of the store opens, the sales person is facing a new challenge. Some customers are pleasant and friendly and know exactly what they want, while others are more difficult, presenting a special challenge to the retail sales person.

It may be an oversimplification to attempt to categorize customers, since there are probably as many types of customers as there are various types of people. Nevertheless, some of the more difficult types of customers are presented here with suggestions as to the way the sales person can meet the challenge of serving them tactfully and satisfactorily. It should be strongly emphasized that this material calls for discretion in its application.

The Impatient Customer   This is the customer who believes that his time is more valuable than any other person's and normally demands immediate attention. If the sales person is busy with another customer, the impatient customer will frequently interrupt the presentation to gain attention and service. This situation requires patience and skill on the part of the sales person, who must avoid neglecting the original customer but at the same time attend to the needs of the impatient one. With such a customer it is usually not enough to suggest that you will be with him in a moment. This will just increase his impatience.

The Argumentative Customer   This classification of customer is the one who likes to argue. In such a selling situation it is important to remember that it takes two people to have an argument, and as a result the sales person should not allow himself to be drawn into a dispute. The technique of handling this customer is to agree with her at first and then proceed to get her to compare type, quality, and other selling features of the merchandise in question.

The Talkative Customer   Some customers tend to enter the retail store and wish to engage the sales person in lengthy conversations which waste both his own time and that of the sales person. With proper encouragement and direction of the conversation the customer will frequently talk himself into buying. Thus, it is essential for the sales person to keep the conversation from wandering and to centre the discussion on the store's merchandise rather than on personal affairs.

The Positive Customer   This customer is characterized by her insistence that she is positive about a particular aspect of the purchase decision. She is certain she wears a particular size garment or that an item in the store was much cheaper at a competing store. When encountered by this challenge, the sales person should generally agree with the customer but then attempt to switch her diplomatically to merchandise that will suit her needs.

The Hesitant Customer The sales person is frequently called upon to assist the undecided customer in making his decision regarding the purchase of an item. By getting the customer to narrow his choice to two or three items and then evaluating each of these in light of his needs, wants, and interests, the sales representative is assisting the hesitant customer in making his final selection. With this type of customer it is important to emphasize the selling points of the merchandise as they relate to the needs and wants of the customer.

The Economical Customer The customer who is seeking the best merchandise possible and the lowest price possible is said to be an economical buyer. Articles which have been reduced in price have great appeal for these customers, providing the sales person can direct the customer's attention to the merchandise value. When dealing with this price-conscious customer the sales person should attempt to lead her to consider the quality of the item in relation to the price as a means of assessing value.

The Timid Customer Frequently a customer finds himself in a shopping environment which is basically foreign to him; for example, when a woman enters an exclusive boutique for the first time or a man shops for a gift in a lingerie store. When this happens, the sales person must be sympathetic and understanding to make the customer feel at ease and win his confidence.

The Suspicious Customer When a customer of a suspicious nature comes into the store, the sales person must patiently present the actual facts about the merchandise which will prove the reliability of the store and its goods. The merchandising of discounted goods, highly promotional items, and constant clearance sales have led to a significant increase in the numbers of suspicious customers. Assurance that the store desires to give satisfaction should be made clear to the customer in an attempt to win her confidence. Guarantees and testimonials of good results with the merchandise are natural parts of the sales presentation to this customer.

The Hurried Customer Much like the impatient customer who demands service immediately, the hurried customer wishes to make his purchase as quickly as possible. The sales person must then establish as rapidly as possible what the customer wants, present the merchandise, and give him only the minimum essentials of information about the item. The key to handling this type of customer is to remain calm and poised in the presentation.

The Looker   This is perhaps the most common type of customer that enters the retail store. Almost as mechanical as the sales person who uses the greeting "May I help you?" is the response of the customer saying "No thanks, I'm just looking". The sales representative must then attempt to determine if the customer is undecided or if the expression is used because she would rather look at the merchandise without being bothered by the pressure and interference of the sales person. With most merchandise lines it is advisable to allow the customer to look at her leisure indicating your desire to assist or answer any questions she might have. The key in dealing with the "just looking" customer is to demonstrate helpfulness without appearing too persistent.

There are many other types of customers that present challenges to the retail sales person. The sales person who realizes that someone will make a sale to these people if she doesn't, is a real asset to the store. Offering such service to the difficult customer will also generally cause this person to return again and again to the same sales person for assistance.

It is the responsibility of the professional sales representative to attempt to establish the mood of the customer at the time of approach, and subsequently to adapt her sales presentation to this mood. It should be recognized that customers are people and thus the mood of a particular customer may vary each time he enters the store. His attitudes will be affected by the weather, family circumstances, and other environmental factors. The sales person who is alert to this fact is able to offer efficient, courteous service to all of the store's customers.

ASSESSING CUSTOMERS

Another basis upon which sales representatives tend to categorize customers is their appearance and mannerisms. In today's free-spirited environment, appearance is often very deceiving; discretion and common sense are mandatory in assessing customers on this basis. As a result, the sales person must not place too

much emphasis on judging the customer by external characteristics, but rather should use this assessment as a guide to the
sales presentation.

Facial Expression As in any face-to-face encounter, each expression of the customer's face should tell the sales person the
reaction being experienced by the merchandise presentation.
By observing facial expressions, the sales person should quickly
sense the customer's likes and dislikes as well as her mood.

Movement The way a customer walks or carries himself as
he enters the store generally indicates to the sales person the
mood of the customer. By observing these movements, customers
can be classified as impatient, nervous, hurried, or timid. The
alert sales person may to some degree determine the type of
customer that has entered the store by paying attention to
movement.

Apparel The sales person who places too much emphasis on
what the customer is wearing as a means of assessing her, may
find he has miscalculated completely in his appraisal. However,
it is essential for the sales person to note what the customer is
wearing to determine her tastes, her style and colour preferences,
and her emphasis on quality. While this analysis may offer some
indication of what merchandise should be shown to the customer,
it should be remembered that this is only one basis of judging
the customer.

Speech By observing the language and the tone of the customer's voice, it is possible to gain some insight into his present
mood, his merchandise awareness, and his desire for more
information.

Age and Size Because people of different age groups react
differently to most merchandise lines, the assessment of the
customer's age can be beneficial in determining her needs in a
sales presentation. Also the ability to accurately assess the
customer's size will be essential in the selling of wearing apparel
and accessories if the sales person is to establish confidence
with the customer.

It must be constantly stressed to sales representatives in the
retail trade that assessing customers on the basis of appearance
is only one of several factors that should be used in understanding the customers. The more experienced the sales person
becomes in the art of retail selling, the more accurately will
she be able to direct her sales presentations to the needs of the
customer on the basis of her assessment.

PROFESSIONAL SELLING

It is often stated that modern merchandising has in fact made personal selling at the retail level obsolete. Retail stores have employed personnel only to take merchandise orders, and other workers who are only capable of handling routine questions, or of completing the transaction at the cash-wrap desk. While this aspect may be true of self-service retailing employed by many mass merchandisers, creative selling still remains an integral part of the independent's merchandising philosophy.

Personal selling in many retail stores still demands the use of effective selling skills to maximize the sales and profitability of the store. This becomes especially true in fashion apparel, technical products, and items of high-unit value. Where customers seek advice and information regarding the merchandise item, personal selling remains a strong element in the merchandising mix. Therefore, personal selling has remained important to the merchandising of furniture, appliances, fashion apparel, home furnishings, sporting goods, cameras, jewellery, cosmetics, and numerous other products.

While retail salespeople have not for the most part been considered as professional in their techniques when compared to manufacturer or wholesaler salespeople, there appears to be a tendency among the more progressive independents to improve this element of the mix. While it is very difficult to pinpoint the exact characteristics required for professional selling, the following elements indicate the philosophy that must accompany the activity.

1. He's customer-oriented rather than self-oriented. He will not knowingly sell you something he knows will not satisfy your needs and wants. In fact he will advise you against buying something he knows will not bring you satisfaction.
2. He's a storehouse of valuable information and advice. People seek him out for the information he can provide. His word is trusted and he helps buyers get maximum utility from their purchases.
3. He will not use high-pressure sales tactics. He depends more upon helpful information and service to secure business. After all, he does not want you to buy unless he can deliver the satisfactions for which you pay.

—Richard J. Stanley, *Promotion*, © 1977, p. 269. Reprinted by permission of Prentice-Hall, Englewood Cliffs, New Jersey.

The professional selling attitude of most salespeople in the retail store tends to be affected by the nature of the average retail sales person's job. In addition to their selling function, most employees are also required to perform housekeeping duties, create displays, or receive, price, and replenish the inventory. While these activities need to be performed, they are not highly productive in terms of sales.

As a result of these activities and the attempt to balance staff requirements with fluctuations in customer traffic to the store, retail selling tends to be characterized by low-productivity and low-wage levels. Subsequently, the most gifted salespeople are not generally attracted to retail selling. Rather, large contingents of part-time and untrained sales staff constitute the bulk of the personnel on the selling floor.

Therefore, the degree and extent of personal professional selling at the retail level will depend on the type and nature of the merchandise, the image created by the store, and the means of merchandise presentation used in the arrangement of items in the layout.

As noted earlier, there has been a return in recent years to a greater amount of personal selling in retail stores where the non-personal form of promotion has not been effective in producing the anticipated results. Thus, in stores where convenience goods are sold, advertising and display may be the most productive means of promotion. But when merchandise is classified as shopping or specialty in nature, personal selling generally assumes a larger role in the promotional effort.

The relationship that generally exists between the availability of salespeople in the store and the image that the customer perceives of the store is best illustrated in Pierre Martineau's observation:

> It is ironical, that at the very time when a better educated and discriminating shopper expects more from the store and the clerk, management is dragging its feet in upgrading salespeople. The stores are more beautiful and interesting; they have escalators, air conditioning, and improved fixtures; they have buyers ranging far and wide to offer the broadest merchandise selection. But what about the salespeople?

—Pierre Martineau, "The Personality of a Retail Store," *Harvard Business Review*, January-February (1958), p. 52. Reprinted by permission of *Harvard Business Review*. Copyright © 1957 by the President and Fellows of Harvard College; all rights reserved.

While this statement appeared 20 years ago, the need for improved training of retail sales personnel in both large and small stores is still evident. It is therefore to the independent retailer's advantage to make the time and effort necessary to train the salespeople well. The primary advantage of small merchants over their large-scale competitors rests in their ability to offer personal service which is generally lacking among the mass merchandisers. To improve the quality of this personal service is consequently to improve the profitability of the retail operation through effective personal selling efforts.

11

RETAIL MANAGEMENT FUNDAMENTALS

It is the objective of this chapter to bring together those concepts which were presented earlier. At the same time, some of the fundamental elements of operating a retail store are presented in an introductory fashion to induce you to seek additional information on these areas. To this end, please review the additional readings in the Bibliography of this book. Successful independent merchants must constantly seek ways to improve their operations—generally by gathering information from what other merchants have attempted, from what trade publications have presented, and from ideas encountered in researching the literature which has been written.

The function of retail management for the independent merchant is defined as the process involved in creatively adapting the controllable elements of the merchandising mix to the uncontrollable environment in which the store operates. The independent looks for the most effective means of directing price, place, products, and promotion at the planned target market.

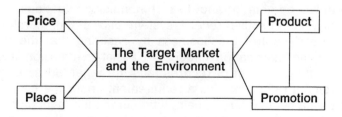

Throughout this book we have sought to explain the principles and techniques involved in each of these elements to provide you with the fundamentals of managing your operation. It is the interrelationship of these four basic elements of the mix that must be directed as a strategy at the target market. The pricing policy of the store will need to be in line with the product assortment in much the same way that the location of the store must indeed be placed where the strategies of price, product, and promotion suggest.

However, in addition to these four basic elements, a number of relevant miscellaneous factors need to be explored in planning for the successful operation of a retail store. While the factors discussed in the remainder of this chapter are neither all-inclusive nor presented in detail, they are offered to assist you in recognizing the need for discovering and researching some of the supplementary aspects of operating a store. The topics which have been selected for discussion here have been included on the basis of the problems encountered by many independent merchants researched by this author.

Some of the topics have been included to motivate you to realize their importance in the overall strategy of the store, while others have been included to suggest that you stay constantly aware of new techniques developing in the field and that you interpret the feasibility of adopting and adapting these tools to your operation.

RECORD KEEPING

Perhaps the least exciting task of operating a retail store is that which demands that accurate information and up-to-date records be kept on the store's operations. Independents who have continually neglected this important function have found their stores in operational and financial difficulty. The more accurate and current the information is on the store's operation, the more likely the firm will be able to react to merchandising situations.

Ideally, an effective record system allows the merchant to operate and control the business by ensuring that the system provides the information needed to assist in decision making. Consequently, this set of records must be regarded as a tool of management rather than as a requirement under the law providing the data needed for the calculation of the firm's income taxes. When the books are properly maintained and the assembled information is effectively used, the independent merchant is able to better meet the needs and wants of the store's target market.

So far we have explored some of the merchandising records

that need to be maintained to assist in the buying and selling functions of the store. By now you should be totally aware of the important role the merchandise plan, the model stock plans, the open-to-buy controls, the inventory records, and the gross margin summary play in the merchandising performance of the store. In addition, similar records must be established to provide the operational controls for the store on a daily basis.

In the retail store, the record system must allow the proper and effective handling of the following three basic factors.

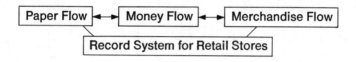

Such retail activities as the merchandise delivered, invoices received, cash and charge sales, payments to suppliers, personnel records, and bank reconciliations need to be recorded and maintained to execute the management function.

It is not the intention of this section to establish a complete set of records for a retail store. Since each store will differ in its needs and in its capabilities for maintaining an adequate record system, this task is better left to the firm's accountant to tailor to the individual needs of the store.

However, as a means of ensuring that effective records are maintained, the following discussion centres on some of the more important records common to most retail stores. It is important to stress at this point that records exhibit their importance only when the information they contain is used to assist in the decision-making process. Maintaining information that is never used becomes nothing more than an exercise in futility. In this context, work closely with your store's accountant to maximize the deployment of the information provided.

Purchase Records Some retail firms place orders with their suppliers on forms prepared exclusively for the store's use, while others choose to use the purchase order form of the supplier or the supplier's representative. Regardless of the form used, the information contained on the record must be complete in all details.

An example of a purchase order is included below in Exhibit 11-1 for your scrutiny. It is essential that the retailer understand and negotiate each item of the order with the supplier before the order is confirmed with a signature. Since this represents a

Exhibit 11-1
Sample Purchase Order

Eddy's Baby Ltd.

— PURCHASE ORDER —

R 187089

| Div. No. | Store No. | Store Event |

SHOW ALL ABOVE NOS. ON ALL INVOICES, CASES, PACKING SLIPS, BILLS OF LADING AND CORRESPONDENCE

STREET ADDRESS ____ Ship to above address unless otherwise stated

CITY & PROVINCE ____

SOURCE NAME & ADDRESS ____

Date of order ____ | Ship on ____

Authorized Signature ____

DETACH AT PERFORATION BEFORE MAILING

WRITE CLEARLY

THIS SECTION FOR RETAIL USE ONLY. NOT TO BE SENT TO SUPPLIER

SHIPPING INSTRUCTIONS

TERMS: | TRADE-DISCOUNT | F.O.B. | INSURANCE OR DECLARED VALUE | Shipment Partial Complete

TRANSPORTATION ALLOWANCE

Eddy's Stock No.	Mfg. Stock No.	Description	Size Colour	Order Quantity	Buying Unit	Cost Price	Unit Selling Unit	Selling Unit	Mark up

TOTAL SELLING $ ¢

binding contract between the store and its supplier, careful attention must be paid to every section on the order form. The upper portion of the order form must be completely filled in before the order should be signed.

The purchase order is generally prepared in duplicate or triplicate, depending on the size and functional organization of the store. The original copy is sent to the supplier, the duplicate is retained in the store's office, and a third copy, if necessary, is maintained in the department. So begins the paper, merchandise, and money flow in a retail operation.

Once the order has been placed, the proper filing of the store's records is essential so that follow-ups can be undertaken in the event that the delivery schedule of the merchandise is not maintained. In addition, the invoice received for the merchandise which has been delivered must be checked against the purchase order to make sure that all items of the purchase have been adhered to by the supplier.

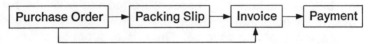

When the merchandise is received by the store, the independent will be confronted by three pieces of paper which need to be reconciled. The purchase order records the contract entered into by the store and the supplier. Upon receipt of goods, a packing slip or shipping record is enclosed with the merchandise, indicating the items in the shipment. The packing slip is then checked against the purchase order to determine if the order is complete. Finally, the invoice is received by the store, indicating the quantity shipped and the amount of money payable to the supplier at the terms previously negotiated. The invoice must then be checked against the packing slip and the purchase order to determine any differences before payment is authorized. Substitute items, back orders, short shipments, damaged merchandise, incorrect order filling, and other purchase variances must be determined and rectified before payment of the invoice.

Invoice Records   Once the merchandise has been delivered to the store and the invoice reconciled with the purchase order and packing slip, the recording of this information is essential. The vital information of the invoice is initially recorded in the purchase journal illustrated in Exhibit 7-6 as part of the retail method of inventory management. The data provided on the invoice must then be recorded in the appropriate accounts payable ledger to indicate the store's liability for payment to the designated supplier. When payment is made, this activity is also recorded in the accounts payable ledger to signify that portion of the debt that has been cleared and that portion which still remains outstanding. In this way, the store's buying relationship and activity with each supplier is recorded and maintained. Such a record is usually maintained on a ledger sheet as illustrated in Exhibit 11-2.

As part of the negotiations with each supplier, the merchant seeks to obtain the most lucrative cash discounts possible in the event that the invoice is paid before the net amount is due. Please refer back to the discussion of the retail method of inventory in Exhibit 7-5 to determine the effect of the cash discounts earned on the store's gross margin and net operating profit.

As a result of the importance of the cash discount to the invoice records, you should establish a system to ensure that payment is made before the time the discount period ends. At the same time, you must note that charges might be made by the vendor for late payment of the invoice. Thus, if a supplier offers you terms of 2/10, n/30 DOI as indicated on the purchase order, then the supplier is allowing you to take a 2% cash discount if the invoice is paid within 10 days (2/10) of the date of the invoice (DOI) with the net amount of the invoice due within 30 days (n/30) of the date of invoice.

While many independents tend to overlook the importance of the cash discount, a 2/10 discount in fact represents an effective interest rate of 36% per annum. If a discount of 2% is being allowed for payment in 10 days instead of the net amount which is due within 30 days, this in fact represents a 2% discount for 20 days (30-10) prepayment. If we assume 360 days in a year, then the 20-day prepayment represents 18 discount periods (360 divided by 20). Therefore, over a year, the 18 discount periods at 2% each will represent an effective discount rate of 36% per annum. At this rate, it may indeed be more economical to borrow funds from the bank to take advantage of the cash discount negotiated.

It is therefore important for you to devise a system that will allow the payment of the invoice at the appropriate time for the cash discount, or for the net amount to be paid so that interest charges will be avoided.

A simple but effective manual system that has been widely used to provide this control is the use of an accordion file

Exhibit 11-2
Sample Accounts Payable Ledger Sheet

Sheet No. ___	
Rating AA	Credit Limit 6
Terms 2/10 n 30 R.O.G.	

Name DUNNVILLE POTTERIES LTD.

Address 240 CHESTNUT STREET, DUNNVILLE, ONTARIO

Account No. KBO875

Date	Particulars	Fol.	Debit	✓	Credit	✓	Dr. or Cr.	Balance	✓
5/3/79	Invoice A36729	PJ3			145 90			145 90	
11/3/79	Invoice A36751	PJ3			42 70			188 60	
3/4/79	CK#5627	CR4	145 90					42 70	

folder similar to that in Exhibit 11-3, with each slot in the file representing each of the 31 days in any particular month. In the event that the last discount day is designated as January 14, for example, the invoice is filed in the slot numbered 11 to make sure that payment is received by the vendor by January 14. Three days are thus allowed for delivery from the retailer to the supplier through the mail system.

Each day the slot for that day is examined to determine what invoices must be paid to gain the cash discount or to avoid interest charges associated with invoice payments made after the net amount is due.

Once the invoice is paid or the information recorded in the accounts payable ledger and purchase journal, the invoice should be retained in a permanent file established for each supplier so that future reference can be made when necessary. These records can be maintained in alphabetical order by supplier.

Exhibit 11-3
Accordion File—To Ensure Invoice Payments

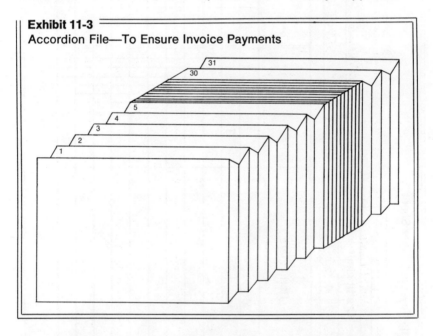

Recording Daily Transactions One of the most important records maintained by a retail store is that which seeks to summarize the daily sales and expenses of the store. This record is usually referred to as a daily sales audit and is concerned with the handling and control of the money flow in the store.

An example of a daily sales audit form is illustrated in Exhibit

Exhibit 11-4
Daily Sales Audit Form

| Date | Cash Register Classified Sales Readings | | | | | | | | Reconciliation | | | | | | |
	Class. #1	Class. #2	Class. #3	Class. #4	Class. #5	Sub Total	Sales Tax	Total	Cash Minus Float	Credit + Cheques	Payouts	Total Cash Reconciliation	Over or (Short)	Credit Card Charges	Bank Deposit
Weekly Total															

11-4. While the form outlines the type of information that needs to be assembled by any retail store on a daily basis, it should be clear that the more sophisticated the cash register system being used, the less the need for detailed manual control.

While any means can be established by the store to record this information, it is essential that a system be employed that will be implemented on a daily basis. The information contained in this record can then be transferred to other journals which will summarize the activity of the store over a longer period of time. As was noted earlier, the more current the information is, and the more complete the records maintained by the store, the more efficient you can be in making merchandising and operating decisions that will ultimately affect the profitability of your establishment.

Additional Records   While we have attempted to outline only a few of the more important operational records that need to be established by the independent merchant, each retailer must seek to develop additional control of the operation with the guidance and assistance of the store's accountant.

The payroll journal, the cash disbursements journal, a cheque register, and other subsidiary ledgers may need to be maintained to provide the store with an accurate and informative bookkeeping system.

ELECTRONIC DATA PROCESSING IN RETAILING

Many of the onerous tasks of accurate bookkeeping have been alleviated by innovations in the application of electronic data processing to retailing. While the mystique of the computer and the speed at which developments take place in this field tend to frighten many small business entrepreneurs, through effective implementation of the information available, merchants can be greatly assisted. To this end, the developments in the system of retail management have been much improved by the point-of-sale recording equipment, namely the cash register.

The computer system offers the independent a management information system that will allow the store effective controls over inventory, operating records, and decision-making variables. While not all independents will find these systems economical for their stores, many would be well advised to explore the potentials of the system, the costs of adapting the new procedure to the store, and, most importantly, the benefits it will provide in the management and operation of the store. Discussions with reputable and experienced merchandising systems' organizations will provide you with the information needed to assess the possibilities for your operation.

Retailers have tended to be rather late in accepting electronic data processing as a merchandise management tool. However, the realization that so much information is available in today's environment has led to a greater use of these devices, for competitive reasons. In fact, a virtual explosion of the application of electronic data processing systems in all sizes of retail stores has taken place in recent years.

The assortments of merchandise available to retail merchants have been expanding at an alarming rate. Consequently, the traditional methods of maintaining an adequate assortment to avoid out-of-stock situations will have to be replaced by something more efficient. The need to adequately record the enormous number of stock keeping units (SKUs) in each selection factor demands a more efficient method of assembling data. One merely needs to visualize the number of selection factor combinations that are potentially available in bed linens to appreciate the usefulness of electronic data processing techniques.

In the same context, probably the most significant problem that the retailer faces is the tardiness of management information. To find out that the store has a stock overage in a particular item at the end of the season merely becomes historical data. Excessive markdowns and lower margins are the result of this form of record keeping. The frequency and reasons for retail bankruptcy explained in the first chapter could probably be reduced significantly if all independents had adequate information early enough to rectify any merchandising mistakes made.

The independent retailer, like the large-scale merchant, is faced today with the inevitable profit squeeze. Declining stock turnover rates, severe price competition, the absence of customer loyalty, increasing rental and labour rates, and the great proliferation of scramble merchandising by many merchants have drastically changed the environment of retailing. The independent seeks to improve the operation by attempting to increase sales volume without a corresponding increase in expenses. To effectively achieve this goal, the retailer must seek to invest inventory dollars in merchandise items that will yield a higher return and/or a faster stock turnover. This placement of inventory dollars can be accomplished by supplying the independent with a reporting technique made possible by current quantitative data on the store's merchandising strategy.

Capturing information at the point-of-sale through the cash register is perhaps the most accurate and logical method for the independent merchant. It has frequently been stated that the future of the retail operation lies at the point-of-sale since this represents the most efficient source of capturing sales, credit, and merchandise information.

There have been significant developments over the past decade in recording the information at the point-of-sale. It is now possible for an operator of a cash register to punch the information from the price ticket into the machine. It is also possible, through the use of an electronic wand hooked to the cash register, to record the data directly from the magnetic price tickets attached to the merchandise. A further development in the recording of information at the point-of-sale is being witnessed at the present time through the use of laser scanning equipment that automatically reads the universal product code (UPC) appearing on the items.

While this development of the UPC and scanning equipment is undergoing experimentation by some supermarket chains, it has had difficulty in being accepted both by consumer groups and by retail organizations. The system teams computer-assisted electronic registers with laser scanners to read the UPC imprinted on the merchandise. As a result of the caution being exercised at all levels in installing this system, we are witnessing a gradual evolution of a new means of capturing information at the point-of-sale.

While the implementation of scanning equipment and the application of the UPC have very little significance at this time for the independent retailer, awareness of new techniques in recording information at the point-of-sale is important to every merchant intent on satisfying customer needs and wants.

For the independent merchant, retail management systems have been developed by such firms as the National Cash Register Company (NCR) and International Business Machines (IBM). Both companies have sought to capture information for retail use at the point-of-sale through electronic cash register systems. Part of the success of these systems for the independent retailer has been the ability of these firms to provide reports to the merchant that will best fit the store's individual needs and its tailored accounting system. Other electronic data processing equipment firms have also engaged in providing management systems for independent retailers via the cash register.

While much discussion centres on the cost and capabilities of the traditional versus the electronic system, the selection of the equipment, the records, and the sophistication will depend on a thorough analysis of the needs of the store.

Finally it should be kept in mind that the equipment comprises but one part of the sales transaction system designed to provide fast and courteous service at the lowest cost to the store, to protect cash receipts, to furnish the data required to control merchandise, to permit auditing of all kinds of sales and to prepare the necessary statistical and managerial reports. It is imperative, of course, that the sales transaction system should be related to other systems of the store to provide overall operating efficiency.

—Delbert J. Duncan and Stanley C. Hollander, *Modern Retailing Management: Basic Concepts and Practices*, Ninth Edition (Illinois: Richard D. Irwin, Inc., 1977), p. 633. Reprinted by permission of Richard D. Irwin, Inc.

Whether a manual or electronic system is used, you should recognize that the need for accurate, current, and complete information is mandatory in operating a retail store in today's competitive environment.

THE STORE'S IMAGE

Perhaps no concept has been repeated more often throughout this book than that associated with the management function of developing an image for the retail store. The need for an efficient bookkeeping system or for the recording of information at the point-of-sale will, in fact, be much less important if the store has not accomplished its primary objective of directing its merchandising strategy at the designated target market.

Because of the great proliferation of retail stores operating in the marketplace, the development and growth of scramble merchandising, and the intensive and extensive diversification of large retail organizations, the need for a well-defined and projected image on the part of the independent merchant is paramount. As such, a concerted effort must be made by you to present the customer with a unified image of your store amidst the massive choices available to the store's target market. It is therefore essential that we understand the complexities of the store image.

Twenty years ago, the subject of building a store image for department stores was focused upon; since that time the concept has permeated all areas of retailing. Pierre Martineau, in a discussion of the personality of the retail store attempted to define the meaning of a store's image in 1958.

What is it that draws the shopper to one store or agency rather than another? Clearly, there is a force operative in the determination of a store's customer body besides the obvious functional factors of location, price ranges, and merchandise offerings . . . this force is the store personality or image—the way in which the store is defined in the shopper's mind, partly by its functional qualities and partly by an aura of psychological attributes. Whereas the retailer thinks of himself as a merchant concerned with value and quality, there is a wide range of intangibles which also play a critical role in the success or failure of his store.

—Pierre Martineau, "The Personality of the Retail Store," *Harvard Business Review,* January-February (1958), p. 47. Reprinted by permission of *Harvard Business Review.* Copyright © 1957 by the President and Fellows of Harvard College; all rights reserved.

While merchants tend to define a store's image in many ways, it is clear that all merchants recognize that the store's image, in fact, represents the way the customer views the store, as Mr. Martineau has suggested. Note that the above definition emphasizes the two important aspects of image as being functional qualities and psychological attributes. This implies that the store's image is derived both from the elements of the merchandising mix and the psychological or emotional characteristics of the target market. Therefore, each retailer must look to the functions of place, price, promotion, and product for the store in relation to the emotional impact they are likely to have on the potential target market. In fact, the store's image is truly the personality that the firm is projecting and the way in which it is perceived by the various market segments making up the potential market.

In this context, let's recall the discussion in Chapter 2 in which we discussed the various patronage and product motives that are exhibited by consumers in their selection of retail stores and merchandise assortments. The merchant who has analyzed these motives and is able to adapt them to the retail store has fulfilled the primary function in developing an effective store image.

Of the many studies which have been conducted as part of retail image research, almost all have concluded that the essential components that must be co-ordinated to project a unified image are those in the following list. Each element plays a crucial role in projecting the store's image, but the relative importance of each will vary with the type of store, the type of customer, and the merchandise assortment presented.

The following factors represent those which have an important role to play in defining the store's image.

1. *Merchandise*
   Price ranges
   Degree of quality
   Selection and assortment
   Style and fashion awareness
2. *Services Provided*
   Guarantee
   Courteous, helpful sales personnel
   Credit, delivery, customer services
3. *Convenience*
   Locational convenience
   Convenience of store layout
   Parking facilities
   Shopping ease
   Other convenience factors
4. *Promotion*
   Sales promotion
   Window and interior displays
   Advertising
   Publicity and community relations
5. *Store Atmosphere*
   Conducive to shopping
   Physical facilities
   Architectural presentation
   Degree of congestion
6. *Institutional*
   Store's reputation
   Reliability
   Knowledge and attitude of sales personnel

In an effort to help the firm survive through the substantial satisfaction of the customer's needs and wants, the independent must effectively communicate the message through all of the elements of the merchandising mix. But, more than projecting a message to the market, it is vital that all elements in the mix are in fact illustrating a unified image to the segment designated as the target. The advertising message must project in the same way that the merchandise assortment indicates to the customer the type of store being discovered. The store's location must convey the same information about the store as does the interior decor. And it is vital that the sales personnel convey the same image in face-to-face contact with the customer. The breakdown of any one of these links can seriously affect the overall success the store enjoys as a result of its image definition.

The independent must view the impact of the store's image as a cumulative attraction that will generate increased volume when all the elements of the mix are pulling in the same direction.

Since the image for a retail store is composed of many parts, care must be taken in establishing a procedure that will encompass all aspects of its development. To this end, the following steps are provided for you to follow:

1. Identify the elements-dimensions that are perceived, sensed, and sought by many potential customers.
2. Determine how your store actually ranks on those dimensions.
3. Determine how other stores rank.
4. Determine the opinions, impressions/image held of your store by different types of customers.
5. Decide what kind of images and impressions you would like to create ideally.
6. Decide what kind of impression-image you should realistically try to convey—taking account of the present image and cost-of-change.
7. Select the tools to employ—taking account of cost-effectiveness and risk . . .
8. Monitor the result.

—Alfred R. Oxenfeldt, "Developing a Favourable Price-Quality Image," *Journal of Retailing*, Winter (1974-1975), p. 12-13. Reprinted by permission of the *Journal of Retailing*, New York University.

The overall implementation of these steps will assist the independent in establishing an image that may set the store apart from the many competitors in the marketplace. Too often, in both large stores and small stores, thousands of dollars are spent on the physical attributes of the store, on advertising campaigns, on merchandise selection, and on other elements of the strategy, only to find that all of this can be damaged by the attitude or carelessness of the sales personnel. It is therefore vital to the success of the independent retailer that there be only one message projected, with all elements pulling in this same direction.

A careful adherence to the steps outlined by Alfred Oxenfeldt should ensure that a unified image is projected.

A note of caution: it is not unusual for the customer's image of the store to be very different from that held by the owner or manager. Some merchants are so close to their operations that they are unable to objectively assess the personality being projected by their stores. It should not be surprising to note that independent merchants are likely to overrate their own operations. The independent often views the operation as much more effective than the competition in meeting the demands of the customer.

A concerted effort must be made by each independent to view the store from the eyes of the customer rather than in terms of defending an ego. Shopping in competing stores in the same area, or in communities quite distant from the store, will often register inefficiencies in the store's operation that are constantly viewed by the target market.

While the independent merchant is constantly faced with the competitive threats of the large-scale retailer, it is in the area of image projection that the small retailer has much to gain. Because of the personal, individual attention given by the owner or manager, the independent merchant is better able to offer the customer the personal service that is generally not available in larger retail operations. By taking advantage of this concept and making sure that it is projected in the store's overall image, the independent is likely to remain a competitive force in the retailing environment.

THE FUTURE OF THE INDEPENDENT RETAILER

Much has been written during the past 25 years regarding the future of the small independent retailer. While some writers have predicted the absolute demise of the independent, others remain optimistic about the potential for growth of the small retailer. The common thread that permeates the view that the independent can survive amidst the increasing competitive threats is the ability of the merchant to establish a philosophy of adopting the new techniques of merchandising and adapting these to the store's organization. Self-service retailing, satisfaction guaranteed as a customer service, the offering of credit facilities, and the adoption of electronic data processing are just some of the techniques that have been increasingly used by the successful independent.

Increases in disposable and discretionary income, the growing demands of the needs and wants of consumers, the mobility and shifting of the population within the urban areas, and the improved modes of transportation are providing expanding markets that will support highly differentiated retail operations of all sizes. Such elements have, in fact, played a significant role in the growth and development of our large-scale retail organizations in their quest for increased market share and profitability. But while these components have motivated the giant firms to become larger, they have also provided a niche in the retailing environment for the small independent. Therefore, the small independent merchant must seek to establish a distinctive operation that will survive and grow in a retail environment which is composed of many different operations both in size and assortment.

Because of certain advantages possessed by independent merchants in meeting the demands of the market, large-scale retail operations have attempted to adopt those techniques of specialization and concentration and still reap the benefits associated with expansion and size. Thus, as large department stores and chain organizations institute specialty departments and classifications, the independent will be required to seek new ways of attracting their target markets by emphasizing their uniqueness.

It is essential to note that rather than direct competition existing between these two sizes of organizations, developers of the planned shopping centres have come to realize that the small independent retail establishments in fact complement the large-scale merchandisers by providing a more complete and attractive shopping environment. To this end, the specialized independent will seek to satisfy consumer requirements that the large stores cannot or do not satisfy. When this has been established, the small retailer will have provided a merchandise complex for a specific target market that will offer the store the means to grow and survive in the marketplace.

This book has been devoted to an explanation of those tools and techniques of retail management that will assist the independent in sharing in the growth of the consumer market and the economy in general. The need to accurately define the store's target market before the application of the merchandising strategy to this customer segment has been indicated as a fundamental requirement for all merchants. Once the market has been defined, it is then possible to adapt the elements of the merchandising mix to this market. This process of developing a strategy for the store has been thoroughly explained to allow you to understand the merchandising and operating principles and controls required in the management of the retail establishment.

In some merchandising fields, independents have sought to join a voluntary chain organization to gain the advantages of size while still maintaining their independence. Such establishments have been developed in hardware, grocery, automotive supplies, and drugs. The growth of such chains as Pro, Home, and Dominion Hardware shows the success these organizations have achieved in their efforts to improve the operating efficiencies of the independent.

In addition, the rapid explosion of the franchise system of distribution, as noted earlier, has assisted many individuals in establishing and operating their own businesses. Such organizations have witnessed tremendous growth patterns in fast foods, service facilities, and automotive repairs. Recent trends indicate that this system is gaining popularity and acceptance in the general merchandise field as well. Whether it is McDonald's, Holiday Inn, Management Recruiters, Mister Transmission, or other franchise organizations, all operate on the premise that the future of the independent retailer can be assured. Franchising is believed to combine the best of the large business—financial ability, specialized management, modern equipment, and mass merchandising—with the best of small business—knowledge of the local community, personalized service, and individual initiative and attention.

While the voluntary chains and franchise operations have improved the chances of success of many independent operations, small retail establishments which have sought to operate on their own have also continued to grow and survive with varying degrees of success.

It is difficult to predict the future under the best of circumstances and with the best of information, but it is my opinion that there is, indeed, a bright future for the independent merchant. To ensure this survival, it is essential that the merchant avoid the pitfalls associated with complacency and maintenance of the status quo. To succeed, grow, and compete effectively the merchant must change the retail operation to meet the constantly changing environment in which the store operates. The potential market in Canada is increasing, providing small merchants with the opportunity not only to survive but, more importantly, to grow, with these changes.

BIBLIOGRAPHY

Bernard, Frank J. *Dynamic Display: Techniques and Practice.* Cincinatti: Display Publishing Company, 1962.

Brink, Edward L., and Kelley, William T. *The Management of Promotion: Consumer Behavior and Demand Stimulation.* New Jersey: Prentice-Hall, Inc., 1963.

Davidson, William R.; Doody, Alton F.; and Sweeney, Daniel J. *Retailing Management.* 4th ed. New York: Ronald Press Company, 1975.

Diamond, Jay, and Pintel, Gerald. *Retail Buying.* New Jersey: Prentice-Hall, Inc., 1976.

Duncan, Delbert J., and Hollander, Stanley C. *Modern Retailing Management: Basic Concepts and Practices.* 9th ed. Illinois: Richard D. Irwin Inc., 1977.

Edwards Jr., Charles M., and Brown, Russell A. *Retail Advertising and Sales Promotion.* New Jersey: Prentice-Hall, Inc., 1959.

Engel, James F.; Fiorillo, Henry F.; and Cayley, Murray A. *Market Segmentation, Concepts and Applications.* New York: Holt, Rinehart and Winston, 1972.

Engel, James F.; Wales, Hugh G.; and Warshaw, Martin R. *Promotional Strategy.* Illinois: Richard D. Irwin, Inc., 1975.

Gist, Ronald R. *Basic Retailing: Text and Cases.* New York: John Wiley and Sons, 1971.

—————. *Management Perspectives in Retailing.* New York: John Wiley and Sons, 1971.

Hartley, Robert F. *Retailing, Challenge and Opportunity.* Boston: Houghton, Mifflin Company, 1975.

Jacobs, Laurence W. *Advertising and Sales Promotion for Retailing.* Illinois: Scott, Foresman and Company, 1972.

Kleppner, Otto. *Advertising Procedure.* New Jersey: Prentice-Hall, Inc., 1974.

Kneider, Albert P. *Mathematics of Merchandising.* New Jersey: Prentice-Hall, Inc., 1974.

Kurtz, David L.; Dodge, H. Robert; and Klompmaker, Jay E. *Professional Selling.* Texas: Business Publications, Inc., 1976.

Larson, Carl M.; Weigand, Robert E.; and Wright, John S. *Basic Retailing.* New Jersey: Prentice-Hall, Inc., 1976.

Macpherson, Mary Etta. *Shopkeepers to a Nation: The Eatons.* Toronto: McClelland and Stewart Limited, 1963.

Markin Jr., Rom J. *Retailing Management: A Systems Approach.* New York: The Macmillan Company, 1971.

Marquardt, Raymond A.; Makens, James C.; and Roe, Robert G. *Retailing Management: Satisfaction of Consumer Needs.* Illinois: The Dryden Press, Holt, Rinehart and Winston, 1975.

Mills, K. H., and Paul, J. E. *Create Distinctive Displays.* New Jersey: Prentice-Hall, Inc., 1974.

National Retail Merchants Association. *The Buyers Manual.* New York: 1966.

Pintel, Gerald, and Diamond, Jay. *Retailing.* New Jersey: Prentice-Hall, Inc., 1971.

Rachman, David J. *Retail Strategy and Structure: A Management Approach.* New Jersey: Prentice-Hall, Inc., 1969.

Redinbaugh, Larry D. *Retailing Management.* New York: McGraw-Hill Book Company, 1976.

Richert, G. Henry; Meyer, Warren G.; and Haines, Peter G. *Retailing Principles and Practices.* 5th ed. New York: Gregg Division, McGraw-Hill Book Company, 1968.

Robinson, O. Preston; Robinson, Christine H.; and Zeiss, George H. *Successful Retail Salesmanship.* New Jersey: Prentice-Hall, Inc., 1961.

Russell, Frederick A.; Beach, Frank H.; and Buskirk, Richard H. *Textbook of Salesmanship.* 9th ed. New York: McGraw-Hill Book Company, 1974.

Shaffer, Harold, and Greenwald, Herbert. *Independent Retailing: A Money-Making Manual.* New Jersey: Prentice-Hall, Inc., 1976.

Stanley, Richard E. *Promotion: Advertising, Publicity, Personal Selling, Sales Promotion.* New Jersey: Prentice-Hall, Inc., 1977.

Stephenson, William. *The Store That Timothy Built.* Toronto: McClelland and Stewart Limited, 1969.

Troxell, Mary D., and Judelle, Beatrice. *Fashion Merchandising.* New York: McGraw-Hill Book Company, 1971.

Wingate, Isabel B.; Gillespie, Karen R.; and Milgrom, Betty G. *Know Your Merchandise: For Retailers and Consumers.* 4th ed. New York: McGraw-Hill Book Company, 1975.

Wingate, John W., and Friedlander, Joseph S. *The Management of Retail Buying.* New Jersey: Prentice-Hall, Inc., 1963.

Wingate, John W.; Schaller, Elmer O.; and Miller, Leonard F. *Retail Merchandise Management.* New Jersey: Prentice-Hall, Inc., 1972.

Wright, John S.; Warner, Daniel S.; and Winter Jr., Willis L. *Advertising.* 3rd ed. New York: McGraw-Hill Book Company, 1971.

INDEX

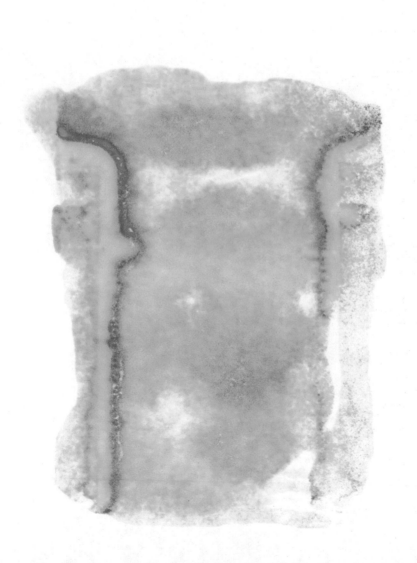

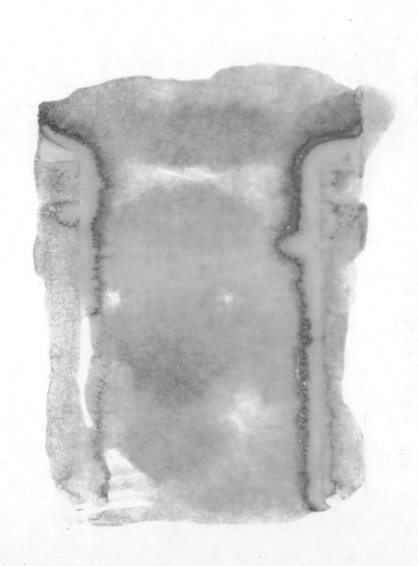